Praise for Reneau Z. Peurifoy, M.A., M.F.T. and

ANXIETY, PHOBIAS, AND PANIC

"A clearly written book that should enable readers to evaluate, understand, reduce anxiety, and change their own self-defeating behaviors."
—*Jean Baer, author of* **How to Be an Assertive (Not Aggressive) Woman**

❁ ❁ ❁

"Excellent . . . complete."
—*Arthur B. Hardy, M.D., founder of TERRAP programs, the nation's largest network of treatment programs for panic disorder and agoraphobia*

❁ ❁ ❁

"The most thorough and practical book available to address this problem."
—*Shirley F. Green, executive director, Agoraphobics Building Independent Lives (ABIL)*

❁ ❁ ❁

"One of the most comprehensive and well-written books on anxiety and panic. It is easily followed no matter what stage of recovery one is at. A superior self-help, too. . . . Outstanding."
—*Anne Barnette, facilitator, Phobia Recovery and Support Group*

❁ ❁ ❁

"A book that cannot help but benefit sufferers of anxiety disorders."
—*Lynn Maguire, Phobia Society of Dallas, Texas*

❁ ❁ ❁

"Lucidly written. . . . One of the better reality-oriented psychological self-help books."
—**Book Reader**

❁ ❁ ❁

"A stand-out reference. . . . A useful manual with a wealth of information that will make a welcome addition to the library of clinician and client alike."
—**The California Therapist**

❁ ❁ ❁

SEE HOW THIS BOOK HAS HELPED OTHER READERS . . .
THEN LET IT WORK FOR YOU!

"Thanks for putting me on the path to conquering my fears."
—*Jon A., DE*

❄ ❄ ❄

"I just want to thank you. Your book has helped me a lot and I have suggested it to many people."
—*Cindy K., CT*

❄ ❄ ❄

"I thought the lessons were excellent, comprehensive and practical. I liked the building process of the program. Each lesson was valuable and had its place in the overall process. I learned something from each step in the program."
—*Kathleen M., VA*

❄ ❄ ❄

"I found your workbook assisted me with the integration of intellect and emotion, and [I] began to gain real insight and relief. The workbook reframed and helped me to incorporate what I knew intellectually with an inner emotional acceptance. . . ."
—*Susan S., NY*

❄ ❄ ❄

". . . Thank you, thank you, thank you for writing that book! You will never know how much you have truly helped me!! . . . The whole entire book is fantastic, and . . . your program has helped me get my life back. . . . Once again, I thank you!"
—*Barbara L., NY*

❄ ❄ ❄

"This book has been very helpful in getting me back on track in my life. The skills are tools for life and really work."
—*Greg K., CA*

❄ ❄ ❄

"Your book has really helped me by giving me a game plan to follow and goals to strive for."
—*Robin E., VA*

ANXIETY, PHOBIAS, AND PANIC

Revised and Updated

Reneau Z. Peurifoy, M.A., M.F.T.

WARNER BOOKS

NEW YORK   BOSTON

Note: The ideas, procedures and suggestions contained in this book are not intended as a substitute for consulting with either a physician or psychotherapist. You should regularly consult a physician in matters relating to your health and particularly in respect to any symptoms that may require diagnosis or medical attention. Likewise, if you feel desperate and are unable to cope with stressful events, you are urged to seek help from a qualified psychotherapist.

Warner Books Edition
Copyright © 1988, 1992, 1995, and 2005 by Reneau Z. Peurifoy, M.A., M.F.T.

The circumstances of certain events depicted and the names of individuals have been altered and/or deleted to protect the privacy of the people involved.

This Warner Books edition is published by arrangement with the author.

Warner Books

Time Warner Book Group
1271 Avenue of the Americas, New York, NY 10020
Visit our Web site at www.twbookmark.com

Printed in the United States of America

First Warner Books Printing: September 1995
Second Edition, Revised and Updated: February 2005
10 9 8 7 6 5 4 3 2

Library of Congress Cataloging-in-Publication Data

Peurifoy, Reneau Z.
    Anxiety, phobias, and panic / Reneau Z. Peurifoy. — 2nd ed., rev. & updated.
        p. cm.
    Includes bibliographical references and index.
    ISBN 0-446-69277-8
    1. Anxiety—Popular works   2. Phobias—Popular works.   3.   Panic disorders—Popular works.
4.   Stress management.   5.   Self-help techniques.   I.   Title.
    RC531.P428 2005
    616.85'22—dc22

                                                        2004006441

Book design and text composition by HRoberts Design

Acknowledgments

There are many people who have made this book possible. First, I would like to thank the clients who have worked with me. Through their struggles with anxiety, they helped perfect the program outlined in these pages. Next, I would like to thank the people who read the various drafts of the manuscript for the first edition. Kris Baxter, Carole Sabo, Joyce Herman, Dorothy Lambert, and Jann McCord labored through the first drafts and offered many suggestions on both content and format.

After the first drafts were revised, Alissyn Link, Lucille De Rose, Jane Fry, Mary Ann Kinyon, Linda Kenney, and my mother, Clara Peurifoy all made extensive suggestions on style and format. Kim and Kevin Thompson managed the actual page layout and production of the first edition. Alissyn Link, Dr. Frank Capobianco, Jane Fry, Nancy Morris-Struben, and Kaaren Smith all helped with the revisions for the second edition. I would also like to thank Shirley Green, founder of ABIL (Agoraphobics Building Independent Lives, which is a large self-help organization in Richmond, Virginia), who has offered much encouragement and support.

In regard to the most recent, revised edition of the book, I'd like to thank the many people who have made it possible. My agent, Barbara Zitwer, worked with my editor, Diana Baroni, to create this update. Melissa Carney, Danielle Seadia, Keiloni Bruner, and Patricia Popp volunteered to read the revised lessons as they were completed and offered many suggestions for improvements. Laura Jorstad, the copyeditor, did a superb job of editing the final text. My greatest thanks goes to God, who has blessed me richly over the years and provided me with the abilities, opportunities, and insights that have allowed me to make this book what it is.

Finally, I would like to thank my wife, Michiyo. Without her support this book would not have been possible. Because her love and companionship have helped sustain me, I dedicate this book to her.

Contents

Preface   xi

The Path to Freedom   xv

Getting Started   xvii

Lesson 1: What, Why, and How   **1**

I'm Not Alone   1

Anxiety and Fear   2

Panic Attacks   3

Medical Causes of Anxiety   4

The Fight or Flight Response   4

Brain Circuits That Manage Fear   7

Personality Traits That Can Contribute to Anxiety   8

Childhood Experiences That Can Contribute to Beliefs and Traits
     Associated with Anxiety   11

What Causes These Conditions to Develop?   16

Recommended Activities   27

Lesson 2: Reducing the Symptoms of Anxiety   **33**

Four Common Roadblocks   33

Four Basic Skills for Reducing the Symptoms of Anxiety   34

Medication   50

Recommended Activities   52

Lesson 3: Understanding and Reducing Stress   **63**
What Is Stress?   63
Basic Stress Management Principles   65
Stress Symptom Inventory   66
Three Guidelines for Periods of High Stress   69
Develop a Lifestyle Based on Stress
    Management Principles   71
Recommended Activities   78

**Lesson 4: Identifying and Reducing the
        Sources of Anxiety**   **81**
Needs and Beliefs   81
How Emotions Are Generated   82
Why Do We Have Emotions?   83
Habitual Thinking Patterns   86
The Cognitive Approach   87
Should/Must Thinking   89
Recommended Activities   96

Lesson 5: Distorted Thinking   **103**
Common Forms of Distorted Thinking   103
Changing the Way You Think   118
Recommended Activities   120

Lesson 6: Learning to Enjoy Being Human   **127**
Characteristics of Perfectionism   127
Challenging Beliefs That Support Perfectionism   130
Changing Perfectionistic Behavior   134
Recommended Activities   143

Lesson 7: Becoming a Positive Realist   **147**
Negative Anticipation: What If?   147
Thinking and Acting Like a Victim   156
Blaming   159
Recommended Activities   163

Lesson 8: The Excessive Need for Approval   **167**
How the Excessive Need for Approval Is Expressed   167
Eliminating the Excessive Need for Approval   170
Recommended Activities   176

Lesson 9: Eliminating the Self-Defeating Behaviors Commonly Associated with Anxiety   **181**
Behavioral Therapy   181
Exposure Therapy   187
Guidelines for Practicing   195
Response Prevention   200
Rapid In Vivo Exposure or Flooding   203
Imaginal Exposure   204
Social Role-Playing   206
Recommended Activities   208

Lesson 10: The Process of Change   **213**
Learned Helplessness, Self-Efficacy, and Change   213
Rationalization and Denial   214
Six Roadblocks to Change   216
Recommended Activities   223

Lesson 11: Feeling Good About Yourself   **229**
Self-Esteem and Self-Acceptance   229
The Development of Low Self-Esteem and Self-Acceptance   231
The Fear of Being Incompetent   233
Eight Approaches for Increasing Self-Esteem and Self-Acceptance   233
Recommended Activities   243

Lesson 12: Making Anger Your Friend and Ally   **249**
What Is Anger?   249
The Threats That Generate Anger and Fear   250
Actions Generated by Anger   251
Appropriate Versus Inappropriate Anger   252
Minimizing Inappropriate Anger   253

A Four-Step Approach for Dealing with Anger   259
Suggestions for People Who Habitually Suppress Anger   260
Suggestions for People Who Anger Easily   263
Dealing with Anger Directed at You from Others   265
The Fear of Losing Control   267
Recommended Activities   271

Lesson 13: Standing Up for Yourself   **273**
Three Basic Types of Behavior   273
Common Irrational Beliefs About Assertiveness   276
Your Rights and Responsibilities   277
The DERN Approach: An Effective Assertive Method for
    Resolving Conflicts   279
"I Language"   288
Recommended Activities   289

Lesson 14: Staying on Track   **295**
Seven Common Tactics That Can Sabotage Your Assertive Efforts   295
Five General Approaches for Resolving Problems and Conflicts   305
When Is an Assertive Approach Most Effective?   308
What to Do When People Fail to Keep Their Agreements   310
Resolving Conflicts with Businesses and Salespeople   312
Recommended Activities   312

Lesson 15: Continuing Your Growth   **315**
Three Plans for Continuing Your Growth   315

Appendix 1: The Six Basic Types of Anxiety-Related Problems   323
Appendix 2: Methods for Developing a Relaxation Response   329
Appendix 3: Guidelines for Selecting a Therapist   343
Appendix 4: Suggestions for People with Sleep Problems   349
Appendix 5: Developing Effective Listening Skills   357

Supplemental Materials   363
About the Author   365
Index   367

Preface

What a pleasure it is to be able to update a work that has stood the test of time. In looking back over the last twenty years, it is amazing to see the advances that have been made in our understanding of anxiety disorders. When I first wrote *Anxiety, Phobias, and Panic,* research into anxiety disorders had just begun. At that time the main focus was panic disorder, and the first edition focused on that problem. With the second edition, I expanded the book to include the other types of anxiety disorders, but many of the examples still focused on panic disorder. Much has been learned over the past ten years, and in this edition I have updated the various lessons to include this, along with more examples of the other types of anxiety disorders.

The evolution of this book began decades ago when I was beginning my career as a therapist. I heard two people on the radio who suffered from what was then called agoraphobia but is now known as panic disorder. Their story intrigued me. I soon discovered that there weren't many people working with agoraphobia at that time. I found a group in another city working with agoraphobia and spent a week there studying their approach. This included visiting support groups they had organized for agoraphobics.

Upon returning to Sacramento, I held two lectures where I shared my newfound knowledge and was surprised to find that enough people attended to enable me to begin two therapy groups of my own. Within two weeks it became evident that the approach I had studied was woefully inadequate. This is when I began developing the program that has evolved into the one described in this book.

I went to a local university and reviewed all of the current research on agoraphobia. This was relatively easy, because the explosion of research that is available today had not yet begun; there also weren't many good books written on the subject. Still, I took what I had found, combined it with material from several workshops I had conducted, and put together a set of twenty lessons. After several years of refining this material, I wrote the first edition of *Anxiety, Phobias, and Panic,* which was published in 1988.

It was gratifying to see not only individuals, but also self-help groups and therapists across the nation use the book as the basic text for their groups and report back how well it was working. This new edition includes many suggestions made by groups using the first edition as well as new insights I have gained while using the original work with my own clients.

As with any author, my work and ideas are an extension of work done by many people. My main goal while writing this book was to produce a practical manual that would help people struggling with anxiety live full and satisfying lives. As a result, I have not used extensive footnotes to credit my sources; I felt it would detract from my overall purpose. Instead, I will discuss a little of my background and acknowledge those sources of inspiration who have most directly influenced this work.

When I was a child, my family had a dog, several cats, and a parrot. I raised chickens and rabbits and collected insects. By the time I entered high school, a keen interest in animal behavior had developed. I was especially fascinated by the work of Konrad Lorenz, the founder of modern ethology (the study of animal behavior). In college I majored in biology and graduated with minors in chemistry and math. I then studied to be a teacher and taught junior high and high school science and math for five years before deciding to become a therapist. During the time when I trained to be a teacher, self-directed learning modules were in vogue. Both this training and my experience as a teacher are reflected in the organization of this work.

During this time I was also actively involved in what was then referred to as the human potential movement. Many of the exercises that are included in the Recommended Activities evolved out of things I learned during this period.

When I began my training to be a therapist, I was especially interested in hypnosis and the techniques of neurolinguistic programming. As my training progressed, however, I was introduced to theory and techniques from most of the major schools of psychology. This opened up many new doors for me. In my work as a therapist, I draw from many different schools of psychology. The strongest source of influence for this work comes from the ideas developed by cognitive psychologists such as Albert Ellis and Aaron Beck. Adlerian psychology provides a strong secondary source of inspiration.

In closing I would like to add that I have always been involved in teaching in one form or another. One of my greatest thrills has always been when a struggling student, a person in therapy, or a workshop participant grasps a new concept or skill that opens up new vistas for that person. My sincere hope is that this work will help you master ideas and skills that will enable you to travel the path to freedom.

Reneau Z. Peurifoy, M.A., M.F.T.

The Path to Freedom
by Reneau Z. Peurifoy

As each day passes,

I am better able to embrace and love myself,
all of myself,
and to more fully embrace and love others;

I am better able to understand
that feelings are friendly,
and this understanding allows them to flow freely through me;

I am better able to think rationally and realistically,
to look at life as a series of choices
and to stop and look before choosing;

I am better able to know
that perfection is a direction rather than a place,
and to laugh at my mistakes and imperfections;

I am better able to be patient with time
and face my world with courage,
knowing that each day

I take another step on The Path to Freedom.

Getting Started

This book describes a self-help program that has been used successfully by many people. For good results, the program has to be used correctly. The following guidelines describe how to achieve the most success possible.

Do not read the book from front to back quickly like a novel. Instead, spend at least one week on each lesson. Since each lesson builds on the ones before, do not skip around unless a lesson directs you to do so. If you wish to preview the program, read the contents and take a day or two to skim through the book. This will give you a general idea of the book's format and the areas in which you will be working. Then start with the first lesson and work through the book in the systematic way in which it is designed to be used.

When you start a new lesson, read the headings to get an overview of the material. Then read it word by word at your usual rate. Read each lesson at least three times; more, if you find the information difficult. The second and third readings will increase your understanding of the material and reveal ideas that were missed during the first reading.

Overcoming anxiety-related problems requires more than a general understanding of ideas. Your goal is to internalize the information and skills presented in each lesson, to make them a natural and automatic part of your behavior. The Recommended Activities play a key role in this process. The more time and energy you spend on them, the more successful you will be.

There may be times when you could spend several weeks on a lesson. While it is important to be thorough, it is also important to keep your momentum going. Spend no more than two weeks on a lesson and do as many of the Recommended Activities as possible. After completing the program, you can spend additional time on those areas where you feel more work is needed.

This may sound like a lot of work; it is. But keep in mind that it took all your life to develop the behaviors and thinking patterns that produced your condition. It will take time, energy, and commitment to learn new and effective ways of thinking and acting. If you work through the material in the manner outlined, chances are excellent that you will be as successful as the many others who have used this program to overcome severe anxiety.

LESSON 1

What, Why, and How

Congratulations! You are about to start a journey along the path to freedom. During this journey you will meet many people just like yourself. Like most who traveled this path before you, your first questions are probably: "What has happened to me?" "Why me?" and "How can I overcome these anxiety-related problems?" This lesson answers the first two questions and starts you on the path that leads to freedom from anxiety-related problems.

I'm Not Alone

People with anxiety-related problems often feel that they alone suffer from this problem. Nothing could be further from the truth. The National Institute of Mental Health (NIMH) ranks anxiety disorders as the most common mental health problem in the United States. The NIMH has found that more than nineteen million adults suffer from anxiety-related problems. While reliable figures for the number of children and adolescents suffering from anxiety-related problems are not currently available, it is now known that they can also develop anxiety-related problems. Anxiety-related problems will also frequently occur with other issues such as depression, eating disorders, and substance abuse. The following table, based on statistics from the NIMH, shows how common the six basic types of anxiety-related problems are:

1

NUMBER OF AMERICANS EXPERIENCING AN ANXIETY-RELATED PROBLEM IN A GIVEN YEAR		
	Population Estimate (in millions)	Percentage
Panic disorder	2.4	1.7
Obsessive-compulsive disorder	3.3	2.3
Post-traumatic stress disorder	5.2	3.6
Specific phobia	6.3	4.4
Social phobia	5.3	3.7
Generalized anxiety disorder	4.0	2.8

One of the big changes that has taken place since I first began working in this field is that most medical personnel are now familiar with the different types of anxiety-related problems that people can experience. As a result, most of the readers of this book who suffer from an anxiety-related problem will have already been diagnosed and read some literature that describes their specific problem. If you have not been formally diagnosed, however, or if you are reading this book because a friend or relative suffers from anxiety, descriptions of each of the above anxiety disorders are given in Appendix 1.

Anxiety and Fear

Anxiety and fear are normal responses to a perceived threat. For the purposes of this program, anxiety and fear are considered as opposite ends of a spectrum. Anxiety is usually triggered by a vague or ill-defined threat, while fear is usually triggered by a well-defined threat, such as a car skidding on wet pavement. This relationship between anxiety and fear can be diagrammed as follows:

Anxiety — — — — — — — — — — — — — — — — Fear
Vague or ill-defined threat   Well-defined threat

Both anxiety and fear trigger unpleasant mental symptoms such as a sense of helplessness, confusion, apprehension, worry, and repeated negative thoughts. Both also trigger physical symptoms ranging from simple muscle tension to a pounding heart. The full range of possible symptoms is listed in the description of panic attacks that follows. (The next two sections describe the different symptoms that characterize anxiety along with some of the medical causes of anxiety. Some find that reading about anxiety-related symptoms makes them overly anxious. If this is true for you, you have been diagnosed by a therapist who understands anxiety-related problems, and you know the specific type of anxiety-related problem you have, feel free to skip ahead to the section titled The Fight or Flight Response.)

Panic Attacks

A panic attack is an intense state of fear that occurs for no apparent reason and is characterized by four or more of the following symptoms:

- Shortness of breath (dyspnea) or smothering sensations.
- Dizziness, unsteady feelings, or faintness.
- Palpitations or accelerated heart rate (tachycardia).
- Trembling or shaking.
- Numbness or tingling sensations (paresthesias), usually in the fingers, toes, or lips.
- Flushes (hot flashes) or chills.
- Chest pain or discomfort.
- Fear of becoming seriously ill or dying.
- Fear of going crazy or of doing something uncontrolled.
- Sweating.
- Choking.
- Nausea or abdominal distress.
- Feelings of unreality (depersonalization or derealization).

An attack with fewer than four of the above symptoms is called a limited symptom attack. Panic attacks can build gradually over a period of several minutes or hours or strike very suddenly. While they can last from a few minutes to several days, most do not last longer than half an hour.

When anxiety or panic is felt regardless of where one is, it is called spontaneous anxiety or spontaneous panic, depending upon the degree of intensity. If the anxiety or panic occurs only in a particular situation, it is called situational or phobic anxiety or panic. If anxiety or panic is triggered simply by thinking of a particular situation, it is called anticipatory anxiety or anticipatory panic.

Medical Causes of Anxiety

The first step in overcoming any anxiety-related problem is to rule out possible medical causes by having a complete examination by a physician. There are many medical conditions that can cause one or more of the symptoms associated with anxiety such as cardiovascular problems, asthma, seizure disorder, diabetes, hypothyroidism, and problems with the inner ear. Medications such as stimulants, thyroid supplements, cold medications, tranquilizers, sleeping pills, certain blood pressure medications, steroids, and, ironically, antidepressants can also cause anxiety symptoms. Sometimes anxiety symptoms are due to unsupervised experimentation with or withdrawal from a medication. Finally, common legal and illegal recreational drugs, such as caffeine, alcohol, and marijuana, provide yet another potential source of anxiety symptoms.

While identifying possible medical sources of anxiety is important, you may find that resolving the medical issue by itself will not end your anxiety-related problems. As you will see later in this chapter, anxiety that starts out as a medical condition often takes on a life of its own and continues long after the medical condition is no longer present. It is essential, then, to work both with any medical condition that might be triggering anxiety as well as with the thinking patterns and behaviors that can keep anxiety active without the initial medical condition.

The Fight or Flight Response

Like all of your body responses, the various anxiety-related symptoms described above are controlled by your nervous system. This system is divided into two parts: the voluntary nervous system and the autonomic nervous system. The voluntary nervous system, also called the somatic system, is composed of the nerves that connect to the muscles that control movement and your various senses. This system sends information from your eyes, ears, and other senses to the brain and controls actions that require thought, such as raising your arm or walking. The autonomic nervous system is composed of all the nerves that connect to your internal organs and glands and controls all the automatic activities that occur in your body, such as digestion and breathing. The autonomic nervous system is itself broken down into the sympathetic and parasympathetic divisions. The sympathetic division, responsible for what is commonly referred to as the fight or flight response, is designed to activate the body quickly and prepare it to fight or flee from danger almost instantaneously. When the danger has passed, the parasympathetic division quiets the body and returns it to normal functioning. These two divisions of the autonomic nervous system can be diagrammed as follows:

Autonomic nervous system

Sympathetic division: regulates your fight or flight response

Parasympathetic division: regulates the "resting" functions in your body such as growth, digestion, relaxed breathing, etc.

When triggered, the sympathetic division of the autonomic nervous system suspends all nonessential activity in the body and increases activity in any system necessary to either fight or flee from an external physical threat. This response involves many complex reactions in the body. Some of the most noticeable changes that take place include the following:

- *Accelerated heartbeat:* This pumps more blood to the muscles for the impending struggle.
- *Deeper and more rapid breathing:* This ensures a large supply of oxygen and is the basis for the panting associated with strong excitement.
- *Increased muscle tension:* This prepares the muscles for any upcoming action.

- *Cold sweat:* This is in preparation for the warm sweat of actual muscular activity.
- *Constriction of peripheral blood vessels near the surface of the body:* This raises blood pressure and is the basis for "blanching with fear."
- *Shivering and raising of hairs:* This conserves heat and protects the body from the increased threat of cold caused by the constriction of the peripheral blood vessels.
- *Dilation of the pupils:* This permits a better view of threatening dangers and is why eyes are said to be "wide with fear."
- *Suspension of digestive activity:* This provides additional blood for the motor muscles.
- *Dry mouth due to decreased flow of saliva:* This accompanies the decreased flow of gastric juices in the stomach as digestive activity is suspended.
- *Tendency toward voiding bladder and bowels:* This frees the body for strenuous activity.
- *Suppression of the immune system and pain response:* This prevents swelling and discomfort, which could interfere with a quick escape.

When the fight or flight response is triggered, it releases increased amounts of adrenaline (epinephrine) and related chemicals into the bloodstream. This response provides the added strength, stamina, and ability to respond quickly that helps soldiers survive in battle, athletes perform better, and people facing dangerous situations respond more effectively. Fortunately, in our modern technological world, we face fewer physical dangers requiring strenuous action than did our ancestors.

The most common threats we face today are psychological threats such as the loss of love, status, prestige, or our sense of belonging and significance. Usually, these losses do not require an immediate physical response. Unfortunately, our bodies respond to any threat as if it does require an immediate physical response. So when you are embarrassed and feel threatened by what others think, your body triggers the fight or flight response and begins gearing up to physically run away or to fight. If you experience a panic attack in this situation, you are actually experiencing an overreaction of the fight or flight response. If you compare the above responses to the list of symptoms of a panic attack given earlier, you will see that each of the symptoms characteristic of a panic attack is simply an exaggeration of one or more of the normal body responses triggered by the fight or flight response.

Brain Circuits That Manage Fear

Information coming into the brain from the senses is processed in two different ways, cognitively and emotionally. Cognitive processing involves conscious thought about what we are experiencing. Emotional processing is designed to alert us to events that are important, whether positive or negative. One of the exciting things that is occurring in research is the pinpointing of the brain circuits where cognitive and emotional processing take place. One of the key structures for processing danger signals at this unconscious, emotional level is the amygdala, two small, very complex almond-shaped structures on either side of the brain. When you experience something fearful or unpleasant, a memory of this is stored in the amygdala. When you encounter this object or situation again, an immediate fear response is triggered. This fear response causes you to experience anxiety and triggers the fight or flight response.

The amygdala is designed to overreact to possible signs of danger. For example, a person living where there are poisonous snakes will quickly learn to associate snakes with danger. The amygdala will then immediately trigger the fight or flight response whenever anything that might be a snake is perceived. After all, if you are walking in the woods, it is better to mistake a stick for a snake than a snake for a stick. Keep in mind that this all occurs very quickly at an unconscious level. This circuitry allows you to react very quickly to danger without the need to consciously think about what is occurring. Unfortunately, events and objects that pose no threat can become associated with danger and trigger a fear response when you encounter them. This unconscious interpretation of harmless everyday situations as danger plays a major role in anxiety-related problems.

Personality Traits That Can Contribute to Anxiety

Research into the personality traits of people who suffer from the various anxiety disorders has had mixed results. There is no well-defined set of personality traits that can be said to produce a particular anxiety-related problem. Instead, there are a variety of ways in which people can develop a wide range of anxiety disorders. With obsessive-compulsive disorder (OCD), physiological factors seem to be far more important than personality or childhood factors. The triggering of post-traumatic stress disorder (PTSD) and specific phobia also seems to be much more dependent upon outside influences than on personality traits. Personality and childhood factors seem to play a larger role in the development of panic disorder, social phobia, and generalized anxiety disorder. In addition, when the traits noted below are present in a person with OCD, PTSD, and specific phobia, they can intensify symptoms and make recovery more difficult.

Several traits that can complicate anxiety-related problems are compiled in the following list. As you read through it, you will probably find that many do not apply to you, or that they describe people you know who do not suffer from anxiety-related symptoms. These are fairly common traits. Still, it is likely that you will find that some do describe you. When this is the case, place a check next to it; this may be an area you need to work on to overcome your anxiety-related problem.

High-Anxiety Personality (HAP) Traits

- High level of creativity or imagination: People suffering from severe anxiety are often very creative with the ability to imagine things vividly. Unfortunately, this creativity can become a powerful force behind negative anticipation or what-if thinking. The more creative a person is, the easier it is for him or her to think of a host of frightening things that could occur in a given situation. A creative mind can also help a person imagine these frightening possibilities in vivid detail.
- Rigid thinking: Rigid thinking is the tendency to perceive life as a series of either–or alternatives. Events are either right or

wrong, fair or unfair. Another characteristic of this type of black-and-white thinking is the presence of many rigid rules. There is usually a "correct" way to do things, and it is upsetting when things are not done in that correct way. In addition, there are often many things that "should," "must," or "can't" be done by oneself or others.

- Excessive need for approval: The excessive need for approval is often referred to as a fear of rejection. A person with this trait depends on others for a sense of self-worth, tends to have a heightened sensitivity to criticism, and often finds it difficult to say no to the demands of others. An excessive need for approval can also create the tendency to take responsibility for the feelings of others and to be overly sensitive to their needs. A person with this trait often makes it his or her responsibility to keep friends and relatives happy.

- Extremely high expectations of self: There is often the expectation of a much higher level of performance and accomplishment from oneself than would ever be expected from others.

- Perfectionism: Perfectionism is actually a combination of three things: the excessively high expectations mentioned above; the tendency to use all-or-nothing thinking when evaluating one's actions; and a tendency to focus on small flaws and errors rather than on progress or overall achievement. This can cause the perfectionist to consider any less-than-perfect achievement as a failure. He or she then tends to personalize the poor achievement so that both the task and the person become failures. One common way in which this is expressed is the "but" habit. A perfectionist often says things such as, "Overall this project was done well, but . . ." The perfectionist then dwells on what was wrong.

- Competent, dependable doer: The interaction of all the above factors often creates a person who is not only competent, capable, and dependable, but also a real doer skilled at getting jobs done and done well.

- Excessive need to be in control: A person with this trait places a high value on being calm and in control. Often there is also a need for events to be predictable. Unexpected changes in a predetermined schedule cause distress because it is harder to be in control when one is not sure what will happen. There may also be a tendency to try to control the feelings and behavior of others. This is not done with the intention of hurting others, but out of fear of losing control.

A person with the need to be in control can experience fairly intense anxiety symptoms but appear normal to the casual observer. Since a person like this usually presents a "proper" image to the world even when there is tremendous self-doubt and turmoil inside, he or she may be considered to be very strong by friends and relatives.

- Suppression of some or all negative feelings: A person with the above traits often suppresses feelings that "shouldn't" be felt because they might cause loss of control or disapproval from others. Anger and sadness are two common examples.
- Tendency to ignore the body's physical needs: This trait is commonly reflected in the attitude that the body is unimportant. Signs that the body is tired, in pain, or in need of rest or care are ignored or given low priority. A person with this trait is frequently only aware of fatigue when the symptoms of exhaustion are present.

I would like to emphasize that the above traits are not necessarily undesirable. This is easiest to see when looking at the opposites for each of the above. Here are a few examples. When used in a positive fashion, creativity is the source of all effective problem solving. The opposite would be someone who is dull and unimaginative. The need for approval is essential for healthy relationships; the opposite would be a person who has no feelings about others. A moderate degree of perfectionism, high personal expectations, and dependability creates a valuable member of society. The opposite would be someone who has little concern about how well a job is done. The ability to maintain control of self and emotions helps a person function well during emergencies and in the midst of chaos. The opposite would be someone who is overly emotional.

As with any given trait a person can possess, there is a healthy range for each of the above. For each trait, some people will be at the low end, some in the middle, and some at the high end. A particular trait creates problems only when it is exaggerated and outside this healthy range.

The key to success is learning how to moderate these traits so they are in the normal range and tap into them only during times when they are appropriate. Learning to use them in this way, and minimizing them during the times they interfere with your life, transforms these traits into valuable assets. In the weeks that follow, much of your time will be devoted to accomplishing this task.

Childhood Experiences That Can Contribute to Beliefs and Traits Associated with Anxiety

Your personality developed from the interaction of seven factors:

- The values and beliefs of the family in which you were raised.
- The methods of discipline used to train and socialize you.
- The role models presented by the adults in your life when you were young.
- Your place within the family constellation (your birth order; the sex of your siblings; and whether or not you had siblings that died, were handicapped, or joined the family as a result of remarriage or adoption).
- The social and cultural influences present while you were growing up.
- Your biological inheritance.
- The meaning you gave to each of the above while growing up.

There are many ways in which these seven factors can interact to produce the HAP traits described in the previous section. In addition, they shaped your beliefs about yourself, relationships, and the world. Experiences and events that can contribute to the development of anxiety-related problems are listed below. Check any that apply to you.

Childhood Contributors to Anxiety
- Substance abuse in the family: Many of the coping skills that help children survive in the home of a substance abuser can

interfere with their lives as they enter into the adult world. The tendency to rely on their drug of choice to avoid feeling the pain associated with normal life problems can be summarized by the saying, *Don't look; don't feel; run away.* While children of drug users may lead drug-free lives as adults, they often still cope with problems by avoiding them. This is especially true when problems arise in interpersonal relationships. Instead of acknowledging and dealing with interpersonal problems directly, they often use work, hobbies, sex, or activities to avoid such problems.

• Child abuse: There are six types of child abuse:
  a. *Physical abuse:* Any nonaccidental injury of a child. This is usually the result of being hit, pushed, whipped, bitten, punched, slapped, or burned.
  b. *Sexual abuse:* Any kind of sexual contact with a child by either an adult or child through the use of coercion, threat, or force.
  c. *Neglect:* The failure to provide basic necessities such as clothing, shelter, medical attention, or supervision.
  d. *Cruel and unusual punishment:* A punishment that is extreme or inappropriate for a child's age or ability to understand. Examples include corporal punishment that results in injury, locking a child in a closet, forcing a child to toilet train at six months, and sitting a child in a corner for hours at a time.
  e. *Emotional neglect:* Failure by a parent to be emotionally available to take an interest in, talk to, hold, or hug a child.
  f. *Psychological abuse:* Any form of recurring communication that causes extreme and unnecessary mental suffering. Examples include name-calling or belittling, blocking a child's efforts to accept him- or herself, and threats of abandonment.

People with anxiety who have also experienced any of the above forms of abuse often find that the habit patterns and beliefs that developed as a result of the abuse contributed to the development of their problem and also hinder recovery.

- Anxious parental role model: When a parent suffers from severe anxiety, has fearful beliefs, or has many of the personality traits listed above, a child can develop many of those beliefs and traits as a result of modeling after the parent.
- Critical parent or family member: Excessive criticism often comes from a perfectionistic parent with unrealistic expectations. A parent like this often demands adult behavior and capabilities beyond the child's ability. Sometimes excessive criticism or teasing can come from a jealous brother or sister. The result for the child is often a poor self-image and the belief in his or her inadequacy.
- Rigid family rules: Growing up in an environment characterized by many rigid rules can set up a pattern of black-and-white thinking that continues into adulthood. Usually the rigid rules in such an environment are imposed by parents, older brothers or sisters, or other family members. A child in a family where there is chaos due to illness, alcoholism, abuse, or some similar factor may develop rigid rules in order to create a sense of security amid the chaos or may need them simply to survive.

  Rigid rules can also come from living with parents who were raised in harsh circumstances. The rigid rules that often helped the parents survive harsh circumstances become stumbling blocks for their children.
- Rigid belief system: A person with rigid thinking often has parents who had a rigid set of values and beliefs. These values and beliefs may have been based on the cultural background or religious affiliations of the parents and expressed in a black-and-white fashion. Parents with a rigid belief system also tend to have rigid rules like those discussed above. Their rigid belief system can become a model for rigid thinking that is passed on to the child.
- Emphasis on appearances or "proper" behavior: A rigid belief system can create a perfectionistic model of a "proper" person and a demand for the child to always act properly. A rigid belief system can also generate a feeling that the family either is or should be better than others. Failure to live up to this ideal image of a perfect person or meet the family's rigid standards can cause the child to feel inadequate and worthless.

- Overprotective parent: An overprotective parent usually attempts to shield the child from life's adversities in the mistaken belief that the child is fragile. Sometimes overprotection is the result of the parent's need to have someone who is dependent. Unfortunately, even when done with the best of intentions, overprotection tends to encourage the belief that taking risks is dangerous and should be avoided. It also keeps the child from learning how to handle adversity and learning that taking risks is a natural part of life.

- Suppression or denial of feelings: A child can be taught to suppress feelings directly by being told things such as, "Don't cry"; "You shouldn't feel that way"; or "Don't be angry with me." A child can also be taught indirectly by watching parents who suppress and deny feelings. Another way to learn that feelings are not important is to have them discounted. This can be done by ignoring a child when feelings are expressed, telling the child the feelings being expressed are not important, or denying the feelings by saying something like, "You're not really angry." When the expression of feelings triggers violence or abuse in others, a child may need to suppress feelings in order to survive.

- Lack of information about bodies and emotions: Many children grow up in families where there is little information about how bodies, emotions, and thoughts are interconnected. This often plays a major role in developing unrealistic expectations about what a person should be able to do or how a person should react to situations.

- Performance-related approval: It is appropriate for a parent to express pleasure when a child accomplishes something difficult and displeasure when a child misbehaves. A child also needs to be shown love and approval just for being part of the family. Some children receive approval only when something is accomplished, such as household chores, high grades in school, or the development of a talent such as music or sports. This type of strict performance-related approval occurs when a parent fails to distinguish between the child's actions and the child's value as a person. Pleasing behaviors are labeled good. Displeasing behaviors are labeled bad.

This is a common experience for people both with and without anxiety-related problems. Strict performance-related approval encourages the mistaken belief that a person has value only when doing something valuable. The negative impact of this experience is increased when there is a perfectionistic parent who not only requires the child to perform in order to be loved, but also demands a level of competence beyond the child's ability.

- Anxiety about separation or loss: A child can experience significant anxiety when separated from a parent for a prolonged time. This is especially true when the child doesn't understand the reason for the separation. Common reasons for such parental absence are extensive travel for business, a prolonged hospitalization, divorce, or death. A parent who is physically present but ignores a child can also cause separation anxiety and a feeling of abandonment.
- A reversal of parent–child roles: When a parent is sick, busy, or absent, a child sometimes assumes the role of a parent in some way. This can range from managing the house to just trying to keep things calm so the parent won't become angry, abusive, or distressed. A child who is required to assume adult responsibilities for which he or she is not ready often needs to develop a rigid set of rules in order to survive. This rigid approach to life is usually carried into adulthood, contributing to black-and-white thinking, the suppression of feelings, the need to be in control, and high expectations of self.
- A family secret: Sometimes a lot of a family's energy is used to keep a family secret hidden. This secret can be something simple or involved such as a premarital pregnancy, alcoholism, legal wrongdoing by a family member, or a family member in a mental institution. This type of family behavior generates the mistaken belief that certain types of feelings are wrong and must be suppressed or hidden from others. Family secrets can also contribute to the creation of an excessive need for approval.

Before going on, take a moment to look at the personality traits you checked in the previous section, and the childhood experiences you checked in this one. You will find that the development of the traits you checked was essential for your survival during childhood. Unfortunately, traits that can help a person during a difficult childhood often interfere with the ability to function as an adult.

The good news is that people have a tremendous capacity to learn and adapt to new situations. You can learn to modify any traits that are contributing to your anxiety-related problems. In fact, you have already taken the first step by gaining some insight into what these traits are and how they developed. Much more will be said about this in the lessons that follow.

What Causes These Conditions to Develop?

Since it is common for a person with a specific type of anxiety-related problem to also have some of the elements of one or more of the other types, it is recommended that you read through this entire section at least once. You may also wish to refer to Appendix 1 for a complete description of the six anxiety-related disorders. Make a note of any areas that describe your background or condition.

Panic Disorder

Panic disorder usually results from a combination of factors. One thing that everyone with panic disorder has in common is an initial panic attack that *seems* to occur for no apparent reason. Take, for example, Brian, who experienced his first panic attack while he was at work. One day he was going through his normal routine when, suddenly, his heart started to pound and he found it difficult to breathe. The sensations lasted only ten minutes but left him shaky and frightened for the rest of the day. Like most people, Brian attributed the physical symptoms to some physical illness and left work to seek a diagnosis from a physician. At the doctor's, Brian was told that he was fine and that the symptoms were just "nerves."

Before going on with Brian's story, let's look at five factors that can cause this initial panic attack; for any particular person, only one may be present, or several may combine to produce the initial panic attacks.

- *Inherited reactive body:* People with panic disorder often have highly reactive bodies that respond more intensely to environmental stimuli such as noise, odors, medications, and temperature variations. This is an inherited trait like eye or hair color. For example, if you give people like this a glass of water with a bitter substance in it, they would be able to discern its taste in smaller quantities than the average person.

  Like all human traits, this type of sensitivity has a positive and negative side. On the positive side, people with this type of body tend to be more aware of their surroundings because more information is coming into the brain. They also are often more intuitive and sensitive to the reactions of others. In fact, this trait is often what others like best about them. It often helps people with this characteristic listen and empathize better as well as notice when something is wrong in another person. People with a less sensitive body often miss the subtle, nonverbal messages of others. People with reactive bodies are also often more emotionally reactive in both a positive and negative way. They can be the life of the party as well as more visibly upset than others when something bad happens.

  A simple way to understand the negative side of this biological trait is to imagine a house where the electrical wiring is inadequate. The electrical system works fine as long as it is not overburdened. When too many electrical appliances operate at the same time, however, the system is overloaded and circuit breakers begin to trip. In a similar manner, it is easier for a person with a reactive body to experience an exaggerated fight or flight response when overburdened with mental, physical, or emotional stress.

  Once panic disorder develops, a person with a sensitive body finds his or her body becoming even more reactive. Another factor to keep in mind is that a person with a body that is not overly sensitive often finds that it becomes overly reactive after a period of prolonged anxiety. It is similar to the way in which a person is more emotionally reactive when sick or tired. The good news is that once a person learns how to manage and reduce the symptoms of anxiety, this reactivity will slowly return to the level it was prior to the development of panic disorder.

- *Stress:* When recalling the time just before the first panic attack occurred, people usually recall a number of factors that were producing a high level of physical or mental stress. Unfortunately, prior to the onset of panic disorder people are often out of touch with their bodies. After the initial panic attack they become overly focused on their bodies. Because they are not aware of how stressed out they are, they continue to do all the things they usually do and often expect to be as effective as they usually are. Much more will be said about this in Lesson 3, on stress management. The result is that their first panic attack really was just a stress response—what Brian's doctor meant when he said his first attack was just "nerves." Unfortunately, Brian didn't really understand what this meant, and the doctor didn't explain it to him or give him any guidelines on how to manage his stress more effectively.

- *Hyperventilation:* Hyperventilation (breathing more rapidly or deeply than is necessary) can produce many of the symptoms characteristic of anxiety and offers a second possible explanation for the initial symptoms that trigger panic disorder. The first major panic attack for many people was actually a hyperventilation episode. For others, like Brian, hyperventilation accompanies most panic attacks and accounts for many of the distressing symptoms experienced. It is quite probable that many people have both the biological sensitivity described above and the tendency to hyperventilate. In some people the tendency to hyperventilate may itself have a genetic component. A more detailed description of the actual mechanics of hyperventilation is given in the next lesson.

- *Medical conditions:* The initial panic attacks that some people experience are triggered by a medical condition. As was mentioned earlier in this lesson, numerous medical conditions and drugs can produce one or more of the symptoms commonly associated with anxiety. Andrea is a good example of this. She had a condition called mitral valve prolapse (MVP). This is a minor defect in the heart valve, and has been associated with panic disorder and agoraphobia. MVP is found in 5 to 15 percent of the population. Normally, no medical treatment is required, and half the people with this condition experience no symptoms. Of the 50 percent who do notice symptoms, the main one is palpitations either in the form of premature contractions of the heart or rapid heartbeat. Other symptoms are breathlessness and vague chest pains. Andrea would experience occasional rapid heartbeat and discomfort in her chest. She had all the HAP traits and soon found herself constantly aware of her heart and breathing and becoming alarmed whenever her heart "did something funny." Fear of the symptoms, which were harmless but misunderstood, soon led her to become so anxious that she began to experience panic attacks   .

Illnesses that are life threatening or that produce unpleasant symptoms can also cause so much anxiety that they begin to trigger panic attacks. For example, one source reports that about 14 percent of cardiac patients suffer from panic disorder. Cardiac patients who have several of the HAP traits described earlier can, like the person with MVP, become so overly focused on their body that they begin to become frightened by normal bodily reactions and trigger the fight or flight response. The more alarmed they become, the stronger the response.

• *Adverse medication or drug reaction:* Many medications and recreational drugs can cause symptoms characteristic of a panic attack. In one case, Kumar, a client of mine suffering from hypothyroidism—a condition where the thyroid does not produce sufficient thyroid hormones—experienced such anxiety. During Kumar's initial treatment, his prescription of replacement synthetic thyroxine was higher than needed, causing many anxiety symptoms. Being an extreme perfectionist with very black-and-white thinking, Kumar's drug-induced symptoms soon triggered internalizing and negative anticipation, which led to the development of the anxiety/panic cycle.

Frank presents another example. While experimenting with cocaine, his heart started pounding so hard it frightened him. After the experience, he became obsessed with the fear that he might have damaged his heart. As he focused more and more on anything that might be abnormal, he became so anxious that he began to trigger panic attacks.

It is important to note that not everyone who has a panic attack like Brian's will develop panic disorder. One of the keys to the development of this problem is how you *think* about your symptoms. As with most people, Brian's initial panic attack was the result of several things interacting. First, he had three of the above factors: a reactive body, stress, and hyperventilation. When Brian recalled the time just before his initial panic attack at work, he explained that he had been going to school full time and working at a tiring job, had recently broken up with his fiancée, and had recently experienced the death of his father. His first panic attack had actually simply been a stress reaction. Brian didn't understand this, however; his beliefs about himself told him that he should be strong and able to continue to do all the things he was doing. He didn't understand that his initial symptoms were simply a very strong message that he was doing too much. Because of this, when his doctor said his symptoms were simply due to "nerves," Brian began to think that this diagnosis was impossible and that there must be something terribly wrong with him that the doctor had missed.

In addition to the above factors, Brian had a high need to be in control of himself, to appear normal, and to avoid anything that might cause others to disapprove of him. This, coupled with his lack of awareness of how stressed out he really was, caused him to worry that the mysterious and frightening symptoms would recur and again produce that terrible sense of being out of control. This fear caused Brian to become very aware of internal sensations such as his heartbeat and rate of breathing. This increased awareness of the body is called internalization or body scanning. As Brian became more aware of his body, he began to imagine what might happen if the frightening sensations were to occur in various situations, a type of worry called negative anticipation or what-if thinking. The combination of not understanding what had happened, internalization, and negative anticipation caused the development of an anxiety/panic cycle, which can be diagrammed as follows:

A normal reaction in the body ➤ The reaction is noticed, causing ➤ The fear triggers the fight
                                                              fear   or flight response
                                                                                                        ↓
                               The increased fear produces a ➤ The increased reaction in
                               stronger fight or fight response ◄— the body produces more fear

Thinking in terms of Brian's brain circuitry, we could say that the sensations associated with Brian's first panic attack—rapid heartbeat, muscle tension, rapid breathing, light-headedness, and so on—had become stored in his amygdala as signs of danger. Thus, whenever he experienced these symptoms—even when they were normal and at a very low level of intensity—they would trigger the fight or flight response, and his attention would immediately be drawn to them. For example, when Brian walked up a flight of stairs shortly after the initial episode of frightening symptoms, he immediately noticed his increased heartbeat and increased rate of breathing. Instead of recognizing these as normal reactions to walking up stairs, the fear response caused him to think, "Oh my gosh, here they (the frightening symptoms) come again!" This triggered the fight or flight response and exacerbated the physical reactions he was noticing. This series of reactions, in turn, increased his fear, producing an even stronger fight or flight response. Within seconds Brian had talked himself into a self-generated panic attack.

As more and more normal situations were associated with danger, Brian began experiencing these self-generated panic attacks regularly and was now suffering from panic disorder. Brian eventually developed agoraphobia and often avoided situations where he feared a panic attack might occur. As Brian's world grew smaller, his tendency to use rigid thinking, need for control, and need for approval became more exaggerated. He was caught in a series of vicious circles (see diagram on the following page).

The rate at which the anxiety/panic cycle develops seems to depend upon what is causing the initial unpleasant symptoms, the intensity of the symptoms, how many of the high-anxiety personality traits a person has, and how exaggerated the traits are. Like many others, Brian, Andrea, and Kumar can remember vividly their first major panic attack and developed panic disorder shortly after it occurred. For others, the anxiety/panic cycle develops over months or years. Sometimes it seems to come and go.

The Development of Panic Disorder

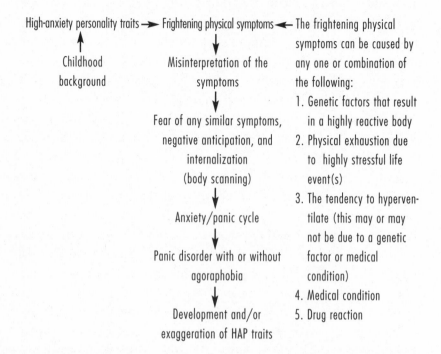

High-anxiety personality traits → Frightening physical symptoms ← The frightening physical

↑ symptoms can be caused by

Childhood   Misinterpretation of the   any one or combination of

background   symptoms   the following:

↓   1. Genetic factors that result

Fear of any similar symptoms,   in a highly reactive body

negative anticipation, and   2. Physical exhaustion due

internalization   to highly stressful life

(body scanning)   event(s)

↓   3. The tendency to hyperven-

Anxiety/panic cycle   tilate (this may or may

↓   not be due to a genetic

Panic disorder with or without   factor or medical

agoraphobia   condition)

↓   4. Medical condition

Development and/or   5. Drug reaction

exaggeration of HAP traits

The tendency for panic disorder symptoms to increase and decrease over time usually occurs in the following manner. Mavis, a successful businesswoman with a very reactive body, had many anxiety symptoms during a period of high stress at work. The symptoms worried her, and she restricted her activities for a while. While Mavis didn't realize it, restricting her activities gave her body a rest. As a result, her body ceased to overreact to normal stimuli. Since the disturbing symptoms were no longer present, she gradually resumed normal activities. Eventually, she again encountered a period of high stress at work. Mavis's reactive body responded with anxiety symptoms that were more severe than the first time, which lead to the development of the anxiety/panic cycle and panic disorder.

From the above it should now be clear that what separates those who do develop the anxiety/panic cycle from those who do not is the way they think about their symptoms. While having a reactive body, a tendency to hyperventilate, a medical condition, or an adverse drug reaction can contribute to the development of an anxiety/panic cycle, the important factor is the way a person thinks about his or her anxiety symptoms. People with some or many of the personality traits described earlier are more likely to overreact to the initial symptoms, begin to watch their body carefully, and worry about what the symptoms mean and what might happen if they cannot be controlled. In essence, anxiety becomes a sort of "boogeyman" that follows them around. They flee from any indication that this boogeyman is coming. Unfortunately, most of the symptoms they flee from are normal. They just don't understand this important point.

Obsessive-Compulsive Disorder (OCD)

Obsessive-compulsive disorder is now understood to be a brain disorder. It is normal to check things. In the morning we all check various things such as our clothes or the door to see if it is locked before we leave. We all have had a thought, melody, or commercial jingle recur in our mind from time to time. These normal responses, however, can become exaggerated and out of control due to faulty circuitry in the brain.

Currently, most experts believe that the problem lies with a malfunction in the part of the brain that acts as a processing center or filtering station for the very complicated messages generated by the front part of the brain where thinking, planning, and understanding occur. Normally, when you decide to do something or are thinking about something, intruding movements and misdirected feelings are filtered out automatically so you can do what you want rapidly and efficiently. Thinking in terms of a car's transmission, there is a quick, smooth shifting of gears. With OCD, though, it seems that these parts of the brain become overactive, much like a car stuck in a ditch. You spin your wheels faster and faster but can't get out of the ditch.

Post-Traumatic Stress Disorder (PTSD)

Of all the anxiety-related problems, post-traumatic stress disorder is the easiest to understand. Anyone who experiences severe trauma will experience some of the symptoms described earlier. The severity of the PTSD and number of symptoms one experiences varies depending upon your background, your personality, and the nature of the trauma. While some will experience more and some fewer symptoms, it makes no difference how strong or capable you think you are: If you are traumatized, you will experience at least some symptoms. Keep in mind that you do not have to experience the trauma directly to experience PTSD symptoms. Witnessing a trauma as well as working or living with someone who has been traumatized can also trigger symptoms.

Juliene was in a severe automobile accident where she was broadsided at an intersection and suffered severe injuries. During the early part of her recovery, she experienced frequent flashbacks where images of the accident would suddenly intrude into her thoughts without warning. Such flashbacks are common when a person experiences trauma. It is as if the mind is unable to absorb all of the events of the trauma at once, so it takes little snapshots of the incident until it has been completely digested.

When Juliene started driving again after her accident, she found that she was very nervous. The sights and sounds of driving had been associated with danger. Because she did not understand that this was a normal reaction, she began telling herself that something must be wrong with her. This triggered increased anxiety. Without realizing it, her negative thoughts and worry about being anxious set up an anxiety/panic cycle that was soon triggered by many different driving-related situations and thoughts.

Specific Phobias

Specific phobias are similarly straightforward. Something occurs that causes an association of a thing or situation with danger in the amygdala. This triggers an unconscious and automatic fear response whenever this thing or situation is encountered.

Mai was traveling in a car when she encountered a locust storm, in which thousands of locusts struck her windshield; this triggered a fear of crickets, grasshoppers, and similar insects. Jason was flying when his plane was struck by lightning; this triggered intense anxiety when he next planned to take a trip that involved flying. When Stamie was young, her brother frequently teased her that there were piranhas in the swimming pool, which would eat her toes. This triggered a fear of water. Bradley was shoved in a laundry chute and covered with laundry by his friends when he was young. This resulted in claustrophobia, the fear of narrow or closed spaces.

Sometimes the initial events cannot be recalled because they occurred when a person was young. The hippocampus plays a key role in creating and storing memories. However, the hippocampus matures slowly. That is why few people have factual memories from before the age of three. In contrast, the amygdala begins to record danger fairly early. It is possible for an unpleasant or fearful experience with a thing or situation to be stored in the amygdala before any conscious memory of the event was recorded. For example, a person could have been bitten by a dog at the age of two. This person could have the fear association stored in the amygdala and become anxious when around dogs while having no memory of being bitten.

Social Phobia

The development of social phobia is usually the result of an interaction between inherited biological traits and early-childhood experiences. It is well established that some traits are present at birth. For example, experiments with monkeys have shown that one biological trait present at birth is the tendency to be shy or bold. At the same time, traits that are present at birth can be changed by experience. Shy monkeys that are paired with nurturing mothers end up doing well and can even become the leaders of their group. If they are taken away from the nurturing mother and raised by one less nurturing, though, they continue to be shy and have difficulty interacting with their peers.

A shy child will often develop social phobia when raised in isolation or by an overly critical or cruel caregiver. Parwindar was a shy only child raised by a single mother suffering from severe depression. She spent most of her childhood playing by herself in the house while her mother lay in bed in another room. Her only experience with other children was at school. Because she had been isolated and was shy by nature, she tended to not interact much with children at school. As her peers developed social skills and comfort with normal social interactions, she fell further and further behind socially. Because there was no one to encourage her, she also felt very inadequate as a person. As an adult, she experienced severe social phobia.

Kao was a shy child raised in an immigrant family. Because he had difficulty with the language and was awkward, other children would tease him. As a result, he stayed by himself when he was at school. In addition, he had a very critical mother. Over time, the teasing and constant criticism Kao faced led to poor self-image and a lack of social skills, which eventually grew into full-blown social phobia.

Social phobia can also be the result of simple modeling. Karynn was a shy child raised by a mother who was kind and loving, but who had social phobia. As an adult, Karynn also had social phobia. In session, she often mentioned that she was just like her mother.

In addition to the generalized social phobia described above, social phobias can also be limited to specific situations such as speaking before groups or eating in public. Marcus had severe presentation anxiety, for example, which began when he was embarrassed while giving a book report in the seventh grade. Up to that point he had found it easy to talk in front of the class. After this event, however, he found getting up in front of people terrifying. Middle school and high school are times when people are often very insecure about themselves and relationships. Because of this, it is common for specific social phobias to develop at these times.

Generalized Anxiety Disorder (GAD)

At this time generalized anxiety disorder is the most poorly researched of the various anxiety-related problems. It is thought to be the result of a combination of inherited biological traits and childhood experiences. Everyone I have worked with who has GAD was raised in a family where the same-sex parent was a worrier. The child learns to worry from the parent. If attention, whether positive or negative, is given to the worry, the child often becomes more of a worrier than the parent. It is also possible that there is an inherited predisposition to be anxious and worry.

Recommended Activities for Lesson 1

How to Get the Most Out of This Section

Each lesson in this book concludes with a set of Recommended Activities. Each activity is something many people have found valuable in overcoming anxiety-related problems. You may find that some of the activities are already a part of your normal behavior and feel very natural to you. Others may seem awkward, uncomfortable, or difficult. This is to be expected, since this program is designed to meet the needs of many people and you are unique with your own personal needs and abilities. Spend less time with activities you find easy and more time with those that seem difficult.

The easy activities probably involve skills you have already practiced. The difficult activities probably involve skills you have not developed and are more important for you. If a particular activity causes undue stress or anxiety, it means you are not ready for it. Skip it and work on it again after a few weeks.

You do not have to apply every idea in this book or do every activity immediately. The point of this program is to learn how to live a comfortable and enjoyable life and do things in a manner that is right for you. People who are successful with this program frequently do not do everything suggested. Still, they usually find they have done *most* of the recommended activities, even though many are not done until long after the last lesson has been read. That is fine. Do things at your own rate.

People who are working through this program will often stop doing the exercises as soon as they start to feel better. This is a mistake. Continue working through the program until you feel that you have mastered all the areas it covers. This will ensure that you master all the skills needed to prevent the return of your symptoms.

No one can say exactly how long it will take for you to overcome your anxiety-related problems. It depends on how severe your symptoms are, how long you have experienced them, and how hard you work on the program. If you have a strong commitment to use the program as it is designed, do the reading, and apply as many of the suggestions to your life as is possible (even though you may think they are silly or may not understand why they are suggested), it is very likely you will succeed.

Rule Out Possible Medical Problems

This lesson stated that the first step in overcoming anxiety-related problems is to rule out all possible medical causes. If you have not had a complete physical examination and discussed your symptoms with a physician recently, make an appointment this week to do so. Be sure to provide your physician with a complete medical history and discuss your diet as well as any medications you are taking. If you find it difficult to talk to a physician, write down the information you believe is important along with the questions you want to have answered. Be sure to take two copies of your notes and questions with you when you go to your appointment. This allows both you and your physician to look at your observations and concerns while you go over them.

If you have been diagnosed with a specific anxiety disorder, it is often a good idea to avoid mentioning this to your physician. I've worked with many clients with medical problems that were overlooked because all of their symptoms were being attributed to anxiety and worry. When these clients went to a new physician and simply described their symptoms, the symptoms were investigated more carefully and the medical problems were then found.

Make a List of Personality Traits and Childhood Experiences That Play a Role in Your Anxiety

Take time to review the sections that describe personality traits and childhood experiences that can contribute to anxiety-related problems. For each one you identify, list ways in which it contributes to your anxiety. When you're done, put this list in a safe place so you can review it as you work through the lessons. When a lesson has a section that addresses an item on your list, spend extra time with that section.

Create a Simple Explanation

After you have read the chapter two or three times, create a short summary of what caused your anxiety-related problem. Write this simplified explanation on a card and read it once a day until you have it memorized. While this in and of itself will not reduce your symptoms, it is a necessary first step. Having a clear understanding of what caused your symptoms takes the mystery out of your condition and helps you shift your focus from "Why is this happening to me?" to "What do I need to do?" Here are several examples.

Brian's Card: A Simple Explanation of Panic Disorder

I underwent physical discomfort due to my sensitive body and the stress I was experiencing. Because I didn't identify the source of my anxiety symptoms accurately at that time, I began watching my body to take note of any sensation that resembled those that originally frightened me. I became trapped in the anxiety/panic cycle. As I work through these lessons, I will learn how to quiet these responses.

Stewart's Card: A Simple Explanation of OCD

The part of my brain that acts as a processing center or filtering station for the very complicated messages generated by the front part of my brain sometimes gets stuck. Instead of filtering out misdirected feelings or thoughts, it starts to feed the same one back to me over and over again. They are like a tic. While they feel real, they are *not* based on reality, but on a biochemical malfunction.

Juliene's Card: A Simple Explanation of PTSD Due to an Accident

I had a terrifying accident. My mind could not process the entire experience all at once. So it took little snapshots of it in order to manage the trauma. I also developed unconscious associations between driving and danger. This unconscious association is what triggers anxiety whenever I approach an intersection or see a car coming in my direction. I maintained and strengthened this association by telling myself I'm crazy and beating myself up whenever I noticed any anxiety symptom. These symptoms are *normal* and will lessen as time goes by and I work through these lessons.

Mai's Card: A Simple Explanation of Specific Phobia

I had a fearful experience when driving through a locust storm. My brain now associates crickets and grasshoppers with danger and triggers anxiety whenever I see one or think about them. This is an unconscious response stored in my amygdala. I can learn to quiet this response by working through this program.

Kao's Card: A Simple Explanation of Social Phobia

I was very shy as a child and didn't understand many things about the new country I had come to live in. Because I kept to myself, I never learned the social skills that most people acquire while growing up. At school I was teased because I was awkward, and at home I was told that I was useless and couldn't do anything right. Because of this, I developed a poor self-image and often put myself and my abilities down. I became afraid of doing anything that might cause others to tease or criticize me. This combination of a poor self-image, negative self-talk, lack of social skills, and anxiety associated with displeasing others causes me to become anxious when I'm around people. I can change these habitual ways of thinking and acting over time by working through this program.

Marquita's Card: A Simple Explanation of Generalized Anxiety Disorder

My mother was a world-class worrier. She regularly warned me about all of the dangers I would face whenever I left home. She also openly worried about any fearful story that was in the news. As I watched her, I began to copy her behaviors. Without realizing it, I was also able to get attention from her when I was concerned about something. The habit of worrying and exaggerating potential threats is now a deeply ingrained habit pattern. I can learn new positive habits that will eventually replace the old negative ones.

Consider Using Supplemental Materials

These lessons can be used by themselves, but you may find supplemental materials helpful. This is especially true if you find it difficult to understand the material or stick with written lessons. Helpful materials are described in detail at the end of the book. You can also find them at www.rpeurifoy.com.

Developing a Relaxation Response

The triggering of deep muscle relaxation through a set method is called a relaxation response. This week, practice developing a relaxation response at least once a day. If you already know how to use meditation, self-hypnosis, biofeedback, or some other method of developing a state of deep relaxation, use it. If not, use one of the methods described in Appendix 2. It usually takes several weeks of regular practice to become skilled at producing a relaxation response, so be patient. It is well worth your time and effort. Many people find that professionally produced audio programs such as those described at the back of the book are very useful when learning how to develop a relaxation response.

Consider Psychotherapy

While many people have used the program in this book to overcome anxiety-related problems without the help of a psychotherapist, others have found it best to use it in conjunction with professional psychotherapy. If you are experiencing extreme difficulty coping with life, find a therapist experienced in working with anxiety-related problems. Guidelines on how to select a therapist are given in Appendix 3.

Be Good to Yourself and Reduce Unnecessary Stress

In the coming weeks you will learn how to relax and calm yourself when you start to become anxious. You will also learn more effective ways to deal with people and situations you encounter. Until you have learned these skills, avoid unnecessary stress. Continue to work and to do what is necessary in your daily routine, but eliminate as many unnecessary activities that produce excessive stress as is possible.

Experiencing severe anxiety over a prolonged period of time is as debilitating as experiencing a severe case of the flu. That is why you are being asked to take a few weeks to allow your body to rebuild its strength and repair itself. Later you will work on problem behaviors, such as avoidance patterns or rituals, that you developed as a result of your anxiety. But first things first. Give your body time to heal while you work on mastering the skills in the early lessons.

Find a Study Partner

If possible, find a friend or relative who will be a study partner and read and work through this book with you. This does not need to be a person with anxiety-related problems, but it does need to be someone you are comfortable with and trust. Discussing the lessons with a study partner will deepen your understanding of the material. This partner will also be able to see things you might otherwise miss and point out times when you forget to use the skills you are learning.

This is a long lesson. Take your time with it. The Recommended Activities in this lesson prepare you for the work in the lessons that follow. It is important to do them before continuing on to the next lesson.

LESSON 2

Reducing the Symptoms of Anxiety

T he four skills for reducing the symptoms of anxiety described in this lesson are an important first step for each of the six types of anxiety-related problems discussed in Lesson 1. They take time to develop. So plan for only modest results at first. Once these skills are mastered and you combine them with the ideas and skills presented in the following lessons, they become a powerful force for managing stress and anxiety.

Four Common Roadblocks

You probably already use some if not all of the skills described in this lesson. However, it is likely that you have also found they do not always work well. The four main roadblocks that prevent people from using these skills effectively are described below, along with suggestions for overcoming them:

- *Inappropriate use:* Skills for reducing anxiety often fail because they are used inappropriately. This roadblock can be overcome by studying the explanations provided in this lesson for how and why each skill works and following the suggestions that are made.
- *Overreliance on one or two skills:* If you only have one or two methods for reducing the symptoms of stress and anxiety,

inevitably there comes a time when these methods do not work very well. Overcoming this roadblock requires the use of several different skills to cope with stress and anxiety. Each skill reinforces the others, making them all more effective.

- *Failure to use at the first signs of distress:* If you treat a wound as soon as it occurs, it usually heals without any problems. If you do not attend to it and allow it to become infected, it causes much discomfort and requires more extensive treatment to heal. The same principle applies to the skills described in this lesson. They work best when used at the first signs of stress and anxiety. When you ignore your body, behavior, and thoughts until you are experiencing severe stress or anxiety, the approaches work poorly. The key to overcoming this roadblock is to use these skills when you first notice yourself becoming anxious.

- *Overreliance on just reducing the symptoms of anxiety:* It is not enough to work only at relieving the symptoms of anxiety. You also need to learn how to eliminate the mistaken beliefs and habitual thinking patterns that cause them. The skills presented in this part of the program are, in a sense, a kind of Band-Aid designed to help you feel more comfortable and regain some control over your body. They are much like medications used to relieve the pain of a broken leg. While this is important, it is also essential to set the leg, put it in a cast, and learn how to avoid injuring it in the future. This is not meant to minimize the importance of the skills you are developing this week. They are an essential part of overcoming severe anxiety. In fact, as you progress through the program and become better able to minimize the sources of stress and anxiety you have control over, the skills described in this lesson become even more effective.

Four Basic Skills for Reducing the Symptoms of Anxiety

Take your time as you develop the four skills presented in this section. Plan to return to this lesson and work with these skills many times as you work through the following lessons. It takes time to master them.

Cue-Controlled Relaxation

At the turn of the twentieth century, a Russian scientist named I. P. Pavlov conducted a classic experiment. He presented a neutral stimulus to hungry dogs, such as ringing a bell, then followed it by giving them food. The food caused the dogs to salivate. With repetition, the neutral stimulus (the ringing bell) would trigger salivation. When an automatic, unconscious response is triggered by a stimulus as a result of this type of conditioning, it is called a conditioned response.

Many human reactions and behaviors are a type of conditioned response learning. Consider the saying, *Mom's cooking tastes best*. Mom could be a terrible cook and her children would be none the wiser, because they have been conditioned to her cooking. This is why food in foreign countries often tastes "funny." The same is true with clothing fashions. Pictures of clothes worn ten years ago look funny because we have been slowly reconditioning ourselves to the fashions of today.

When a person experiences high anxiety, the various sensations and events present during the time that the person is anxious tend to become conditioned response stimuli. Lesson 1 discussed the important role that the amygdala plays in the development of these types of responses. For example, if a person has panic attacks while driving, the sights and sounds that occur while experiencing the panic attacks become associated with danger. The result is that simply being in a car may trigger mild anxiety symptoms.

The same is true for the other types of anxiety-related problems. The anxiety symptoms associated with obsessions or compulsions become automatic conditioned responses that are further ingrained each time an obsessive thought occurs or a ritual is performed. Likewise, a person with GAD associates worries with real danger more and more over time.

Anxiety generated by this form of conditioned response learning plays an important role in maintaining anxiety-related problems. Even though you may consciously understand the dynamics that caused the original symptoms and are confident that there is no danger, you will still continue to experience anxiety generated by conditioned response learning. This type of conditioned response learning can be reversed through a process called desensitization (explained in detail later in the program). Cue-controlled relaxation can also help to reduce anxiety generated by conditioning.

Cue-controlled relaxation refers to relaxation triggered by a cue in a conditioned response manner just as Pavlov's dogs were conditioned to salivate to a bell ringing. The actual cue can be anything. Commonly used cues include a word such as "relax," an imaginary scene, or a simple physical cue like putting your thumb and finger together.

The first step in developing cue-controlled relaxation is to learn a method that enables you to produce a relaxation response such as those described in Appendix 2. The second step is to decide on a cue and begin associating it with the relaxation response you are practicing. For example, you might place your thumb and two fingers together while practicing your relaxation response exercise. With time, the act of placing your thumb and fingers together would act as a cue or trigger for the relaxation response. This type of cue is often referred to as a relaxation response anchor because the response is anchored to it.

At first, the anxiety triggered by conditioned response learning will be much stronger than the relaxation generated by your relaxation response training. Two things cause this. First, as Lesson 1 discussed, we are designed to overreact to danger. It is better to mistake something neutral as dangerous than to be harmed. Second, you have been unconsciously reinforcing the conditioned response anxiety you experience for a long time. Even with practice, your cue-controlled relaxation will, by itself, probably not eliminate all of your anxiety. With practice, however, it will reduce it. When used in combination with the other skills in this and following lessons, cue-controlled relaxation will become an even more effective tool for reducing anxiety.

Diaphragmatic Breathing

Hyper (too much) *ventilation* (air movement) is simply over-breathing. It occurs when a person breathes more rapidly, more deeply, or both than is needed to meet the body's demands for oxygen and removal of carbon dioxide. Breathing in this fashion causes the level of carbon dioxide to drop in the bloodstream. Forceful hyperventilation can reduce the carbon dioxide level in the blood by 50 percent in as little as thirty seconds. Most people would think this is good since they were taught in school that carbon dioxide is a waste product. However, carbon dioxide is very important in maintaining a proper acid–base or pH level in the blood and is the chemical used by the body to regulate breathing.

Hyperventilation raises the pH level in the nerve cells, making them more excitable, and it also tends to activate the fight or flight response. This sets off a chain reaction of activity in the body that can produce any of the following symptoms:

- Heart palpitations, tachycardia (racing heart), heartburn, or chest pain.
- Numbness or tingling of the mouth, hands, or feet.
- Dizziness, faintness, light-headedness, poor concentration, blurred vision, or a sense of separateness from the body (depersonalization).
- Shortness of breath, apparent asthma, or a choking sensation.
- Difficulty swallowing, lump in the throat, stomach pain, or nausea.
- Tension, muscle pains, shaking, or muscle spasms.
- Sweating, anxiety, fatigue, or weakness.

Most of the above symptoms can develop in less than a minute. While they can be uncomfortable, none causes lasting harm. Most people who hyperventilate do not realize they are hyperventilating. Instead of reporting a problem with hyperventilation, they complain of various specific or vague symptoms from the above list. Hyperventilation can occur with any of the following:

- When at rest, you breathe with your upper chest instead of with your diaphragm.
- When you breathe through your mouth either from habit or because of physical or medical problems.
- When you sigh or yawn because you have been holding your breath.

Let's look at each of the above individually. Humans have two basic breathing patterns. In thoracic or upper-chest breathing, the chest lifts upward and outward, and breathing tends to be shallow and rapid. In diaphragmatic breathing, the inhalation tends to be deeper and slower. When the lower lungs fill with air, they push down on the diaphragm and cause the abdominal region to protrude, making the stomach appear to be expanding and contracting with each breath.

Upper-chest and diaphragmatic breathing have their own purposes and functions in everyday life. During strenuous exercise, your body uses upper-chest breathing to provide the large amounts of oxygen needed. In contrast, relaxed diaphragmatic breathing is your body's normal breathing pattern when physical activity and the corresponding need for oxygen are low. A healthy breathing pattern during moderate, everyday activities usually involves movement in both the upper chest and diaphragm.

Many people with anxiety-related problems use upper-chest breathing as their primary breathing pattern. Many others find they quickly convert to upper-chest breathing whenever they become anxious. The reason for this is unknown. It is known, however, that upper-chest breathing is a normal but usually brief response to any threatening or anxiety-provoking situation. It is triggered by the fight or flight response and is your body's way of preparing for the strenuous activity of fighting or running away from danger. One possible explanation for habitual upper-chest breathing is that a person who continually feels threatened by normal, everyday situations is simply triggering this breathing pattern via the activation of the fight or flight response.

Another possible explanation involves our culture's obsession with thin bodies and flat stomachs. During adolescence, when there is much concern about physical appearance, many people develop the unconscious habit of constantly tensing their abdominal muscles in order to meet this ideal image. Since it is impossible to use diaphragmatic breathing when the abdominal muscles are tensed, the body begins to use upper-chest breathing as its primary breathing pattern. Wearing tight-fitting clothes that restrict the movement of the diaphragm can also contribute to upper-chest breathing.

Another common form of hyperventilation is due to mouth breathing. People with allergies, asthma, or obstructions are often forced to breathe in this manner because it is difficult to breathe through their nose. When excited, stressed, or doing mild exercise, these people will sometimes experience mild hyperventilation symptoms.

Hyperventilation associated with breath holding is yet another common form of hyperventilation. People who tend to hold their breath when anxious often find themselves yawning or sighing. Any deep yawn or sigh will cause the carbon dioxide level to drop markedly. This in itself can produce subtle symptoms of hyperventilation. If this habit is present along with a tendency to use upper-chest breathing as a primary breathing pattern, it can trigger more severe hyperventilation. This is especially true if the initial vague symptoms are noticed and cause alarm. That is why the tendency to constantly internalize (described in the first lesson) plays such an important role in many forms of severe anxiety.

Hyperventilation can play a role in increasing anxiety in any of the various anxiety-related problems. A person with social phobia, for example, might hyperventilate when anxious. This increases the sense of discomfort produced by conditioned response anxiety triggering additional fear. The same would be true for someone with PTSD when a flashback is experienced. Hyperventilation is especially important for people with panic disorder, because it often underlies panic attacks that seem to strike out of the blue with no apparent reason. It only takes minor degrees of hyperventilation to trigger the effects of increased heart rate, constriction of blood vessels, and a rise in the blood's pH level. The symptoms these reactions produce are noticed and trigger the anxiety/panic cycle, which then results in the "mysterious" panic or anxiety attack.

While hyperventilation plays a major role for many people with panic disorder, this is not true for everyone, especially those with a medical condition. For example, a person with mitral valve prolapse might find that it is the unpleasant "skipped" beat of the heart that is noticed and triggers a panic attack. The type of internalization associated with the anxiety/panic cycle makes a person very sensitive to any internal sensation considered unusual or a sign that the dreaded anxiety or panic attack is about to occur. The following three tests can provide a good indication of whether or not hyperventilation plays a role in your anxiety symptoms.

First, become aware of your normal breathing pattern. Place one hand on your chest and one hand on your stomach. Take a slightly deeper breath than you normally do and see which hand moves the most. If most of the motion is in the hand on your chest, you are an upper-chest breather and the chances are very good that hyperventilation is a major contributor to your symptoms. If most of the motion is in the hand on your stomach, you are using diaphragmatic breathing. While this is very good, it does not rule out the possibility that some form of hyperventilation plays a role in your anxiety symptoms.

Second, count your breathing rate. You can do this yourself or have someone else do it at a time when you are unaware it is being counted. A normal breathing rate at rest is eight to sixteen breaths per minute. One study of people with panic disorder found an average resting breathing rate of twenty-eight breaths per minute.

Third, deliberately hyperventilate in order to consciously experience its effects. Breathe sixty times a minute (once every second) for one to three minutes. Everyone who attempts this test will notice feelings of dry mouth and throat, and many people will report some light-headedness, slight changes in vision, numbness, and tingling. If you begin to experience feelings you associate with anxiety or panic, hyperventilation probably plays a role in your anxiety symptoms. *If at any point during the test, the feelings you experience become very uncomfortable or make you overly anxious or panicky, stop the test.* This test is perfectly safe for the vast majority of people reading this book; however, there are some medical conditions such as angina (heart pain) and seizures (epilepsy) that can be made worse by hyperventilation. If you are in doubt about whether this test is safe for you, consult your doctor.

The recommended activities for this lesson include an exercise on diaphragmatic breathing. Many people find the ability to use diaphragmatic breathing is one of their most effective skills for controlling the symptoms of severe anxiety.

Coping Self-Statements

The various situations in which you find yourself usually resemble past ones in one or more important ways. The feelings and thoughts triggered by a particular situation are the result of both your conscious and unconscious interpretation of the situation. This interpretation is usually based upon automatic, habitual thinking patterns. The key to changing this type of learned habit pattern lies in the fact that thoughts are really silent sentences you say to yourself. Since your emotions are partly controlled by your conscious interpretation of the situation, statements that calm you when you feel afraid or anxious also help you reinterpret the situation so it is not as frightening. These types of statements are called coping self-statements because you say them to yourself and they help you cope with a given situation more effectively.

Consider the last situation you were in that produced anxiety. Recall what you said to yourself. If you think about it for a moment, you will probably find that the thoughts or statements you repeated to yourself are the same ones you say to yourself in many similar situations. Furthermore, they are probably statements that increase your level of anxiety. It is as if your particular set of negative statements have been recorded and are being played over and over inside your head. While the specific things people say to themselves varies depending upon which type of anxiety-related problem they have, common examples of negative self-talk include the following:

- This is terrible.
- I can't handle this.
- Why is this happening?
- This is all wrong.
- I can't stand this.
- I can't make it through this.
- Is this ever going to end?
- This is so stupid. Why can't I handle even this simple thing?
- I'm not doing this right.
- I can't breathe.
- I'm dying.
- I shouldn't be feeling/acting this way. (This usually refers to a symptom associated with anxiety such as difficulty in breathing, a racing heart, an obsessive thought, or worry.)
- I'm never going to get better.
- I can't do this.

Decreasing the amount and intensity of this type of negative self-talk is one of the keys to reducing anxiety. One way to do this is to repeat coping self-statements whenever you become tense or anxious. At first, this may have only a small effect; with practice, however, you create a set of positive messages or "tapes" that eventually replace the old negative messages. Over time, as you repeat these messages, you gain confidence that they are true. Specific coping self-statements for each of the six basic types of anxiety-related problems are listed in the following sections. One of the keys to overcoming your symptoms is learning to use them to challenge fears, help you stay focused on the task at hand, remind you to use your anxiety-reducing skills, and concentrate on problem solving rather than on your symptoms or inadequacies.

Overcoming Panic Disorder

Keep in mind that panic disorder begins to develop when you experience unpleasant symptoms and tell yourself lies about what the symptoms mean. Panic disorder is maintained by a combination of conditioned response anxiety, internalization (constantly watching your body for signs of the boogeyman, anxiety), negative anticipation, and the negative habit pattern of repeating lies about what the body sensations that are noticed mean. Two lies that play a key role in maintaining panic disorder are "Anxiety is dangerous," and "I won't be able to function when I become panicky." The truth is, anxiety is not dangerous; it is just a very unpleasant bodily sensation. Likewise, a person with panic disorder always finds a way to get to a safe person or area when a panic attack is experienced. Here are several coping self-statements that can be used to challenge the negative self-talk common to people with panic disorder:

- Anxiety is *not* dangerous—just uncomfortable. I've survived feelings like this and worse before.
- I can be anxious and still function effectively; I just need to stay focused on the task at hand.
- The scary things I have thought about my symptoms are lies—anxiety is a nuisance and no more.
- There is no need to fight what I am feeling. Even though it's uncomfortable, it's just adrenaline and will pass.
- I must check my breathing, then focus on and describe what is going on around me. Externalize and distract.
- My current symptoms are just a type of conditioned response. They will become less as I desensitize myself.

- The symptoms are now occurring because I'm just like Pavlov's dogs—instead of salivating, I get anxious when certain "bells" ring. This conditioned response is normal and will fade with time.
- What I'm feeling is just an unpleasant body sensation. It is *not* dangerous. I don't have to let it stop me. I can continue to function even though I don't like what I'm feeling.
- My body may be reacting strongly right now but it doesn't really matter. It's just an old habit pattern that will pass with time.

Overcoming Obsessive Thoughts of OCD

Jeffrey M. Schwartz, M.D., an associate research professor of psychiatry at UCLA School of Medicine, has developed an effective four-step approach for overcoming the obsessive thoughts typical of OCD:

Step 1: Relabel. When an obsessive thought occurs, recognize that it is caused by a problem with your brain. While this problem is often described as a chemical imbalance, it may also involve other aspects of brain structure. It is similar to a person with a tic. The tic is harmless but will occasionally cause muscles to fire when they are not supposed to. In a similar way, a thought sometimes comes to your mind that has no basis in reality. This is something that surveys show occurs in about 80 percent of the population and is most likely due to automatic associations produced in the brain. For example, while driving, you see a truck and the memory of an accident involving a truck and car that you saw in the news might flash in your mind; or you imagine what it would be like if the truck ran into you. With OCD, these normal random and irrational associations are seen as real possibilities, and the brain quickly becomes overly sensitized to them so that they trigger increasing levels of anxiety when they occur. The more a person gives in to the compulsive ritual used to calm the anxiety caused by the obsession, the more the brain's sensitivity to the perceived threat is increased.

When these biologically driven thoughts occur, relabel them as obsessions and compulsions. For example, Stewart experienced obsessive thoughts about germs, which he relieved by repeated hand washing. When the thought that he just touched something that was contaminated would occur, he began saying to himself, "My hands are not really dirty. It is just my obsession with dirt and washing my hands." When the thought that he needed to wash his hands occurred, he would say, "I don't really need to wash my hands, I'm having a compulsive urge to perform the compulsion of washing my hands." The same approach can be used with any other obsession or compulsion such as checking, counting, or ordering.

Step 2: Reattribute. This step usually is done along with the first step. In it, you remind yourself that the intense urge to perform a ritual to relieve the anxiety is being driven by a malfunctioning of your brain. Because of this, at least for the short term, there is nothing you can do to make the thoughts and urges go away. The key is to remember that *you don't have to act on them.* They are false messages from the brain that are being generated by a medical condition called OCD. Since you cannot make them go away, the best option is to do another behavior. Trying to make them go away only increases your anxiety and stress and makes OCD thoughts and urges worse. Acting on the urge will give momentary relief, but it also strengthens the faulty response, causing the urge to become even stronger the next time the obsession occurs. Refusing to act on the urge actually changes the way your brain functions and makes the feeling lessen over time.

Stewart would follow the statements given in the first step with statements such as, "The urge I'm feeling to wash my hands is coming from my OCD. I don't have to act on it," or "This is not me, this is my OCD causing me to think and feel this way."

Step 3: Refocus. Refocusing is the process of shifting your attention to something else, even if for only a few minutes while you delay responding to the urges generated by your obsessions and compulsions. Refocusing is the most difficult part of this four-step process. It takes considerable effort and, at first, may produce a high level of discomfort. It's the only way to change the way your brain is functioning, however, and it will reduce the pain you're experiencing in the long run. More is said about this in Lesson 9 when response prevention is discussed more fully.

Something that will help you refocus is to decide to delay

responding for a set period of time. Begin by delaying acting upon a compulsion for fifteen minutes. If this seems like too much, choose a shorter period of time such as ten or five minutes. During this time, find something constructive or pleasurable to focus on that is unrelated to your obsession or compulsion, such as a task for work, a hobby, playing a computer game, or taking a walk. The key is to never perform a compulsion without some delay.

At the end of the time period you have set, reassess the urge. Note whether there has been any change in intensity. Even when there is only a small decrease in intensity, it will help give you the courage to wait longer. Over time, you will find that the longer you wait, the more the urge will lessen in intensity.

When an urge becomes so strong that you perform the compulsion, be kind to yourself. Remind yourself that using the four steps to change your thoughts and feelings will take time. During times when you give in to an urge and perform a compulsion after a time delay, be sure to relabel the behavior. For example, you might say, "I'm not checking the lock because I forgot to lock it. I'm checking it because I've given in to my OCD. While the OCD won this time, I'll wait longer next time."

Step 4: Revalue. This step is really a long-term goal that flows out of the first three steps. Over time, you learn to put less and less importance on obsessive thoughts or urges that occur. OCD thoughts, while annoying, are not important. Two things that help in this process are learning to both anticipate and accept obsessive thoughts and urges.

To anticipate means that you are prepared for obsessive thoughts and urges to recur because you understand that they are being driven by faulty brain functioning. As you come to expect that your symptoms will recur, they no longer surprise you.

Acceptance refers to the development of a calm attitude toward your obsessions. It is similar to when an annoying car alarm goes off. You can choose to dwell on how terrible it is to listen to all that racket, or you can choose to ignore it and focus on other activities. In a similar way, you come to accept that this is just the way you were born. Just as some people have asthma or other biological problems, you have a brain that sometimes malfunctions and produces obsessions and compulsions. When you notice that you are belittling yourself because you have obsessive thoughts or perform a compulsive ritual, remind yourself that they are simply due to faulty brain functioning and that you are learning to work around them. It also helps to remind yourself that your obsessions and compulsions will eventually lessen in intensity as you practice these steps.

Overcoming PTSD

People with PTSD often feel that their symptoms are a sign of weakness. It is important to realize that *everyone* will experience PTSD symptoms when traumatized. One of the most powerful statements for countering these feelings when they occur is to remind yourself that "I am a normal person who has been in an abnormal situation." A good statement to use when flashbacks are experienced is: "My mind is just taking snapshots of the incident and trying to make sense out of something that is actually senseless." If sensations or images of the trauma are intense, remind yourself that it is over and you are now safe. Juliene, the person described in Lesson 1 who had experienced a traumatic car accident, would tell herself, "The accident is over. It's in the past and I'm now safe. I'm just sitting in my car and driving normally. I'm just experiencing feelings from the past. They are just conditioned response feelings triggered by the accident. They have nothing to do with what is going on right now." The statements given in the section on panic disorder can also be very useful.

Overcoming Specific Phobias

The coping self-statements listed in the section on panic disorder work well for people with specific phobias. In addition, it is important to develop coping self-statements that address the specific fearful thoughts associated with your phobia. For example, Stamie, the person described in Lesson 1 with a fear of water that had developed as a result of her brother's teasing, found the following statements useful: "There are no piranhas in the water. My fear is simply a conditioned response caused by my brother's teasing when I was young. The water is safe and nothing bad will happen if I put my feet into the pool."

Overcoming Social Phobia

The central fear underlying social phobia is the belief that other people are watching you and judging you in a critical way. The key to challenging these types of thoughts is to realize that things in the adult world are very different from when you were young. The vast majority of adults around you are too busy thinking about their own lives to spend much time or energy thinking about you. In addition, most of the adults you encounter will treat you with the same kindness you extend to others. If you make a mistake or do something stupid, it's not that important to them. Unfortunately, many people with social phobias react to others as if they are still in grade school or junior high school. At that time children are very concerned with their status in the social group and can be very cruel to one another. While there are a small number of adults who still react that way, most have grown up and will treat you in a mature manner.

Overcoming GAD

The key to working with GAD is the Four-Step Analysis used to evaluate fears and worries described in Lesson 7. In addition to using this technique, remind yourself that your predictions rarely come true. When you worry, your reasoning is based on emotion rather than fact.

Distraction

Distraction is the process of shifting or diverting your attention from one activity to another. It is also referred to as redirection or refocusing. Distraction uses an important principle: Shifting your attention *toward* something neutral or positive is always easier than shifting it *away* from something negative. Trying to reduce anxiety by thinking or saying phrases such as, "Don't be anxious," "I must not be anxious," or, "Don't think about that," rarely works. The process of telling yourself not to be anxious or to not think about something focuses your attention and energy on your anxiety and thoughts even more and usually intensifies them. The five forms of distraction described in this section provide a more effective way to reduce anxiety by redirecting your attention toward neutral or positive activities.

One important feature of most forms of distraction is externalization. Externalization is the act of focusing your attention on sensations originating outside your body. It is the opposite of internalization, the focusing of your attention on sensations originating inside your body as described in Lesson 1. Distracting your attention away from your body and focusing externally is especially important for people with panic disorder because it prevents the initial alarm reaction that triggers the anxiety/panic cycle. Using distraction after the cycle has been triggered helps calm you by interrupting negative self-talk and breaking the cycle of escalating fear over self-generated symptoms.

The following forms of distraction are listed from simpler to more complex forms. The simpler forms are fairly easy to learn and use but only work moderately well when anxiety is high. They also are most effective when used to cope with an anxiety-producing situation that lasts only a short time, such as crossing a bridge, waiting in line, or using an elevator. In addition, they work well for people with OCD who are delaying responding to an obsessive thought. The complex forms take longer to master, but are more effective since the more interesting or demanding an activity is, the more distracting it is. They become easier as you challenge the lies you have believed about your condition and begin to accept what your condition really is and what it isn't.

One word of caution needs to be made for people with OCD. Several of the simple forms of distraction are similar to compulsive rituals used to relieve the anxiety of obsessions. If you have OCD, do not use any form of distraction that resembles rituals you use. The more complex forms of distraction such as conversation, work, or play are usually more effective.

Simple Externalization

Simple externalization is the use of one or more of your senses to focus on some external sensation. Some common types of simple externalization are listed below. They work best when done systematically. For example, if you are using the design on a wall to distract yourself, don't just look at it, but identify where the design repeats itself and all the variations it contains.

- *Observing carefully:* Read signs; examine the design of a nearby wall, clothing, or carpet; observe the intricate activities of people around you; or observe surrounding scenery.
- *Listening attentively:* Listen to random conversation or background noises such as a ticking clock or a passing plane.
- *Feeling textures:* Feel the texture of clothing, paper, a gum wrapper, or the steering wheel of the car you are driving.
- *Tasting or smelling:* Taste and smell gum or candy you carry with you; note the various odors surrounding you.
- *Doing repetitive activities:* Count floor tiles, lights, or cracks; tap a finger rhythmically; fold a piece of paper in a systematic manner.
- *Changing your surroundings or activities:* If you're inside, go outside; if you're sitting, go for a walk; if you're in the living room, go into the kitchen.

Simple Tasks That Require Concentration

Simple mental activities that require concentration—such as recalling the words to a song, determining how much a total purchase will cost, balancing a checkbook, timing an event like a trip to a friend's house, or recalling an event that arouses positive emotions such as happiness, satisfaction, or joy—are often difficult to do when you are very anxious. With practice, however, they become effective distractors.

Conversation

Conversation is an effective form of distraction that can be used almost anywhere. Talking over the telephone can be just as effective as talking with someone in person. Even a stranger such as a person standing in line next to you can offer distraction. Conversation works best as a distractor when you are an active speaker rather than as a passive listener. It is also best if the topic of conversation is unrelated to your anxiety symptoms or to the situation generating the anxiety.

Work

Many people use work as a form of distraction without even knowing it. Work can be mental or physical and can involve household chores or work related to a job outside the home. Work is most distracting when it is interesting, pleasurable, or involves competition. Activities that have become automatic because you have done them often do not work as well as those that demand more attention. One way to increase the distracting quality of routine work is to do it in a somewhat different manner. For example, you can change the order in which you do the various steps of a given chore.

Play

Play includes anything that is both interesting and pleasurable. Working crossword puzzles, playing video games, dancing, and working at hobbies are examples of play that can be used to distract yourself. Activities requiring physical activity are usually more distracting than games where you are passive. Also, the more pleasure you derive from an activity, the more distracting it is. The key element is that the activity holds your interest.

Play can often be combined with other forms of distraction. For example, you can make a game out of simple externalization by trying to connect the dots on acoustical tile to form faces or make up stories about people around you. You can create simple games that require concentration such as guessing the number of telephone poles on a stretch of road. At first, it may be difficult to be playful and find humor in anxiety-producing situations. With practice, however, it becomes easier.

Medication

A wide range of medications have been developed to treat anxiety-related problems. While they can play an important role in treating many anxiety-related problems, by themselves they will not cure the vast majority of such problems. Panic disorder offers a good example of this. Medications will not prevent a person from experiencing panic attacks, but they can reduce the overall level of anxiety a person is experiencing. For many, this helps reduce the number and intensity of panic attacks. The antidepressants are also very effective in reducing depression. This can often be helpful when a person has not yet developed effective skills to deal with anxiety and is facing stressful life events. With OCD, medications can greatly reduce the intensity of the thoughts and urges that a person experiences, making the skills presented in this program easier to learn and use.

On the negative side, it often requires much trial and error to find the right medication and correct dosage for a particular person. There are sometimes problems with side effects and withdrawal. In addition, relapse rates for people who are only receiving medication and not learning the skills presented in this program are very high.

In short, medications have a definite role in treating anxiety—but they are not for everyone. The primary goal of this program is to present skills and methods for changing the way you think and act that will allow you to overcome anxiety-related problems and live a normal life—without the need for medication. Many people find that using medication in the early stages of a program like this is helpful. Others find it is not. If you are currently taking medication to relieve your anxiety symptoms, the chances are excellent there will come a time when you will no longer feel the need for it. Many people who once relied on medication to relieve their anxiety symptoms have found that the approach used in these lessons eliminated the need to continue on such drugs.

Here are some general guidelines you need to know if you are currently using medication or are considering using it:

- Make sure the medication is prescribed by a professional experienced with anxiety-related problems who has conducted a careful assessment of your individual needs.
- Some medications take time before results are seen. Discuss this with the physician prescribing the medication.
- Medications often have the potential for side effects. Talk to your physician about this so you will understand what to expect.
- Make sure the physician who prescribes the medication monitors you to ensure its safe and effective use.
- If the medication is producing side effects that are more troublesome than the anxiety symptoms it is meant to relieve, consult with your physician immediately.

One word of caution is needed concerning the discontinuation of medications. After being taken daily, many medications can produce undesirable and even dangerous effects if stopped abruptly. So when you do wish to discontinue or lower the dosage, it is imperative that you discuss it with the professional who prescribed the medication and has been monitoring its use. In addition, there are some medications, depending upon the length of use and dosage, that can produce some anxiety symptoms as they are discontinued. These withdrawal symptoms can usually be avoided if the medications are discontinued gradually. If you do happen to experience symptoms while discontinuing a medication, however, use coping self-statements to remind yourself that it is just the medication.

If you are interested in learning more about the medications used to treat anxiety-related problems, there are a number of excellent sources of information available. Here are two specific sources that have a wealth of information that is updated regularly:

Anxiety Disorders Association of America
8730 Georgia Avenue, Suite 600
Silver Spring, MD 20910
(240) 485-1001
www.adaa.org

National Institute of Mental Health (NIMH)
6001 Executive Boulevard, Room 8184, MSC 9663
Bethesda, MD 20892-9663
(301) 443-4513 or (866) 615-NIMH (6464)
www.nimh.nih.gov

Recommended Activities for Lesson 2
Begin Developing Cue-Controlled Relaxation

Continue practicing a relaxation response exercise at least once a day. Have more than one practice session a day if it is practical. If you have not yet tried all the approaches described in Appendix 2, decide now when and where you will try each one. Also, if you have not yet tried taping the scripts, select one and tape it this week. Then use it as directed.

As you practice your relaxation response, begin using a cue that will become associated with the response. Three common types of cues are listed below. Decide which type you like best and begin using it. Be sure to use the same cue each time you practice.

- Word cues: Any word repeated over and over as you relax will work. Common word cues include "relax," "peace," "calm and controlled," and "one."
- Imaginary cues: Imagine any scene or image you find relaxing, such as a mountain meadow, the beach, or a forest.
- Physical cues: Physical cues work best if they involve an action that is out of the ordinary. At the same time, they need to be inconspicuous enough that you can use them in public. Three common physical cues include touching the thumb and first two fingers of either hand, touching an elbow, or touching the back of a wrist.

It may take several weeks for you to develop the ability to produce a state of deep relaxation through a set method. It may take a little longer for the association between your cue and the relaxation to become firmly established. Once you are able to trigger a relaxation response, though, you will find it a valuable skill.

Develop Relaxed Diaphragmatic Breathing

This lesson discussed in detail the importance of learning relaxed diaphragmatic breathing for people with anxiety-related problems. Some people master this skill in one or two days. A few take several weeks. If upper-chest breathing is your normal breathing pattern, continue practicing the exercise until diaphragmatic breathing becomes your normal method of breathing. If diaphragmatic breathing is already your normal method of breathing, practice this exercise for at least one week.

Exercise

Do this exercise twice a day, once at night before you go to bed and once in the morning right after you awaken. At these times you are wearing loose-fitting clothes and can easily lie down. This is especially important if diaphragmatic breathing is difficult for you.

Lie down, place one hand on your abdomen over your navel, and breathe in such a way that it moves up and down in a relaxed manner. Your chest may move a little while you do this; however, most of the movement needs to be in the abdominal region. If you are unable to tell what your chest is doing, place your other hand on it so you can feel how much it is moving in relation to your abdomen.

Most people are able to breathe in this manner fairly easily. If you have difficulty, try sucking in the abdominal region as you exhale (breathe out). Then simply relax and do nothing as you inhale (breathe in). Your abdominal region will naturally expand outward on its own.

Each practice session needs to last only about a minute, just long enough to take four or five relaxed and comfortable diaphragmatic breaths. *Do not* make this hard work. It is also important to avoid overbreathing. The type of diaphragmatic breathing you are practicing is a very gentle and relaxed form of breathing. This is very different from the type of diaphragmatic breathing associated with yoga, playing a horn, or singing, which takes in large quantities of air. If you breathe too deeply or too rapidly instead of taking slow, gentle breaths, you might produce a sense of light-headedness or one of the other symptoms characteristic of hyperventilation. If this occurs, it means you are working too hard at the exercise. Take smaller and more relaxed breaths.

Your goals are to be able to tell when you are breathing with your diaphragm without the need to place a hand on your abdomen; to know what a comfortable, relaxed diaphragmatic breath feels like; and to breathe in a gentle, relaxed manner with your diaphragm without effort whenever you wish.

After you can breathe with your diaphragm while lying down, practice two or three times a day while standing. An easy way to remember to practice is to take three or four relaxed diaphragmatic breaths just before you sit down for your regular meals. After you have practiced diaphragmatic breathing while standing and are able to breathe in this manner without effort, begin practicing while sitting. People who are upper-chest breathers usually find that sitting is the most difficult position in which to breathe with the diaphragm. This is especially true for very heavy people. With practice, however, most people find that diaphragmatic breathing eventually becomes easy even while sitting. If you have difficulty, wear loose-fitting clothing.

From now on, whenever you begin to feel anxious or panicky, check your breathing. Taking three or four slow, relaxed diaphragmatic breaths helps quiet the fight or flight response.

Severe hyperventilators are frequently told to carry a paper bag and breathe into it whenever they experience the symptoms of severe hyperventilation. This technique is based upon the fact that the level of carbon dioxide in the blood is the means by which your body regulates its breathing. As the oxygen in the bag is used up and replaced with carbon dioxide, you breathe in more carbon dioxide, and this slows your breathing.

The paper bag technique works. However, many people find it embarrassing to use it in public. Others find that by the time they use the paper bag, they are already experiencing severe symptoms. Furthermore, this technique only removes the symptoms; it does not deal directly with the cause of the symptoms: the tendency to hyperventilate.

Becoming skilled at relaxed diaphragmatic breathing enables you to stop hyperventilation symptoms before they become serious. Taking several relaxed diaphragmatic breaths whenever you are in an anxiety-producing situation is also a good way to prevent hyperventilation symptoms from the beginning. This is especially true for people who are upper-chest breathers or breath holders.

If hyperventilation plays a major role in your anxiety-related symptoms, it is often useful to have several hyperventilation sessions. During each session, hyperventilate, wait until the symptoms disappear, then repeat the process again two or three times. Doing this over the course of several days helps you recognize the symptoms of hyperventilation when they occur. It also shows you that you can control them and that they are harmless. If hyperventilating is very frightening for you, do this exercise with someone you trust. It also helps to start very slowly. Stop at the first signs of hyperventilation until you become accustomed to them. Then increase the symptoms each time you practice until you recognize them for what they are, simply unpleasant body sensations that are harmless. If you have any medical condition, be sure to talk with your doctor before doing this exercise.

List Coping Self-Statements on a Card and Memorize Them

Because your thinking is so automatic when you're anxious, it is often difficult to think of effective coping self-statements. The best way to overcome this problem is to prepare several coping self-statements and write them down on a card or piece of paper. Examples of cards created by the individuals who were introduced in Lesson 1 are shown below. These were the statements they used when first learning these skills. Keep in mind that they are only examples.

If you like any of the examples, you can use it exactly as written. If any of the examples do not fit your personality or life situation, change the wording or create new ones that do apply to you. It is important that your statements have power and meaning for you and fit your unique situation.

After you have developed your list, practice reciting it until you can recall the statements from memory without much effort. Then, when your anxiety is triggered, you can use a small part of your mind to repeat the coping self-statements while most of your mind stays focused on what you are doing. It helps to revise your statements periodically so they don't become stale. Eventually, you will find yourself creating and using coping self-statements spontaneously.

Brian's Card: Coping Self-Statements Used with Panic Disorder

- Anxiety is not dangerous—just uncomfortable.
- I can be anxious and still function effectively.
- Trigger your relaxation response, take three or four relaxed diaphragmatic breaths, then distract yourself.
- Remember that the scary things I have thought about my symptoms are lies—anxiety is a nuisance and no more.
- The symptoms are now occurring because I'm just like Pavlov's dogs—instead of salivating, I get anxious when certain "bells" ring. This conditioned response learning will fade with time.

Stewart's Card: Coping Self-Statements Used with OCD

Step 1: Relabel. My hands are not really dirty. These thoughts are just my obsession.

Step 2: Reattribute. While these thoughts feel urgent, they are due to a medical condition. I don't have to act on them.

Step 3: Refocus. I will treat these thoughts like a car alarm going off outside. I'll wait for fifteen minutes before I decide to act on these thoughts. Now, find something else to focus on during this time.

Step 4: Revalue. I know these types of thoughts will continue for a while. I don't have to be concerned about them. There are lots of minor biological quirks like this that people have. I'm okay even though I have this little one.

Juliene's Card: Coping Self-Statements Used with PTSD Due to an Accident

- I am a normal person who has been in an abnormal situation.
- Sometimes my mind takes snapshots of the accident to try to make sense out of something that is actually senseless.
- The accident is over. It's in the past.
- I'm safe now.
- I've learned how to drive more defensively now so the chances of something like that happening again are very low.

Mai's Card: Coping Self-Statements Used with Specific Phobia

• That cricket is not a danger to me. The cricket doesn't bite and is not poisonous. It cannot harm me in any way.
• I'm simply responding to a conditioned response that developed when I got caught in a locust storm.
• That incident happened long ago and will most likely never happen again. It was a very unusual event. While I was frightened, no harm came to me then, and no harm will come to me now.
• I have choices now. I don't have to run even though my body is reacting to the old conditioned response.
• I feel like I'm in danger, but the reality is that I'm safe and no harm is going to come to me. These feelings are from the past. They are not based on present reality.

Kao's Card: Coping Self-Statements Used with Social Phobia

• I'm not in junior high school anymore. I'm in the adult world.
• These people are adults with lives of their own. They really don't care what I'm thinking or doing. I'm not the center of their lives.
• I'm not going to be teased like I was in grade school or junior high school.
• These people are adults and are going to treat me with the same kindness I show to others.
• I don't think less of others when they make mistakes. These people see me the same way. If I make a mistake, they probably won't even notice. If they do, it won't matter to them.
• My social skills will become more comfortable as I practice them.

Marquita's Card: Coping Self-Statements Used with Generalized Anxiety Disorder

- The terrible things that I think will happen, rarely do.
- When I look at my past, I see that things usually work out fine.
- I am thinking just like my mother. But now, I can see how irrational her thinking was. These worries are just as unfounded as hers were.
- Instead of getting caught up in the what-ifs, I can use the Four-Step Analysis to evaluate the validity of this worry right now.
- Remember: Feelings are not facts. They are just feelings. Most of my worries are based on emotional reasoning.

Basic Skills Checklist for Anxiety-Producing Situations

Many people forget to use these skills when in the middle of an anxiety-producing situation. This tendency can be overcome by carrying a card that lists these skills similar to the sample shown below. Sometimes a support person can help by reminding you to look at your card and use your skills.

Basic Skills Checklist

- Use the cue that triggers your relaxation response.
- Take three or four *relaxed* diaphragmatic breaths.
- Use your coping self-statements to challenge your negative self-talk.
- Distract yourself with one or more of the following: Simple externalization; simple tasks that require concentration; conversation; work; and play.

Remember: These skills work best at the first signs of anxiety. If you wait until you are experiencing severe symptoms, your skills will be less effective.

A Special Word to Those Suffering from OCD and GAD

If you suffer from OCD, go to Lesson 9 *after you complete this lesson*. Work through that lesson, then return to Lesson 3 and continue working through the program. If you suffer from GAD, go to Lesson 7 *after you complete this lesson*. Work through that lesson, then return to Lesson 3 and continue working through the program. If you suffer from any of the other anxiety-related problems, you will probably find it most effective to continue working through the lessons in order.

Eliminate Caffeine

People with anxiety-related problems tend to be more sensitive to both human-made and natural chemicals. Because of this, caffeine —a stimulant and the world's most widely used mood-altering drug— can be a major source of anxiety. In fact, coffee can actually trigger panic attacks in some people with panic disorder. Even people who are not naturally overly sensitive to chemicals find the extra stress produced by anxiety-related problems can make them more sensitive to stimulants such as caffeine.

When you are having a problem with anxiety, it does not make sense to put anything into your body that can increase anxiety. While you are working through these lessons, eliminate caffeine from your diet by drinking decaffeinated coffee, herbal tea, and caffeine-free soft drinks. Read the labels of over-the-counter medications and be aware of any hidden caffeine they may contain.

If you are currently drinking several cups of coffee or other beverages that contain caffeine each day, you may find that stopping all caffeine at once may produce mild withdrawal symptoms such as headaches. When this is the case, it is often best to gradually cut down on your caffeine intake over two or three weeks.

Some people who have overcome anxiety-related problems find they can resume drinking moderate amounts of caffeinated drinks without experiencing any negative side effects. Many others find they are caffeine-sensitive and that it is best to continue to avoid caffeine. By the time you overcome your anxiety-related problems, you will know which approach is best for you.

Continue to Eliminate Unnecessary Stress

People with anxiety-related problems often use large amounts of energy in self-defeating behaviors such as negative self-talk. Additional energy is lost through increased body tension. This leaves less energy for dealing with the everyday stresses of life. The result is that a daily routine that seemed easy to deal with before the anxiety-related problem developed often becomes difficult.

Lesson 1 asked you to be good to yourself and reduce as many sources of unnecessary stress as possible. Your body needs time to begin healing itself from the ravages of the anxiety and stress it has been under and to replenish its supply of energy. This does not mean you are to avoid life; it does mean you need to use common sense in choosing activities. Continue to do this for the next few weeks as you learn your basic anxiety-reduction skills.

For Those Who Are Having Difficulty Sleeping

Sleep is essential for good mental and physical health. If you are having difficulty sleeping, read Appendix 4: Suggestions for People with Sleep Problems. Developing skills that help you sleep well helps to reduce anxiety. It also makes it much easier to understand the ideas in these lessons and apply them to your life.

> If you have not already begun doing the exercises in the Recommended Activities, begin now. Also, be sure to reread the lesson so you understand it fully.

LESSON 3

Understanding and Reducing Stress

Peeople with anxiety-related problems tend to be poor at managing stress. The overview of stress and stress management in this lesson will greatly improve your skills in this area. These skills also provide a firm foundation for the skills presented in the lessons that follow. Be patient as you study.

What Is Stress?

Stress is simply another word used to describe the triggering of the fight or flight response. The effects of stress can be positive or negative. One example of positive stress is the excitement an experienced musician feels just before a performance. In this case, the fight or flight response helps improve the performance. Another example is the excitement of being in love.

Negative stress can be short term (such as the fear, pressure, and need for quick decisions produced when a car suddenly swerves into your path) or long term (such as the stress you might feel in a complex, high-pressure job). Too much stress, especially over a long period of time, can drain energy, cause undue wear and tear on the body, and make you vulnerable to illness and premature aging. Pictures of presidents before and after four years of one of the most stressful jobs on the planet provide a vivid example of this fact.

Stress can be divided into two major types: physical and psychological. Physical stress is created by physical demands on the body such as those caused by accidents, illness, chemical toxins, a demanding work schedule, or prolonged psychological stress. Psychological stress is created by mental or emotional demands on the body. Psychological stress can simply be the result of physical stress. It is, however, more often caused by mental or emotional demands from personal beliefs, family, work, or friends.

This lesson focuses on psychological stress. The four basic types of psychological stress are defined as follows:

- *Pressure:* An internal or external demand to complete a task or activity either within a limited time or in a specific manner.
- *Frustration:* The blocking of needs or wants.
- *Conflict:* The need to make a choice between two or more competing alternatives.
- *Anxiety/fear:* One of two basic emotional responses to a perceived threat (the other is anger).

There are three important points about stress that need to be understood in order to develop a complete approach to stress management. First, stress involves the triggering of the fight or flight response and the release of energy that is not actually needed to cope with an external situation. As explained in Lesson 1, this is what generates the symptoms of anxiety.

Second, your body responds to any thought as though the thought concerns an event occurring in the present. It does not matter whether the thought is about the past, present, or future. This is why a vivid thought accompanied by strong emotion about a past negative experience or a possible future problem triggers the fight or flight response.

Third, people who experience the prolonged stress of severe anxiety usually have beliefs, attitudes, and habitual thinking patterns that tend to perpetuate the stress. This important point is dealt with in detail later in the program.

The process of reducing daily stress is usually referred to as stress management. The word *management* is of particular importance.

Your goal is not to eliminate stress. This is impossible if you are to live a normal, healthy life. Your goal is to manage stress so it does not prevent you from living the life you want.

Basic Stress Management Principles

People with anxiety-related problems usually understand the three basic stress management principles discussed in this section. Unfortunately, they usually do not apply them to their daily life. Embracing these ideas and applying them to daily life is one of the keys to overcoming anxiety.

Accept Your Body as a Machine with a Limited Supply of Energy

The first step in stress management is to treat your body as a machine that needs regular rest, maintenance, and care in order to work properly. When you wake up each morning, you begin your day with a limited supply of energy. It is as if your body starts with a charged battery and tank full of fuel. The exact amount of energy you have each day varies and is different from what other people have. Once this supply of energy is used up, it can only be replaced by taking time to rest and nourish yourself. If you fail to do this, your body starts to break down.

While almost everyone with anxiety-related problems has an intellectual understanding of the concept of the body as a machine with a limited supply of energy, few actually apply it to their lives. Sometimes, childhood training leads to the belief that the body is unimportant. An excessive need for approval, rigid thinking, high expectations of self, or a tendency to suppress some or all negative feelings can also cause people to ignore the needs of their bodies.

Learn to Recognize the Early Signs of Stress and What They Mean

In order to apply the concept of the body as a machine, you need to know when stress is beginning to have a negative effect on you.

Learning to recognize and pay attention to these early warning signs allows you to know when you are running low on energy and apply the ideas that are discussed in the next section. The Stress Symptom Inventory that follows is designed to help you identify your own unique set of warning signs. Complete it before going on with this lesson.

Stress Symptom Inventory

Think of several times when you have experienced excessive stress and check any of the symptoms you experienced during those times of high stress.

Physical Symptoms

❑ Appetite change	❑ Increase of accidents	❑ Restlessness
❑ Colds/flu	❑ Increased alcohol, drug,	❑ Teeth grinding
❑ Digestive upsets	tobacco use	❑ Tension
❑ Fatigue	❑ Insomnia	❑ Weight change
❑ Finger drumming, foot tapping, etc.	❑ Irregular breathing, hyperventilation	❑ Others:
❑ Frequent sighing, yawning	❑ Muscle aches	❑ _____
	❑ Pounding heart	❑ _____
❑ Headaches	❑ Rash	❑ _____

Mental

❑ Boredom	❑ Lethargy	❑ Weird or morbid thoughts
❑ Confusion	❑ Low productivity	❑ Whirling mind
❑ Difficulty in thinking clearly	❑ Negative attitude	❑ Others:
	❑ Poor memory	❑ _____
❑ Dull senses	❑ Reduced ability to	❑ _____
❑ Forgetfulness	concentrate	❑ _____

Emotional

❑ Anxiety	❑ Increased use of profanity,	❑ Nervous laugh
❑ Bad dreams or nightmares	put-downs, or sarcasm	❑ Short temper
❑ Crying spells	❑ Increased emotionalism	❑ The blues
❑ Depression	❑ Irritability	❑ Others:
❑ Discouragement	❑ Little joy	❑ _____
❑ Frustration	❑ Mood swings	❑ _____

Spiritual

- ❏ Apathy
- ❏ Cynicism
- ❏ Doubt
- ❏ Emptiness
- ❏ Inability to forgive
- ❏ Loss of direction

- ❏ Loss of faith
- ❏ Loss of meaning
- ❏ Martyrdom
- ❏ Need to prove self
- ❏ "No one cares" attitude
- ❏ Pessimism

- ❏ Sense of helplessness
- ❏ Sense of hopelessness
- ❏ Others:
- ❏ _____
- ❏ _____
- ❏ _____

Relational

- ❏ Avoidance of people
- ❏ Blaming
- ❏ Distrust
- ❏ Fewer contacts with friends
- ❏ Increased arguing or disagreements

- ❏ Intolerance
- ❏ Lack of intimacy
- ❏ Lashing out
- ❏ Less loving and trusting
- ❏ Lowered sex drive
- ❏ Nagging

- ❏ Resentment
- ❏ Others:
- ❏ _____
- ❏ _____
- ❏ _____
- ❏ _____

You probably noticed that many of the items in this inventory apply to you. This is even true for people who do not suffer from anxiety-related problems. If you go back through the items you checked, however, you will find several that would be especially important warning signs. Put a star beside three to six symptoms that you feel would be the most important indicators for when stress is beginning to affect you in a negative way. Do not be surprised if your key indicators change from time to time. The way stress affects you varies depending on its source and your current physical condition. For example, those symptoms associated with stress due to a heavy workload may vary from those due to the emotional distress of marital problems.

One of the lessons that people with anxiety-related problems need to learn is that the early symptoms of stress are simply messages telling you that you have not taken care of some important need. This need may be physical, mental, emotional, spiritual, or relational in nature. Understanding and accepting this idea helps you avoid exaggerating the importance of anxiety symptoms when they occur. The next step is to identify what that need is and decide on the best way to take care of it.

For example, Audrey found it difficult to say no when others asked her to do something. She often found that she would experience stress and anxiety symptoms when she had agreed to do something she really didn't need or want to do. Instead of recognizing that the symptoms she was experiencing were simply a message that she was not setting appropriate limits with others, she saw the symptoms as an indication that her anxiety-related problems were getting worse.

Over time, she learned to recognize the early signs of distress that indicated that she was not taking care of herself. She would then reevaluate whether she had committed herself to something she really didn't want to do. This, in turn, helped her to avoid becoming stressed to the point where she experienced excessive anxiety. The idea that symptoms are simply messages is something that will be discussed more fully in the lessons to come. For now, become skilled at recognizing the early signs of stress.

Build Stress Tolerance with a Balanced Diet and Exercise

Two basic ways to increase your body's physical ability to tolerate stress are to eat a balanced diet and to exercise regularly. A balanced diet builds stress tolerance in three ways: It increases physical endurance, increases resistance to disease, and promotes increased emotional stability. Unfortunately, the first thing to suffer during a period of high stress or anxiety is usually the diet. The triggering of the fight or flight response by stress or anxiety can decrease appetite. Sometimes people learn that eating will quiet this activation of the fight or flight response causing nervous eating. In addition, people often choose to eat junk foods that have a low nutritional value but a high emotional value—chocolate, candy, or foods with lots of sugar or fat, such as a highly sweetened breakfast cereal or potato chips. The lack of proper nutrition will increase the effects of stress and anxiety. The ingestion of excessive amounts of sugar can also produce mood swings.

It is not necessary to become a food fanatic to prevent these negative effects. Food by itself will not make you stress-free or eliminate your anxiety. Still, it is very important to your health and moods. Keep in mind the concept of the body as a machine that needs proper fuel to run efficiently. If you are not sure what a balanced diet is, there are many excellent books on nutrition available at your local bookstore. Choose one that is by a recognized doctor or nutritionist and avoid anything that looks like a fad diet.

Within any reasonable diet there is plenty of room for "fun" foods. However, your ability to tolerate foods with a low nutritional value is greatly reduced during times when you are experiencing severe anxiety or stress. During times of high stress and anxiety, pay extra attention to what you eat. In addition, when you know you will be facing an activity that is stressful, pay extra attention to your diet the day before as well as during the day of the activity. This prepares your body to cope more effectively with the additional stress.

Regular exercise increases your ability to tolerate stress in two ways. First, the triggering of the fight or flight response by stress causes your muscles to become tense. Engaging in light to moderate exercise helps your muscles relax completely once you complete your exercise. This post-exercise relaxation can greatly reduce symptoms caused by chronically tensed muscles.

The second benefit of exercise is that a strong body can carry more stress than one that is out of shape. As with diet, you do not need to become an exercise fanatic to reap the benefits of exercise. Simple stretching or walking, when done regularly, can be very beneficial. It is usually recommended that an exercise routine be done a minimum of three times a week for at least twenty minutes. This will strengthen your muscles so they can tolerate the muscle tension produced by stress more effectively. Regular exercise has also been shown to help give you a more positive outlook. If you do not already exercise on a regular basis, it is important to check with your physician before starting or drastically changing your exercise routine.

Three Guidelines for Periods of High Stress

Everyone faces periodic times of high stress. The excessive stress during a time like this may be due to an unusual event such as a major illness in a loved one or losing one's job. The stress may also be due to many normal events that all happen at one time. For example, Brian, who was introduced in Lesson 1, had his first panic attack shortly after he received a promotion that required him to move to a new town. At the same time, his wife gave birth to their first child. Both of these are normal events. However, stress associated with leaving his support network, moving, facing a new stressful job, and adjusting to a new baby all added up to produce a simple stress reaction that he did not understand. Recurring times of high stress are also common in many types of jobs such as the end-of-the-year rush for retailers or the pressure of meeting tax deadlines for accountants.

The following guidelines are based on the basic stress management principles outlined earlier in this lesson. Following them during times of high stress enables you to reduce the effect of the stressors you are facing and function more effectively in all areas of your life.

Set Priorities and Reduce Your Overall Activity

Whenever you are facing more stress than usual, reduce your activities. This is not a time to try to beat old performance records and do extra things. It is a time to do less by setting priorities, establishing realistic short-term goals, and delegating more responsibility to others. This does not mean you avoid all activity. Instead, it means you apply the concept of the body as a machine with a limited supply of energy to your current situation. Since stress drains your energy, you have less energy during times of high stress than during times of low stress. Setting priorities and reducing your overall activity is one way to use the limited amount of energy you have wisely.

This is often difficult because stress affects the way you think. Your thinking tends to become more black and white. Small things that don't have much importance when you are feeling good often take on an exaggerated importance when you are stressed. This, in turn, can cause you to waste time and energy on things that are not that important. In order to combat this tendency, you may have to stop periodically during times of high stress and ask yourself, "What really needs to be done now? What can I let go of until some other time?"

Spend Extra Time with Decisions

It cannot be said too many times: Stress interferes with your ability to think. The greater the stress, the more likely it is that you will make poor decisions. Whenever possible, avoid making major decisions during times of high stress. Wait until you are feeling less stressed. When a major decision must be made during a time of high stress, do two things. First, take more time to make the decision. Slowing down the decision-making process helps you use your reduced ability to think more effectively. Second, consult with people you trust and who are objective. They may see problems or options you didn't think of because of your reduced ability to think logically.

Plan Ahead and Take Action During Times When Stress Is Low

Often, you know ahead of time when a period of high stress is coming. This may be a job where there is a large increase of work at regular times. It may also be a onetime event such as a wedding or family reunion. When you know that a stressful event is coming, plan ahead, make decisions, and take action in advance while you are feeling good. This reduces the amount of thinking and action you must take during the time of high stress. For example, if an important function at work is coming, plan to do routine things in advance. Also plan to let go of little things during the time of high stress. Having a plan like this helps you concentrate on what is important and let go of things that are less important.

Many people take action or make decisions only when pushed into a corner or prodded by discomfort. Then they wonder why they make so many poor decisions and act ineffectively. Developing the habit of planning ahead and taking time when you are not stressed to face important issues and take action results in better decisions and more effective behavior.

Develop a Lifestyle Based on Stress Management Principles

Earlier in this lesson, it was pointed out that the symptoms of stress and anxiety are often just a message that some important need is not being met. Unfortunately, it is often difficult in our fast-paced, modern world to develop a lifestyle that balances our various physical, mental, emotional, relational, and spiritual needs. People in our modern society tend to live in a manner where important needs are often ignored. This is especially true for people with anxiety-related problems who usually have lifestyles that are out of balance.

The following section describes activities and attitudes in seven key areas that can insulate you from the effects of stress. You probably already do some of them. If there are several areas that are not part of your current lifestyle, you may feel overwhelmed at the thought of trying all the suggestions. This is a normal reaction. It often takes many weeks or months to develop some of these areas, such as emotional or spiritual support. During the time you are working with this lesson, select one or two areas that are not currently part of your lifestyle. Put most of your time and energy into these. Do not be concerned if you are only able to work on these one or two areas at this time. As you proceed through this program, there will be many opportunities to return to this lesson and work with those approaches you skip at this time.

Relaxation

Taking time to relax is not only important, but also essential for physical and mental health. Develop the habit of scheduling regular time for relaxation. While you are developing this habit, remind yourself of the concept of the body as a machine with a limited supply of energy. Scheduling regular times for relaxation is the same for your body as performing regular maintenance on a car.

There are many different ways to relax. Some are passive, while others are active. The specific activities you choose are not as important as choosing activities you enjoy and that leave you feeling more at ease and refreshed when you have finished them. Here are some commonly used forms of relaxation:

Passive Forms of Relaxation

- Biofeedback.
- Diaphragmatic breathing.
- Hot tubs, showers, and baths.
- Massage and body work.
- Meditation and prayer.
- Movies and theater.
- Music (both as background and just sitting and listening).
- Reading.
- Relaxation response exercises.
- Self-hypnosis.
- Sleep.
- Television.
- Yoga.

Active Forms of Relaxation

- Avocational classes such as photography or cooking.
- Dancing.
- Hobbies and crafts such as art, fishing, gardening, or woodworking.
- Individual sports such as tennis or golf.
- Informal afternoons or evenings with friends.
- Jogging, swimming, and other forms of exercise.
- Road trips and vacations.
- Shopping.
- Team sports such as baseball or basketball.
- Video games.
- Walks.

Since an activity that relaxes one person might cause anxiety or distress in another, you need to select activities that match your personality and current abilities. Use the above lists as a starting point and identify several activities you find relaxing. During this and coming weeks, find ways to make the activities you identify a regular part of both your daily and weekly routine.

Decompression Routines

People with most of the high-anxiety personality traits tend to plunge from one activity into another. They do not allow time for the mind and body to recover in between. This tends to exaggerate the effects of stress, especially when an anxiety-related problem is present. Learning to take time to develop and use decompression routines is one way to overcome this tendency.

A decompression routine is any sort of ritual or routine used to unwind after a stressful event or day. In a sense, it is a specialized form of relaxation. Many people find solitary activities such as reading, working at a relaxing hobby, or just sitting work best. Others prefer activities involving children, spouses, or friends. Many of the activities suggested in the previous section can be used as part of a decompression routine.

Avoid using chemicals such as alcohol or marijuana as part of your decompression routine. Using the so-called recreational drugs to self-medicate in an attempt to relieve stress and anxiety usually creates additional problems. Many people suffering from alcoholism and other forms of chemical dependency began by using chemicals to relieve the symptoms of anxiety.

When I first began working with Brian, the person with panic disorder you met in Lesson 1, he told me that he never took breaks and often worked through lunch. He would then go home and immediately start working on projects around the house. After we discussed this, however, he developed the following decompression routines. First, he began taking his breaks in the morning and afternoon. Often he'd walk to the break room and read a paper for a few minutes before returning to work. He also started taking his lunch break. If the weather was good, he'd walk outside and sit in a small park nearby. When he got home, he took time to sit and read or listen to music for a short period before starting work around the house. These short breaks actually helped him work more efficiently as he found he was actually getting more accomplished than when he worked nonstop.

Play

Play is essential for good mental and physical health. Lesson 1 describes how the fight or flight response dampens your immune system and restricts normal bodily functions such as digestion. Like the other long-term approaches mentioned in this section, play takes you out of fight or flight mode and returns your body to a resting mode. This reduces physical tension and helps your body to resume normal repairs and functioning.

Unfortunately, many people feel it is childish and therefore undignified to play. Play can include a broad range of activities such as romping with the kids, talking with a friend, playing cards, shopping, or having lunch with someone you enjoy. Many of the activities mentioned under the heading Relaxation can be a type of play. Play can also involve exercise such as dancing or softball. In either case, play produces a form of mental and physical release that allows for increased relaxation afterward. The essential point is to do something that is both entertaining and fun on a regular basis.

Humor

A good sense of humor is one of your greatest allies in overcoming the effects of stress and anxiety. People with anxiety-related problems tend to magnify small and insignificant events so they become major anxiety-producing issues. Maintaining your sense of humor helps to keep things in perspective. Humor helps you see your limitations as simply an aspect of your humanness instead of as a sign of inadequacy.

From now on, whenever you notice that you are taking your circumstances, your work, your progress, your flaws, or your problems too seriously, find something to laugh about. This does not mean ridiculing or putting yourself down, but enjoying the comical aspect of life in a good-natured way.

Emotional Support

People are social beings who need emotional support in order to maintain mental and physical health. Loneliness and isolation are two of the most destructive forms of stress. Unfortunately, people suffering from severe anxiety often do not have a strong emotional support system. There are many possible reasons for this. Those who have come from a family that lacked intimacy may not know how to form healthy, nurturing relationships. Many of the high-anxiety personality traits discussed in Lesson 1 will also interfere with a person's ability to form a strong emotional support system. For example, those with an exaggerated need for approval will keep busy by trying to be supportive of others but will tend to not allow others to support them. They may even feel guilty whenever they become aware of their need for emotional support. They don't realize that receiving from others is just as important as giving. In fact, people cannot truly give unless they know how to receive.

The Recommended Activities for Lesson 1 suggested finding a study partner to provide emotional support as you go through the process of overcoming anxiety-related problems. Other sources of emotional support include family, friends, co-workers, church membership, specialized support or self-help groups, clubs, service organizations, professional therapy, and pets.

Another aspect of emotional support is that it can be conditional or unconditional. Conditional support means it is given as long as you behave in a certain way. Frequently, this is the type of support given by friends and co-workers. It may or may not be the type of support you receive from your family. There is nothing wrong with this type of support; still, it is useful to have at least one source of unconditional support. This refers to support that is available regardless of how you are feeling or what you have done. Pets are a common source of unconditional love and support. This is why they are so treasured by their owners. Sometimes unconditional support can also be found in churches, clubs, or community organizations.

If you are unable to find people who can provide emotional support, you may need to find it with a good therapist. A skilled therapist can offer many types of help. However, one of the most valuable aspects of therapy is often the unconditional emotional support it provides. Many people find therapy is the one place where they can really be themselves and have someone listen to what they say. The healing quality of this aspect of therapy is often as valuable as any of the therapeutic approaches used. Having one person to talk with honestly and openly removes the burden of carrying your secrets alone. It also helps you feel better about yourself and be more honest and open in all your other relationships. If you decide to seek the help of a therapist, refer to the guidelines for selecting one in Appendix 3.

Spiritual Support

Spiritual support refers to having something in your life that helps you make sense out of the world in which you live. It helps you give a positive meaning to events within the context of a universe much larger than yourself or your immediate surroundings. It is especially important when you encounter misfortune. Clarifying your spiritual or philosophical beliefs can also provide the key to accepting uncertainty and finding peace when you make mistakes or fail to meet your goals.

There are many ways in which you can fulfill the spiritual side of yourself that is so often neglected in our modern world. Traditional religions are the most commonly used form of spiritual support. Philosophy, taking time for private meditation, or reading inspirational books are other common sources. If you already have a strong source of spiritual support, you are deeply aware of the strength and serenity it provides. If you have a strong source that has helped to strengthen you in the past but that you have neglected to use at this point in your life, renew your relationship with it. You might also find it beneficial to talk to people you know who have a strong spiritual side about how they developed this area of their lives. If you do not have a strong source of spiritual support, take time this week to consider how you might fulfill your need to see events in a larger context and feed your inner need for personal meaning.

Traditions and Routines

The ability to use the various approaches described in this lesson does not just happen by itself. It requires structure. One important way to create this structure is to develop traditions and routines that make the above approaches part of your everyday life. If you do not create structures in the form of traditions and routines, these approaches will probably not become a regular part of your life.

Take time this week to schedule activities that are fun and regenerating. Continue to do this on a regular basis. For example, do something fun with your partner or significant other at least twice a month (preferably once a week)—a special dinner, a visit with good friends, a movie at a theater, or a rented movie at home. If you have children, have special time with each child daily if possible but at least once a week. Special time is one-on-one time where you do something together you both enjoy for at least fifteen minutes. Other traditions might include engaging in a relaxing activity at a particular time or the scheduling of time for a daily decompression routine after work.

Developing traditions and routines that reinforce the use of the various concepts presented in this lesson play a key role in the process of overcoming anxiety-related problems. Once you've overcome your anxiety-related problems, traditions and routines that incorporate the activities discussed in this lesson into your daily life will help prevent your anxiety-related problems from recurring.

Recommended Activities for Lesson 3

Continue Developing Cue-Controlled Relaxation

Continue practicing your relaxation response exercise once a day. Be sure to continue associating the same cue you selected last week with the deep relaxation you are practicing. If you have not yet begun this activity, do so this week. Appendix 2 describes four different methods for producing a relaxation response. Try each one several times and decide which works best for you. Your goal is to master at least one technique that produces physical relaxation. The Recommended Activities in Lesson 2 describes how to associate a conditioned response cue with relaxation in order to develop a cue-controlled relaxation response.

Continue Practicing Diaphragmatic Breathing

Continue practicing diaphragmatic breathing until you have accomplished the following:

- You can tell how you are breathing without the need to place a hand on your lower abdomen; you have developed the ability to use your internal sensors to "feel" when you are using diaphragmatic breathing.
- You can take a *relaxed* diaphragmatic breath whenever you want without effort.
- When you are relaxed, your normal method of breathing is relaxed diaphragmatic breathing.
- You usually continue to use diaphragmatic breathing (as opposed to upper-chest breathing) in anxiety-producing situations.

While some people reach the above goals very quickly, others take three or four weeks, occasionally longer. It all depends upon what type of breathing pattern you used when you began practicing and how consistent you are while practicing.

One word of caution concerning the use of diaphragmatic breathing during times when you are anxious: Do not become overly concerned about how you are breathing. Watching how you breathe tends to interfere with the natural process and may make you more anxious. To avoid this, simply take three or four relaxed breaths and move your attention to your coping self-statements and distractors. Your breathing will then readjust on its own.

Examine Your Diet

This lesson pointed out the importance of eating a well-balanced diet. It also provided general guidelines to follow. This week, examine what you have been eating. If you are not sure what constitutes a well-balanced diet, you may find it useful to read a book on nutrition. Your physician may know of one he or she can recommend. If you have any medical problems or questions, it is best to consult your physician before making any major changes in your diet.

There is one important guideline to follow concerning your diet: Stay away from books or nutritional counselors recommending unusual or fad diets. Your goal is to develop the habit of eating a well-balanced diet based on sound nutritional principles.

Consider Exercise

If you do not currently engage in regular exercise, plan to make exercise a part of your weekly routine. Any aerobic exercise done at least three times a week for at least twenty minutes each time can help increase your ability to tolerate stress and reduce anxiety. You do not have to become an exercise fanatic or purchase expensive equipment. You also don't have to start doing this all at once. Begin with just five or ten minutes. There are many good, commonsense books available on exercise. There are also many good exercise programs on television. Some people find that joining a health spa helps them keep their commitment to exercise regularly. Whatever you decide on, consistency and moderation are the keys to success.

Before starting a new exercise program or drastically changing your current one, it is best to check with your doctor. This is especially true if you have any physical condition that an inappropriate exercise program could affect adversely.

Begin Applying Stress Management Principles to Your Life

Decide when and how you will apply the stress management principles outlined in this lesson to your life. Be sure to review this lesson periodically to see if there are any additional ways in which you can apply these principles to your life.

Helping Others

One common tendency among people with a strong need for approval is the need to "help" others with their personal problems. If this is true for you, refrain from this while working on this program. At this time you simply do not have the time or energy to spare. Devote your time and energy to the work of learning new ways of thinking and acting. After the old anxiety-related patterns have been overcome, you will have the extra time and energy needed to help others. You will also have a whole new set of skills and insights that will make you a more effective resource.

Spend at least one week with this lesson. It takes time to absorb new ideas and apply them to your life.

LESSON 4

Identifying and Reducing the Sources of Anxiety

I n this lesson you learn how most of the anxiety you experience is
generated not by events, but by the meaning you give to events.
Since much of your thinking is simply a learned habit pattern, this
is something that, with time and a sound plan, you can learn to control. This lesson also describes why we have emotions and how they
are generated. It then describes a powerful method for reducing one
of the most common sources of anxiety—should/must thinking.

Needs and Beliefs

The first step in understanding your emotions is to learn a little
about your psychological needs. While different people often identify different needs, examples of needs that are frequently described
include: the need to give and receive love, the need to belong and feel
significant, the need to feel secure, the need to explore and learn, the
need to create, the need for relationships, and the need to find purpose and meaning in life. As a child you learned to satisfy these needs
by imitating the behaviors of adults, by being taught directly through
the way you were disciplined and trained, and by experiencing the
consequences of your actions through a process of trial and error.
These can be described as follows:

- *Beliefs about yourself:* These beliefs, sometimes referred to collectively as your self-concept or self-image, include beliefs about your personal value or worth, your talents and limitations, and your place in the world.
- *Beliefs about others:* These beliefs include all your beliefs about human relationships such as how others should be treated, what form romantic relationships should take, and what type of behaviors can be expected from the various people you meet.
- *Beliefs about the world:* These beliefs include beliefs about the meaning and importance of everyday events, as well as beliefs about abstract concepts as God, patriotism, and morality.

Many of the basic elements of your core beliefs were established by the age of seven. Because young children lack many adult reasoning skills, have very little life experience, and tend to accept what adults say without much questioning, many of the beliefs you arrived at as a child were irrational and unrealistic. While it is possible to examine these beliefs as an adult and replace unrealistic and irrational beliefs with more realistic and rational ones, many people fail to do so in at least some key areas of their lives. Either they do not understand the importance of these beliefs, or they are so busy with the demands of life that they never take time to examine their beliefs in a systematic manner. The tragic result is that many people go through their entire life basing many of their actions on core beliefs developed when they were children. When you think of human behavior in these terms, it is easy to understand why there is so much pain and suffering in the world. You also begin to see the source of much anxiety.

How Emotions Are Generated

Most of your emotions are the result of the interpretations you make of events taking place around you. The only exceptions are emotions that result from interference with the normal functioning of the brain or central nervous systems due to things such as illness, injury, mood-altering drugs, and genetic defects. Putting these exceptions aside, the process that generates most of your emotions can be diagrammed as follows:

Event ⟶ Interpretation ⟶ Emotion ⟶ Action

Because the process of interpreting events takes place so rapidly and usually unconsciously, you are often aware only of the event and the emotional reaction you have to the event. While this is the source of many problems, it is also essential to your survival. You could not function effectively if you had to evaluate and assign meaning to everything going on around you in a slow, deliberate manner.

An example of the mind's ability to interpret and assign meaning to events quickly and automatically is the seemingly simple act of driving a car. This is actually an extremely complicated process that requires you to judge distances, decide what the actions of pedestrians and other drivers mean, and make many other interpretations every second. The mind does all of this so quickly, you are usually unaware of the fact that the process is even occurring. Instead, you listen to the radio, talk to a passenger in the car, or do something else unrelated to driving.

The mind's ability to interpret events quickly and automatically has led to the widespread misconception that people and events generate emotions. Most people don't realize that it is the meaning they assign to people and events that actually generates emotions. Commonly used statements such as "He made me angry," "She made me sad," or "That really made me happy" not only reflect this mistaken belief but actually reinforce it.

If this mistaken idea were true, a specific event would generate the same emotion in everyone experiencing it. Instead, consider how different people react to a rainstorm. Some feel depressed by the lack of sunshine or become angry as they think about the inconvenience caused by the rain. Others feel happy as they look forward to being inside a warm, cozy house or because the rain brings needed water. Even though these people are all experiencing the same event, their emotions are different because each one interprets it differently.

Why Do We Have Emotions?

The exact way in which the biological mechanisms of emotions work is poorly understood by scientists at this time. It is clear, however, that emotions are part of an intricate inherited biological mechanism designed to help us survive.

In animals, emotions have two primary functions: They prepare the animal for action by activating the fight or flight response, and they focus the animal's attention on whatever has triggered the emotion. In higher animals, the bodily expression of the emotion also serves as a form of communication. For example, fear prepares an animal for immediate action and causes changes in posture, eyes, ears, or other body parts that communicate danger to other animals both within a species as well as in other species. This, in turn, triggers a similar response in them. Think for a moment of how a dog, a cat, or even a pet bird reacts when frightened. It is usually easy to tell by the animal's reaction.

Emotions also serve these two functions in humans. Since babies do not have verbal language, parents rely on the facial expressions and behaviors generated by a baby's emotions to understand the needs of a child. Likewise, emotional expression in adults is usually a more powerful form of communication than verbal expression. It should also be noted that while the facial expressions generated by emotions in people can be modified somewhat by learning, the expression of strong emotions show a remarkable consistency around the world. The facial expressions generated by emotions are also basically the same in both sighted people and those who have been blind since birth. It has also been noted that several basic emotions and emotional expressions emerge in an infant at fairly consistent times.

While humans and animals seem to share the same genetic aspect of emotions, there is an important difference between animals and humans. Emotions in animals are controlled by instinct or a combination of instinct and simple types of learning. In humans there are no true instincts. Babies are born with an innate startle response and fear of falling. Other fears emerge at predictable times, such as separation distress at four months and stranger distress at seven to nine months. By the time you become an adult, however, your entire emotional mechanism is controlled by a complex set of beliefs and learned response patterns. It is similar to the biological mechanisms that operate voluntary muscles in your arms and legs. These are also complex biological systems that, when functioning normally, are ultimately controlled by thoughts and learned response patterns.

In simplistic terms, emotions work in the following manner. A part of your mind constantly evaluates events in terms of your needs and wants. This process of assigning meaning to events is usually done automatically and unconsciously. If a need or want is or may be satisfied, you experience the various positive emotions such as joy, excitement, or satisfaction. If a threat is present, you experience anger (ranging from irritation to rage) or fear (ranging from apprehension to panic). If you encounter a loss, you experience sadness, grief, or depression, depending on the nature of the loss. Of course, events are often complex. They can satisfy some needs and frustrate others. This is why we often experience mixed emotions. This process of interpreting needs and wants can be diagrammed as follows:

When emotions focus your attention and motivate you to take actions that help you respond effectively to opportunity, loss, and danger and achieve your life goals, they are self-fulfilling emotions. Unfortunately, emotions often do not work in this manner. Sometimes we experience self-defeating emotions that interfere with our ability to be effective in relationships, work, and play and prevent us from reaching our life goals. Emotions can become self-defeating if they occur when there is no apparent reason for them, if they occur at an exaggerated level of intensity, or if they last for an extended period of time. Examples include becoming anxious when no threat exists, becoming enraged over a minor incident, and remaining depressed for days over a minor loss or disappointment.

If the function of emotions is to help protect you and satisfy your needs, why then do you experience self-defeating emotions? The answer is simple. Every person has at least some, and in most cases many, beliefs and habitual thinking patterns that are irrational or unrealistic. This causes the automatic evaluation process to misinterpret events and either exaggerate threats and losses or see them when they are not actually present. This, in turn, triggers inappropriate emotions and self-defeating behaviors.

This automatic aspect of your mind is like a computer. It has the ability to examine vast amounts of information coming in through your senses and make split-second decisions about whether or not an event satisfies or threatens your needs and wants. In the computer field there is a saying: *Garbage in, garbage out.* This refers to the fact that a computer fed inaccurate information or given a faulty program makes faulty calculations.

In addition to faulty thinking patterns, Lesson 1 described how we also may have unconscious conditioned responses that trigger inappropriate responses. The rest of this lesson focuses on inappropriate emotions triggered by faulty habitual thinking patterns.

Habitual Thinking Patterns

One of the wonders of the human mind is its ability to learn an action so well that it becomes automatic. Some actions that took years to learn—such as dressing yourself—are now so automatic you don't think about them. The way in which you think, the words you use, and the events you choose to remember and focus on are all automatic habit patterns and differ little from all of the other automatic behaviors you learned while growing up. In fact, you spend most of your day on "automatic pilot." Unfortunately, just as you developed many irrational beliefs, you also developed many irrational ways of processing information that are now part of this automatic thought process that, in turn, contributes to your anxiety.

A key component of this automatic thought process is self-talk—the silent conversations that everyone has inside when thinking. Another key part of this internal automatic thought process involves the memories you choose to recall and the events on which you choose to focus. While you have a wide variety of memories from which to choose, you usually recall those that reinforce your current state of mind. When you are sad, you recall sad memories. When you are happy, you recall pleasant ones. You also have a set of memorized stories and explanations you recall for specific events and situations. For example, when you are asked to say something about yourself, your work, or your childhood, you probably recall the same set of stories and explanations each time. In the same way, you have a selective point of view and notice only certain aspects of daily life. You may only be aware of flaws and errors, or you may be aware of opportunities and the positive aspects of the situations in which you find yourself. All of these are, in turn, shaped by the core beliefs described earlier in the lesson.

Your automatic self-talk, selective remembering, prepared stories and explanations, and selective points of view make up your habitual thinking patterns. The interpretation process that generates your emotions is, for the most part, based upon a combination of these automatic, habitual thinking patterns and your beliefs. By changing them, you can change the way you interpret events and dramatically and positively alter your experience of life.

The Cognitive Approach

The ideas you are studying this week come from an approach to psychology called cognitive therapy. The word *cognitive* refers to thinking or thought. Therefore, a cognitive approach involves learning how to change the way you feel and act by changing the way you think. The process of changing the way you think is called cognitive restructuring.

The primary skill used by the cognitive approach is rational self-talk. This skill can help you change the way you feel and act by changing the way you interpret events; perceive the world more rationally and realistically; increase your sense of personal power; and take advantage of opportunities and choices you were unaware of in the past. The seven different types of rational self-talk commonly used to accomplish these goals are listed below. The coping self-statements described in Lesson 2 use ego strengtheners, questioning, and redirecting statements.

- *Ego strengtheners:* Statements that offer self-encouragement or remind you of specific positive abilities you possess.

- *Substitution:* The substitution of words or phrases that characterize rational thinking for ones characteristic of irrational thinking.
- *Questioning:* The use of questions to direct your attention to key issues or to emphasize the irrational nature of a particular form of self-defeating thinking. Questioning is usually followed by a rational challenge, objective evaluation, cost–benefit analysis, or redirecting statement.
- *Rational challenge:* The use of memorized statements or rational arguments to correct faulty assumptions that underlie specific types of irrational thinking or self-defeating behaviors.
- *Objective evaluation:* The objective analysis of your current situation, thoughts, or behavior. The goal is to take yourself off automatic pilot and use your ability to discriminate and reason in a more deliberate manner. This helps you replace automatic thoughts and behaviors that are self-defeating with thoughts and behaviors that are self-enhancing.
- *Cost–benefit analysis:* The listing and evaluation of advantages or disadvantages for a particular belief or behavior. This is often part of an objective evaluation and helps you become more realistic when irrational thinking has caused you to view the world in an unrealistic and self-defeating manner. It also helps correct irrational beliefs that support an unrealistic view of the world.
- *Redirecting statements:* Statements that redirect your attention and energy into more rational and productive activities. Redirecting statements usually follow one of the above approaches.

The above terms will be used throughout the rest of the program. People with a strong analytical bent often find it useful to memorize the above terms; others do not. These terms are listed in parentheses in the examples of rational self-talk that are given in this and the following lesson. If you find it useful to label the different types of rational self-talk, refer back to this section. If you find the labeling of self-talk confusing, disregard this section. Your main goal is to learn to recognize faulty self-talk and be able to challenge it effectively. If the above labels help you move toward that goal, use them. If not, use whatever is most helpful for you to master rational self-talk.

Should/Must Thinking

Should/must thinking refers to the transformation of personal choices, wants, or preferences into universal absolutes. This is usually done by using words and phrases such as "should," "must," "ought," and "have to." When you use should/must thinking, three things tend to occur. First, you focus your attention on the undesirable aspects of problems and the discomfort you are experiencing rather than on finding possible solutions. Second, you tend to waste time and energy criticizing and condemning the person or thing that is breaking the should/must rule. Third, you lose some contact with reality as you enter the fantasy world of how things "should" be.

One evening, Donna had an experience that illustrates these three aspects of should/must thinking. While going to a friend's house for a casual dinner party, she was caught in a traffic jam. Because Donna had the rule, "I must always be on time," she reacted with the following self-talk: "Oh no! I'm not going to make it on time. I can't be late. This is terrible! I must be on time." Donna's should/must rule created the false belief that there was only one possibility in this situation. Donna had to be on time. Nothing else was acceptable. This kept her mind focused on the undesirable aspects of an event she had no power to predict or prevent. She was unable to adopt a problem-solving approach and consider practical and positive ways of dealing with the problem of the traffic jam.

Soon, Donna found herself condemning the person who broke the should/must rule—in this case herself. "Boy have you blown it. You can't even get to a simple dinner party on time. You should have known better than to leave when you did." She also spent time condemning people and events that contributed to the problem: "Stupid drivers. Why can't people drive like they're supposed to? And why can't they do something about this road anyway?" Because most should/must rules like this come from childhood, Donna, like many people, found her internal self-talk sounding like a critical parent.

When you say something should or must exist and it actually does not, to some extent you are denying reality and entering a fantasy world.

Donna's fantasy held that there was no substitute for being on time. In the real world, she is occasionally going to be late. As reality intruded upon Donna's fantasy, she experienced tremendous anxiety along with resentment toward anyone or anything that delayed her further. She even found herself driving recklessly—risking her life, her automobile, and the lives of other drivers. As she arrived late, Donna punished herself with self-condemnation for breaking her should/must rule.

From the above, you might assume that all should/must thinking is undesirable. Not always. Should/must thinking is often essential for survival when living in harsh circumstances with limited choices. For example, if you live in a totalitarian society where the secret police might imprison you for incorrect words or actions, you need rigid rules about what you say and do. Likewise, it is also valuable for a child growing up in a dysfunctional household to develop rigid rules about how to act around a parent who is drunk or has a volatile temper. Indeed, the harsher the environment you were raised in, the more should/must thinking you will tend to engage in. Unfortunately, a person raised in a harsh environment will tend to continue thinking in a rigid way as an adult even when circumstances may now be quite different. It is also common for a child raised by a parent who came from a harsh environment to adopt the parent's rigid thinking patterns by simply modeling after the parent.

The key to challenging should/must thinking is training yourself to accept reality and focusing on the choices that are available to you in a given situation. The following types of rational self-talk can be used to do this.

Substitution

Whenever you catch yourself saying or thinking "I should," "I must," or "I have to," re-state it using phrases such as "I like," "I want," "I choose," "I have decided," "I would like," "I prefer," or "It would be nice." These types of phrases help you become more aware of the fact that life is a series of choices and you are choosing to act in one way or another. There is nothing you have to do in life. You choose to do things that bring something desirable or help you avoid something undesirable. Here are several examples:

SOME SAMPLE SUBSTITUTIONS	
If You Say or Think:	**Restate or Rethink It As :**
I have to be on time.	I like to be on time.
	I want to be on time.
	I prefer to be on time.
The lawn should/must be cut every Saturday.	I like to cut the lawn every Saturday.
	I choose to cut the lawn every Saturday.
	I have decided to cut the lawn every Saturday.
He should be polite.	I would like it if he were polite.
	I would prefer it if he were polite.
	It would be nice if he were polite.
They should be fair.	I would like them to be fair.
	I want them to be fair.
	It would be nice if they were fair.

Questioning

Ask yourself, "Who says I should/must . . . ?," "Why should/must I . . . ?," or "Where is it written that I should/must . . . ?" This exposes the arbitrary nature of should/must rules and the fact that they are actually personal values and preferences rather than universal absolutes. Follow this type of questioning with one or more of the following approaches.

Objective Evaluation

List the choices that are available and choose the one that seems best for you. Your goal is to choose thoughts and actions that are appropriate for the situation you are facing instead of blindly following an arbitrary set of should/must rules that probably do not reflect reality. For example, Donna can acknowledge that she is going to be late and decide what her choices are. She can call ahead to let someone know she is going to be late. She can just arrive late and make the best of the situation. She can also decide whether or not she needs to leave earlier next time in order to arrive at the time she wants to arrive.

Cost–Benefit Analysis

Some should/must rules concern behaviors or values that are valuable and that you may want to keep. In order to determine this, make a list of the advantages and disadvantages of acting in this way or having this value. This can be either a mental list or something you do on paper. If you decide a particular rule is useful, be sure to rephrase it using the language described in the first approach in this section, Substitution.

Rational Challenge

When you identify a should/must rule you want to eliminate, challenge the rule with logical arguments whenever you notice yourself thinking or using automatic behavior that reflects it. Include reasons in your arguments as to why the should/must rule is no longer useful along with a clear statement of a more desirable rule or value. Often a self-defeating rule is something that a parent, teacher, or relative frequently said when you were young. When this is the case, it is helpful to recall where the rule came from and remind yourself that you are no longer a child. Instead, you are an adult who is fully able to take responsibility for making your own rules and decisions.

After learning the above rational cognitive skills, Donna again found herself in a traffic jam. This time it occurred while she was driving to work. As is often the case, her first reaction was to react with her old pattern of should/must thinking. However, she quickly recognized what she was doing and used the following rational self-talk to challenge the old patterns.

> Wait a minute. Here I am getting upset about being late again when there's nothing I can do about it. I like to be on time (substitution). However, there is no way this is going to happen today. My boss understands the problems with traffic in the city and doesn't really mind my occasionally being a little late. In fact, he often complains about this same stretch of road. It looks like I'll only be about ten minutes late and it's been some time since the last time this happened. When I get to work, I'll just explain what happened (objective evalua-

tion). Now let's just relax and listen to the radio and get to work as soon as I can (redirecting statement).

When reading the various examples of rational self-talk in this and following chapters, remember that there is no single correct form of rational self-talk for a given situation. The various cognitive approaches can blend together in many different ways. Different people often use very different forms of rational self-talk for the same situation. As you gain experience, finding the right combination of approaches that fits your beliefs, personality, and the specific should/must rule you are challenging becomes automatic. Here is another example of rational self-talk applied to a different situation:

> *Example:* Jim has just finished dinner and catches himself thinking, "I should do these dishes now that dinner is over."
>
> *Jim's rational self-talk:* He notices what he is thinking and has the following internal dialogue: "Who says I should do these dishes now? Where is it written that they have to be done immediately after dinner (questioning)? I guess Mom always told me to do them as soon as I got up from dinner. Well, I'm an adult now and can make my own rules and decisions (rational challenge). Let's see, I can do them now, stack them and do them later, or soak them and do them tomorrow. I guess I really don't want to leave them until tomorrow. I also want to just sit and relax for a while (objective evaluation). I think I'll choose to leave them for now and do them later (substitution)."

Circular Questioning

Circular questioning is a common form of should/must thinking where you ask yourself over and over questions that are either irrelevant or have an answer you already know but are unwilling to accept. Common examples include "Why am I like this?" "Why can't I change?" "Why did that happen?" "How could he/she do that?" and "How could that happen?" Circular questioning like this usually occurs when a should/must rule has been violated. Your mind becomes "stuck" because you refuse to accept some aspect of reality and slip into the fantasy world of your should/must rules.

Why am I like this? usually means "I should be different and can't stand the way I am." *Why can't I change?* usually means "I have to change" or "I can't change and it's awful." *Why did that happen?* usually means "That shouldn't happen." *How could he/she do that?* usually means "He/she should have acted differently and it's terrible that he/she acted in that manner." How *could that happen?* usually means "That shouldn't have happened."

The first step in challenging circular questioning is to identify the should/must rule that has been violated. This can usually be done by simply changing the question into a should/must or can't statement. Occasionally there is an additional should/must rule implied by your statement that also needs to be challenged. *Life should be fair* is an example of a common should/must rule that can generate circular questioning like the above examples. This and other common underlying irrational beliefs will be explored more fully in later lessons.

Once you have identified the should/must rule that is generating your circular questioning, challenge it with the rational self-talk approaches described in the preceding section.

> *Example:* Jeff lives with Mark, who is often inconsiderate. When his friend acts thoughtlessly, Jeff usually begins thinking "Why is Mark like this? How could he be so inconsiderate?" over and over as he becomes anxious and upset.
>
> *Jeff's rational self-talk:* "Wait a minute. Here I go with the 'hows' and 'whys' again. Actually, I'm saying Mark should be different from the way he is and it's appalling that he isn't (change the questions into a statement). While I would like Mark to be different, it is a fact that he is who and what he is. He is frequently very inconsiderate and I need to decide how I am going to respond when this happens (objective evaluation). Now, what are my choices (redirecting statement)?"

Can't Thinking

The use of the word *can't* to describe a need, want, decision, or choice is another common form of should/must thinking—for example, saying "I can't go to the store," when you actually mean "I don't want to go to the store," or "I shouldn't go to the store."

As long as you either "must" or "can't" do something, you create the illusion that you have no responsibility or control over that area of your life. This causes you to also lose your ability to change and exert power in that area of your life. You are failing to recognize that life is a series of choices. You choose to do or not do something because it brings you pleasure or helps you avoid discomfort. As soon as you begin to realize that you are choosing to do or not do things, you begin to take back the power you need to change the way you live and create the life you want.

Changing the words you use is an easy way to begin taking back the power you need to change your life. Whenever you catch yourself saying or thinking "I can't," change it into, "I don't want to," "I choose not to," "I don't like," or "I don't feel like." For example:

CHANGING CAN'T THINKING	
If You Say or Think:	**Restate or Rethink It As :**
I can't go to the store.	I choose not to go to the store.
	I don't want to go to the store.
	I don't feel like going to the store.
I can't drive.	I don't want to drive.
	I choose not to drive.
	I don't like to drive.

People with anxiety-related problems frequently avoid situations associated with anxiety or panic. If this is true for you, it is important to keep in mind that you have not really lost any of your former abilities. You still can do anything you have done before. You could probably do even more if there were sufficient reason. Consider a situation in which someone you love is seriously ill or dying and you are the only person who can help. You would be able to go wherever you need to go and do whatever you need to do to save this person's life. You might experience anxiety or panic either while you were helping this person or afterward, but you would do it.

Right now you may be choosing to avoid some situations and activities because you do not want to experience the anxiety they produce. This is something everyone does and is perfectly all right. As you continue to work through these lessons as instructed, you will eventually change enough of your attitudes and master enough of the skills to manage your anxiety and overcome your current avoidance patterns. Until then, you are choosing to avoid some situations because you do not want to experience the discomfort associated with them. Do not condemn yourself for doing this. Techniques for overcoming avoidance patterns are presented later in the lessons. Your task right now is to work at changing the way you think so you will be ready to apply those skills.

The Locus of Control

All of the forms of should/must thinking described in this lesson place the locus (or center) of control outside you. When you use them, you tend to act and feel like a child who has a critical parent watching over you and waiting to punish you if you break one of the rules. When you start to use the rational self-talk described in this and following lessons, you bring the locus of control inside yourself.

Eliminating should/must thinking does not mean you do not have rules. It is good to have guidelines for your life. Donna, the person described earlier, still has the rule that she likes to be on time. This is a useful rule in her life. When being on time was a rigid should/must rule, it ruled her like a tyrant and often caused much unnecessary distress. After learning about should/must thinking, Donna is now in control of the rule rather than it being in control of her.

Recommended Activities for Lesson 4

Continue Developing Cue-Controlled Relaxation

Continue practicing your relaxation response at least once a day. When you experience more stress then usual, schedule an extra session. Also, be sure to continue to associate the same cue you selected while doing Lesson 2 with the deep relaxation you are practicing.

After three weeks of daily practice, some people still find it difficult to produce a state of deep relaxation. If this is true for you, reread the instructions in Appendix 2 carefully. If you have not been practicing daily, decide now when and where you will practice and make a firm commitment to do this important activity. If you have tried only one approach, use each of the other methods described in Appendix 2. Be sure to have at least three practice sessions with each method. If you have not yet tried taping the scripts, do so and use them as instructed.

If you have done everything suggested above and are still finding it difficult to produce a relaxation response, consider buying a professionally produced relaxation CD. The basic set of CDs that accompanies this book is designed to help people with anxiety-related problems develop cue-controlled relaxation. They work well with people having difficulty developing deep relaxation. Information on how to obtain them is at the back of this book. Relaxation or stress-reduction CDs are also available in book- and music stores. You may find it necessary to try several in order to find one that suits you. When you find one that works well for you, begin associating a cue with it as explained in Lesson 2.

Begin Making a Record of Your Self-Talk During Times When You Are Anxious or Upset

As described in this lesson, self-talk plays an important role in the interpretation process that generates your emotions. Start recording your thoughts in a notebook or binder. Spend five minutes every other day recalling times during that or the previous day when you were anxious, angry, hurt, or depressed. Take a moment to mentally place yourself back into the event and recall what you were thinking or saying to yourself. Record your thoughts in the notebook.

Since much of your thinking is automatic, the first step in changing how you think is to identify precisely what you are thinking and saying to yourself. This record of your thoughts will be an initial snapshot of your thought process that will be analyzed in the following lessons.

Reevaluate Your Should/Must Rules

Make a list of your personal should/must rules. Take several days to list things you catch yourself thinking or saying that contain the word or idea of "should," "must," or "have to." Don't forget that circular questioning and can't thinking are simply disguised forms of should/must thinking. Here are some examples:

- I should be calm when I go out.
- The house has to be cleaned by 11:00 A.M.
- Why can't I get to places on time? (This means "I should always be on time.")
- How could that person say such a rude thing? (This means "People shouldn't say rude things.")

After a few days, go through your list and evaluate the advantages and disadvantages of each should/must rule. Make a conscious decision about whether you want to keep, change, or eliminate any of the rules you have been following. Whenever you find yourself saying, thinking, or basing your actions on a rule you want to eliminate, use the various rational self-talk skills to challenge it. Practice using accurate and positive language when thinking or speaking about rules you decide to keep.

Be Patient

Remember that you progress at your own rate. You are currently at the beginning of this program and have much to learn. Whether or not you overcome the behaviors and symptoms associated with anxiety at the end of the fifteen lessons depends on many things:

- How much time and effort you put into working through the lessons.
- How carefully you follow the instructions in the recommended reading.
- How severe your symptoms were when you began.
- How long you have experienced your symptoms.
- Your own individual personality.

- The strength of your commitment to change and overcome your old patterns.
- How much time and energy you put into practicing the activities you are asked to do.
- Whether or not there are any complicating factors such as a poor marriage, difficult life events, or medical conditions.

The above combination of factors is different for every person using this program. Some people overcome all the symptoms associated with anxiety in a few months. Others need to work on these skills for a year or more. Some people simply have more work to do to unlearn old patterns and develop new ones to replace them. How long it takes is not important. What is important is that you spend the time and energy required to reach your goal and use the lessons as they are intended to be used. If you are doing this, you will overcome the old patterns that generate and maintain your anxiety.

One common error many people with anxiety-related problems make is to have the goal of eliminating all anxiety. This is impossible. The only people who never experience anxiety are psychotic, brain damaged, drugged, or dead. Anxiety is a natural part of living and is often the most appropriate response to a real threat.

You are working toward two different goals: minimizing the overall amount of anxiety you experience, and managing the anxiety you do experience more effectively so it does not limit or interfere with your ability to enjoy life. Because this requires learning new skills as well as changing old thinking patterns and old attitudes, it is a gradual process. You are not in competition with anyone; just move along at your own rate, one that is right for you.

Reward Your Successes

You will progress more rapidly if you develop the habit of rewarding yourself whenever you experience success with the skills you're developing. This does not mean you wait for your skills to work perfectly. Learn to congratulate yourself whenever a skill works, even if it is only a partial success. The easiest way to do this is with statements such as the following:

- I did it!
- The skills I'm learning worked. I was able to do it!
- Even though there was some anxiety, I didn't let it stop me.
- Wait until I tell my friend/spouse about this!
- It wasn't as bad as I expected. It was actually much easier.
- I did well.
- It's getting better each time I use my skills.
- I'm really pleased with the progress I'm making.
- When I used my skills, it was easier than I thought it would be.
- I've just taken another step forward.

Saying complimentary statements like the above is often difficult for people with many of the high-anxiety personality traits. If this is true for you, make a deliberate effort to learn how to compliment yourself.

Negative Friends

At one time or another, everyone has known a negative person. This is someone who is always noticing flaws and dwelling on problems, illnesses, or unpleasant symptoms. Keep the following points in mind when you are around a negative person.

- When you are anxious or tense, you are more susceptible to the negativity of others.
- You are working on changing your habitual ways of thinking and acting. People with a negative outlook will slow you down and may even sabotage your work.
- Negative people are very energy draining. At this time you need to devote all of your energy to the task of overcoming your anxiety-related problems. You don't have energy to spare.

While working with these lessons, you may find it important to "let go" of negative friends and spend as little time with them as possible. The easiest way to let go of a negative friend is through "creative neglect." Simply be busy or unavailable whenever the negative friend wants to talk or spend time together. After overcoming your anxiety-related problems, you may resume these friendships.

Sometimes the negative person in your life is a relative, co-worker, or someone else you need to deal with on a regular basis. Here are three guidelines for dealing with negative people who are difficult to avoid.

- *Keep time spent with this person to a minimum:* Maintain as much emotional and physical distance as possible. This is especially important if the person is a parent, since the parent–child relationship can be a very strong force and pull you back into old patterns very quickly. When you visit a negative parent, go for just an hour at most a day. Two short visits are often easier to handle than one long visit. It is also useful to plan some neutral event as the focus of the visit such as a dinner, a game, or an outing to some event. You can then redirect the flow of conversation away from "hot" topics to the neutral event.

    If you are visiting negative parents or relatives out of town, do not spend the night in their house. Stay in a motel or hotel so you have a safe place you can retreat to. If you are staying for more than a day, plan one or more activities that take you away from them for a few hours.

- *Use decompression routines:* After you have been in contact with a negative person, do an activity that helps neutralize this person's negative influence as soon as possible, such as spending time alone, reading the lesson on which you are currently working, doing a relaxation response exercise, working on an enjoyable hobby, reading something inspirational, praying, meditating, or talking with someone who is positive and uplifting. This last suggestion is especially useful when you are dealing with a negative parent or parent figure. A short conversation or meeting with a positive support person is often enough to counteract the negative impact of time spent with a negative parent. In extreme cases a visit to a therapist might be needed to undo the impact of a strong negative experience.

- *Develop defense mechanisms for dealing with negativity:* One approach that is useful when dealing with negative people is to be "unconscious." The best example of being unconscious is the reaction many children have toward their parents when the parents are nagging or scolding them. Just as a child can become parent-deaf, you can learn to be deaf and unconscious to the negativity of others. This becomes easier as the weeks go by and your skills in other areas increase.

Another approach is to use your imagination. Create an imaginary fence around yourself. Then imagine the negative thoughts and actions coming from the negative person bouncing off this imaginary shield. You can use this simple method to protect yourself whenever you are around a negative person. You can also imagine a trusted support person or religious figure standing next to you. You can even imagine how a person you respect would deal with the situation and pretend that you are this person.

As you work your way through this program, you may discover other ways to reduce the influence negative people exert on you. When you do, be sure to write them down so you can refer to them when you are not thinking clearly and are going to be around a negative person. You may also find that as you change, the way you are treated by negative people may also change.

> Spend at least one week with this lesson and read it at least three times. If you feel the urge to move ahead before a week is over, use the time to review and practice the skills presented in the previous lessons.

LESSON 5

Distorted Thinking

W
ith this lesson you have reached an important milestone in your quest to conquer anxiety. As you combine the knowledge and skills in this lesson with what you have already learned, you will begin to see your rate of progress increase more rapidly.

Common Forms of Distorted Thinking

The following forms of thinking are called distorted thinking because they cause an irrational or unrealistic interpretation of events. This creates a distorted view of the world, yourself, or your place in the world, which can cause inappropriate emotions and self-defeating behaviors. From time to time you use most, if not all, of these forms of distorted thinking. This is especially true whenever you experience excessive stress, hunger, fatigue, or illness. As you read through the lesson, put a check by those forms that are most typical of the way you think and speak. Spend most of your time and energy with the ones you checked as you reread and study this lesson.

Each of the following descriptions includes an explanation of how rational self-talk can be used to challenge that particular form of distorted thinking. In the examples for this and following lessons, the specific types of rational self-talk used are labeled in parenthesis with the terms that were introduced in Lesson 4. Make periodic reviews of the descriptions in The Cognitive Approach in Lesson 4 until you are comfortable with them.

If you are an analytical type of person, you will probably become fairly skilled at labeling the various types of distorted thinking and the various types of rational challenges that can be used to challenge them. Some readers, however, look at the labeling and analyzing of distorted thinking and rational self-talk as just too confusing. If you are one of those, don't be concerned. Many people never become skilled at applying the various labels and terms but *do* become skilled at recognizing when they are using distorted thinking and challenging it with rational self-talk. While learning to identify and label distorted thinking makes it easier to change your thinking, it is not the only way to do so. If you do your best with the exercises in this and the next few lessons, you will gain skill in recognizing the types of distorted thinking you use, whether you are able to label them or not. As you learn to recognize and challenge your distorted thinking, you will be pleasantly surprised at what a powerful tool this is.

Should/Must Thinking

Lesson 4 defined should/must thinking as the transformation of personal choices, wants, or preferences into universal absolutes. This is usually done by using words and phrases such as "should," "must," "ought," and "have to." Lesson 4 also discussed two common variations on should/must thinking called circular questioning and can't thinking. There is one other common form of should/must thinking called all-or-nothing thinking.

All-or-nothing thinking—sometimes called dichotomous thinking—is the evaluation of personal qualities and events in terms of black-and-white categories. The words that are most frequently associated with this type of thinking are "right," "wrong," "good," and "bad." All-or-nothing thinking is based on rigid should/must rules that force everyday experience into absolute good and bad categories. This creates a distorted view of the world that generates increased anxiety and depression. Everyday events are rarely completely good or bad.

All-or-nothing thinking plays a major role in perfectionism because it magnifies the importance of mistakes and imperfections. It

contributes to a poor self-image since any personal flaw or error causes you to view yourself as inadequate and worthless. All-or-nothing
thinking also causes your experience of the world to be negative since
events in an imperfect world are rarely good enough to be considered
positive.

The most effective rational self-talk approach to use when correcting
all-or-nothing thinking is a rational challenge, followed by redirecting
statements. Concentrate on finding examples that contradict the black-
and-white categories you have created. Challenge any should/must or
can't rules you identify as part of the all-or-nothing thinking and remind
yourself that this is a perfectionistic form of thinking.

> *Example:* Choy was in the process of overcoming social phobia
> and experienced a moderate amount of anxiety during part of a
> social event. She reacted by thinking: "I'm really blowing this. I
> wish I could do things right."
>
> *Choy's rational self-talk:* "Wait a minute. What do I mean, 'I'm
> really blowing this'? And what do I mean by 'doing things right'?
> (challenging questions). I'm really not doing that bad even though
> I'm somewhat uncomfortable. In fact, I have actually enjoyed part of
> this event (objective evaluation). There is no one 'right' way to act.
> There are many ways to act and feel at an event like this. When I say
> 'I wish I could do things right' I'm actually saying I should be calm
> and confident in this situation. While I'd like to be calm and confi-
> dent, the truth is I am still learning how to manage my anxiety and it
> will probably be some time before I become calm in a situation like
> this. That is okay. The way I am *acting* is just fine even though I may
> not like the way I am *feeling*. This anxiety only means I still some-
> times become anxious in this type of situation. That is normal and to
> be expected for someone in my situation (rational challenge). Now,
> let's practice using my small-talk skills (redirecting statement)."

Overgeneralization

Overgeneralization is the changing of a single negative event into
a never-ending pattern of defeat or misfortune. This is usually done
by using words like "never," "always," and "every."

The best way to reverse an overgeneralization is to remind yourself that a single negative event is just that—a single negative event and nothing more. Recalling at least one event that contradicts the negative overgeneralization also helps. Some people find their rational self-talk is strengthened if they begin with a question that emphasizes the extreme nature of the overgeneralization such as "Is it really true that I *always* . . . ?"

> *Example:* Andy was planning an outing but woke up to bad weather and began thinking: "Why does it always rain when I plan something? I guess I can't do anything right."
>
> *Andy's rational self-talk:* "Does it really always rain when I plan something? And do I never do anything well (emphasizing the overgeneralization with a question)? I guess this is an overgeneralization. Actually, this is the first time this year I've planned an outing and it rained. I also have to admit that the last outing I planned went very well (objective evaluation)."

Labeling is a common form of overgeneralization in which you define yourself or your behavior in terms of a simplistic and usually negative label. Labeling is usually the result of internalizing labels that were used by adults or other children to describe you when you were a child. As you matured, these labels are internalized and became a habitual, automatic response that now occurs when flaws are noticed or when a mistake is made. Here are some common negative labels. Check any you frequently use for yourself.

Common Negative Labels

aggressive	childish	critical
arrogant	cold	cruel
bitchy	competitive	demanding
born loser	compulsive	disgusting
bossy	conceited	dull
castrating	controlling	dumb
chauvinist	crazy	egotistical

emotional	nitpicking	stubborn
failure	nosy	stuck-up
frigid	overemotional	stupid
harsh	parental	superman/woman
hostile	passive	thoughtless
hysterical	petty	too idealistic
illogical	pig	too sensitive
immature	repulsive	troublemaker
impolite	rotten	ugly
incapable	self-centered	unassertive
insensitive	selfish	ungrateful
irrational	self-pitying	unimportant
irresponsible	shrill	uninteresting
klutz	silly	weak
lazy	sissy	willful
mean	slow	wimpy
nagging	softy	

Sometimes seemingly positive labels can be as bad as negative ones. For example, a "nice guy" might allow himself to be taken advantage of rather than risk losing his positive self-image. Other examples of labels that seem positive but can create similar problems are gracious, good parent, good person, and in charge.

Labeling like the above usually is nonproductive and inaccurate. Furthermore, since these types of labels are usually emotionally loaded, they generate strong negative feelings that often paralyze you or trigger self-defeating behavior.

Several types of rational self-talk can be used to combat labeling. Start with substitution. Dismiss the label for what it is—an inaccurate overgeneralization—and substitute more accurate, opposite, and positive words to describe yourself. The use of ego strengtheners is a good idea if you've been very hard on yourself. Finally, make an objective evaluation of the event or situation. If your labeling is in response to a mistake that you have made, use redirecting statements to remind yourself of the only two constructive alternatives you have: if possible, do something practical to correct your error, and decide how you can reduce the chance of this event or error from recurring in the future. If your labeling is in response to a personal flaw or shortcoming you have noticed, use a rational challenge and remind yourself to separate your actions from your worth as a person.

> *Example:* Pat is a shipping clerk who has sent a shipment to the wrong location. She catches herself dwelling on how she is worthless and always making a mess of things.
>
> *Pat's rational self-talk:* "Wait a minute. I am not a worthless screw-up! I am simply a human being who has made a mistake (substitution). People do this all the time. Actually, I'm a very good worker who is just as accurate and productive as the other clerks (ego strengtheners). Now, exactly what went wrong? It seems I punched the wrong code into the computer when I coded the address labels. I guess the first thing I need to do is make sure that shipment gets rerouted. I can now just look at this as a lesson telling me I need to be more careful when I input information into the computer. When I make a mistake like this in the future, I also need to remind myself that everyone makes mistakes from time to time. In fact, I correct mistakes like this that others have made all the time (objective evaluation)."

Magnification/Minimization

Magnification refers to two different types of exaggeration. The first, called catastrophizing, is the act of turning small personal flaws, minor negative experiences, or errors into major catastrophes. The second type of magnification is the exaggeration of someone else's achievements or abilities.

One common type of catastrophic self-talk involves phrases such as, "I can't stand this," or "I can't take it." These are inaccurate phrases. You may be unhappy, uncomfortable, and may even be responding ineffectively; however, since you are not dead or comatose, you are "standing it." Another common type of catastrophic self-talk is the labeling of events as terrible, awful, or horrible when they are actually only inconvenient. Words like these rarely describe everyday events or personal limitations accurately. When these types of catastrophic exaggerations become habitual reactions to everyday inconveniences, they trigger exaggerated emotional responses and unnecessary anxiety. More importantly, they paralyze you and prevent you from solving your problems and improving the situation.

One effective type of rational self-talk to use with catastrophizing is the substitution of more accurate language for the catastrophic descriptions. Sometimes a direct rational challenge or objective evaluation is also helpful. Remind yourself that you can stand events. An event may be inconvenient or a disappointment and may even involve discomfort or negative consequences; however, most events are only a tragedy when you define them as such, exaggerate their meaning, and magnify your limitations.

Example: Fred is having difficulty with an algebra assignment when he thinks: "This is awful. I can't stand not knowing how to do this."

Fred's rational self-talk: "What am I saying? It is true this is difficult and I am finding it frustrating. However, it is certainly not 'awful' (substitution). Saying I can't stand not knowing how to do this is also untrue. Even if I never figure this out, I'm not going to die (rational challenge). I always have the choice of quitting if I decide this frustration is more than I choose to endure. But now that I think about it, it's really not that bad. In fact, it's relatively minor compared with events that are truly awful. I am willing to experience some frustration in order to pass this class and receive my degree (objective evaluation)."

Exaggerating the achievements or abilities of others creates the illusion that your own achievements or abilities are of little value. It can also cause you to give up working toward developing a skill or ability since magnifying similar abilities or achievements in others makes them appear unattainable. All of this lowers self-esteem and can produce anxiety, depression, and self-condemnation.

When you catch yourself magnifying the abilities or achievements of others, evaluate their abilities objectively and use ego strengtheners to remind yourself of your strengths and abilities. Redirecting statements can also be used to channel your energy into a different and more positive activity. Sometimes it helps to use a rational challenge.

Remind yourself that anyone with average intelligence who is free from brain damage and physical disabilities can learn any skill if an effective method is used and enough time and energy are devoted to it. This does not guarantee that you will become an expert, but you can at least achieve an average level of skill. In most human activities, from job skills to interpersonal skills, this is all you need to be successful.

> *Example:* As Fred works on his assignment, he thinks: "Bob and Kay both seem to pick this stuff right up. In fact, everyone in the class seems to do better than me (this last statement is both a magnification and an overgeneralization)."
>
> *Fred's rational self-talk:* "Hold on. Here I go again. I know I may never be as good at algebra as Bob and Kay. They are the best students in the class. However, I can do well enough to pass the class and that is all I need for my purposes (objective evaluation). Come to think of it, I received Bs on my first two quizzes. That was better than many of the other people in class. So I guess I can do just fine (ego strengtheners). Now let's take another look at this problem and come up with the best way to solve it. If I can't figure it out on my own, I'll ask Bob for help (redirecting statements)."

Minimization is the devaluing of personal strengths, abilities, and achievements as well as the mistakes and imperfections of others. Minimization and magnification usually occur together. For example, when you magnify another person's positive qualities and achievements, you also tend to minimize this person's negative qualities and failures. Likewise, when you magnify your own faults and errors, you usually minimize your strengths and successes.

When you catch yourself minimizing your own positive qualities and achievements, combat it with an objective evaluation and ego strengtheners. Identify specific personal strengths and achievements and affirm their importance and value. When you find yourself making others perfect by minimizing their mistakes and shortcomings, make an objective evaluation of their skills and accomplishments and identify specific shortcomings and flaws. At the same time, identify areas where you have skills and talent.

Example: While at a company dinner Margaret, a successful manager, found herself thinking: "Mary is such an excellent office manager. Her unit always runs so smoothly. I wish I had one-tenth of her ability."

Margaret's rational self-talk: "There I go putting myself down again. All my evaluations have very high ratings and I've been told many times how productive my unit is. I guess I really am a pretty good manager (objective evaluation/ego strengtheners). I also know that while Mary can do some things better than me, there are other things I can do better than her. Her unit also has its occasional problems and glitches just like mine. Last week's foul-up with the Mondale account is a good example (objective evaluation). So I guess we're both good, each in our own way (ego strengthener)."

Minimization is often called discounting and sometimes becomes so extreme that neutral and even positive experiences are interpreted as negative ones. When a person with this tendency cannot twist a positive event into a negative one, the person reduces it in importance by saying something such as, "This doesn't really count since it was just a fluke and wouldn't happen again in a million years." This type of discounting plays a major role in maintaining a poor self-image and is commonly associated with both depression and anxiety. With time and practice, the pairing of an objective evaluation with ego strengtheners will successfully overcome this type of minimization.

Example: Fred receives a compliment after helping out a friend at work and thinks: "Jim is probably just being nice and doesn't really mean it. He probably wouldn't even say that if he really knew how I was feeling today."

Fred's rational self-talk: "Wow! There I go discounting a perfectly wonderful compliment. If Jim had done the same for me, I would be genuinely grateful. So why shouldn't Jim respond in the same manner? I guess he really is sincere (objective evaluation). While it feels funny, it's nice to be complimented like this. I deserve it (ego strengtheners)."

Personalization

Personalization is the assuming of responsibility for a negative event when there is no basis for doing so. Personalization can be a major source of guilt. The key flaw in personalization is the confusion of influence with control. While you may exert much influence in some situations, your ability to control people and events usually exists only in your mind. Personalization usually leads to self-blame and negative self-labeling.

Personalization can be successfully challenged as follows. List the factors that could have caused the negative event for which you are assuming responsibility and assess the amount of influence you have over each factor. After you have evaluated all the factors you can think of, rate the degree of control you feel you have over the event. If you have difficulty with this process, ask someone you trust to help you. With practice, you will be able to list many factors for a given event and evaluate them objectively on your own.

> *Example:* Meera offers a mild constructive criticism to a friend, Jim, who becomes angry even though the criticism is valid and worded positively. Meera responds by thinking: "Now there I go again hurting someone. When will I learn to just keep my big mouth shut. It's all my fault that Jim is so upset and will not enjoy the rest of this event."
>
> *Meera's rational self-talk:* "It looks like I'm falling into the personalization trap. Now, what are some factors that could have caused Jim's anger? What I said is certainly one factor. Jim has been under a lot of pressure from work lately and he also tends to be overly sensitive at times. I also know that people are always interpreting what events mean and sometimes interpret them incorrectly. So how much influence do I really have over these factors? I have complete control over how I say things; however, I have no influence over Jim's work or the way he interprets events. I also know the way I stated the criticism was positive and would have been received well by most people I know. I guess Jim is reacting badly for reasons over which I have no influence (objective evaluation). I guess my next step is to decide whether I want to do something about what happened or just forget about it (redirecting statement)."

Mind Reading

Whenever you assume that you know what other people are thinking or feeling with little or no evidence to support the assumption and no attempt to confirm or deny the assumption, you are mind reading. This type of distorted thinking is a major source of discord in relationships and helps maintain a host of irrational beliefs.

When you catch yourself mind reading, ask the question, "What evidence do I have to support my assumption?" If there is little or no evidence, decide how evidence could be obtained. During an objective evaluation of someone's behavior, it often helps to ask yourself, "Would this mean the same thing if I did it?"

> *Example:* Barbara walks by a friend who is reading a book and says, "Good morning." The friend, Jack, does not say anything and Barbara begins thinking: "I guess Jack is angry with me. I wonder what I did?"
>
> *Barbara's rational self-talk:* "Stop right there. What evidence do I have to support my assumption that Jack is angry with me? All that happened was I saw him reading, said 'Good morning,' and he did not respond. When I don't respond to someone, does it always mean I am angry? Sometimes, but not always. Jack was reading a book. I guess sometimes I get so involved in what I am doing I don't hear what people are saying (objective evaluation). I guess I could just ask Jack if he heard me. If he did, I could ask why he didn't respond (redirecting statements)."

Fortune-Telling

When you make a negative prediction and then convince yourself it is an established fact, you are fortune-telling. Essentially, fortune-telling is the confusion of a possibility with a probability. This type of negative prediction often becomes a self-fulfilling prophecy.

When you notice yourself making a negative prediction, stop and evaluate the prediction objectively. Ask yourself: (a) "What is the probability (or possibility) of this occurring?" and (b) "What facts do I have to support the estimate I have just made?" If this type of evaluation is difficult for you, ask someone you trust to help. It also helps to remind yourself that there is no way for you to know what will happen since you are not omniscient. A prediction is merely a guess about what might happen. The fewer facts you have, the poorer your guess.

Example: Gary is considering taking a new job. He has no experience in this field and begins to think: "I've never really done that type of work before. I bet it will be hard to learn. What if I can't catch on to what I am supposed to do? I don't think I can do this job. What am I going to do?"

Gary's rational self-talk: "It seems I am acting as if I knew what was going to happen when I'm just guessing. What is the probability of my not being successful at this job (question a)? Right now I feel that it is fairly high; but what facts do I have to support the guess I have just made (question b)? Actually, very few. The closest job I've ever had to this one was my last job. I was pretty good at it. I also know that I learn things fairly quickly even though I am somewhat of a perfectionist and often don't give myself credit for what I have accomplished. I guess the chances of my succeeding are really very good. The probability of my being unable to do the work is low (objective evaluation)."

Accepting Questionable Sources as Authoritative

This refers to the acceptance of a person's opinion or advice as reliable and authoritative even though it is colored by personal interest, ignorance, lack of experience, or prejudice. If you frequently accept questionable sources as authoritative, develop the habit of making an objective evaluation of the opinions and advice you receive. Do this by asking yourself: (a) "What experience or training makes this person an expert in this area?" and (b) "Does this person have any biases or interests that might influence the opinion or advice being offered?" After evaluating the source, you are ready to make an objective evaluation of the opinion or advice given.

Example: Sharon was planning to take dance lessons. Her friend Ann told her she would not do well because she had poor timing and lacked coordination. Sharon began thinking: "I guess I'll have to give up my plans to take dance lessons."

Sharon's rational self-talk: "Wait. What makes Ann an expert (question a)? Does she dance well? No. Has she ever taken dance lessons herself? No, not to my knowledge. Does Ann have any biases or interests that influenced this advice (question b)? Yes. She is very negative and always tells people they won't succeed (evaluation of the source). Now, let's look at what Ann actually said. I really don't need excellent timing and coordination for the kind of dancing I want to learn. All I want to do is have some fun and be able to hold my own on a dance floor. I don't think you need to have more than average ability to do that. I don't think Ann's opinion is at all valid (objective evaluation of the opinion)."

Emotional Reasoning

Emotional reasoning is using emotions as objective evidence of a truth or to validate a belief or thought. Decisions or evaluations are based solely on your emotional reaction without an objective evaluation of the facts involved. For example, you feel awkward in a situation and use this emotional response as the sole basis for deciding that you do not belong there and should leave. Emotional reasoning is sometimes called analogical reasoning because the analogy between one's emotions and objective reality is taken as fact even though it may not be true.

Lesson 4 described how emotions provide important information because they are triggered by needs and wants being met, frustrated, or threatened. It also noted that some emotions are triggered by mis-interpreting events. One way in which this occurs was described in Lesson 2's discussion of conditioned responses where normal events become identified as threats. Lesson 4 also described how irrational beliefs and faulty habitual thinking patterns can distort events and cause negative emotions when no threat or loss is present. Emotions generated by conditioned responses and distorted thinking feel just as strong and seem just as valid as emotions generated by real threats and rational thinking. This is why it is self-defeating to follow emo-tions blindly, as is characteristic of people who frequently use emotional reasoning. The information provided by emotions is important but it needs to be evaluated objectively for an accurate understanding of what it means.

From the above it might seem that all decisions should be made on the basis of pure logic. This is not true. In fact, people who actively suppress their emotions and try to rely only on logic often experience just as many inappropriate emotions and self-defeating behaviors as emotional reasoners. The reason for this is simple. Because emotions signal when a need or want is being satisfied, frustrated, or threatened, suppression of emotions tends to block awareness of when needs are not being met.

When an important need is not met, it eventually generates one or more of the following: a physical reaction due to the constant triggering of your fight or flight response; an inappropriate emotional response—the three most common ones being anger, anxiety, and depression that is either too intense for a given situation or occurring for no apparent reason; or self-defeating behaviors.

Popular self-help books often state that it is important to be "in touch" with your emotions. Unfortunately, this often means that it is important to be more emotional or use emotional reasoning. The healthy management of your emotions involves the following three steps:

- Accurately identifying the emotion you are experiencing.
- Accurately identifying the need or want that is generating the emotion.
- Developing a plan that meets the need or want in an appropriate and realistic way.

Because effective decisions are usually based on both emotion and reason, the most effective rational self-talk approach to use with emotional reasoning is an objective evaluation that involves the above three steps. Whenever you experience strong emotions, first label the emotion. Then identify the need or want that is generating the emotion. Only then can you objectively consider the situation and decide on the best course of action. Sometimes emotional reasoning takes the form of a recurring pattern involving a certain type of emotion in a certain type of situation. When this is the case, it can also be helpful to recall past situations in which you experienced similar emotions and decide whether the emotions were the result of rational or irrational thinking.

Emotional reasoning is often accompanied by other types of distorted thinking. Identify the types and use rational self-talk to correct them. Take a few minutes to calm down before doing this. As you examine your thoughts, relabel magnified emotions more accurately.

Example: Charles has a high-stress job. One day he begins to feel very anxious and somewhat confused and thinks: "I feel like I'm going crazy! Why can't I even handle simple things? I'm really beginning to crack up!"

Charles's rational self-talk: "Wait a minute. I think I'm using emotional reasoning. Let's calm down and use those three steps I read about. The emotion I'm feeling is anxiety (identify the emotion). That means some need or want is threatened in some way. That's easy to identify. I want to do well and I'm afraid I might do poorly. I'm also afraid that this might cause people to think poorly of me and laugh at me. This is just my old excessive-need-for-approval 'button' getting pushed again (identify the need or want). Now, let's come up with a plan to deal with these fears. I do feel somewhat disoriented, but that is really not being crazy. I'm just overstressed right now and exaggerating the importance of what I'm feeling. I've handled many situations far more difficult than this in the past and am really doing fairly well at this one. Because I'm tired and overworked, I'm just not doing as well as I usually do. I am not going to lose my job. As far as people laughing at me or thinking poorly about me, most of the people in this office are reacting the same way and are sympathetic. In fact, some have said I'm doing very well (objective evaluation/relabeling). As I think about it, this is something I have often done in the past. Whenever I get overstressed, I begin to think there is something wrong with me emotionally when I'm really just tired (recalling a past event and identifying the pattern). I need to cut back on my outside activities and get some rest. Then I'll feel like my old self again (redirecting statements)."

The past example demonstrates the many different forms of rational challenges discussed in this lesson. Depending upon your personality and how you think, what you say to yourself when you use rational challenges may be shorter. That is fine as long as it is effective for you. At the same time, if you are using short rational challenges and finding that they have little effect, you may find it more effective to be more thorough.

Changing the Way You Think

Changing behavior is essentially a three-step process. First, you identify precisely those behaviors you want to eliminate. Second, you identify precisely those behaviors you want to do. Third, you practice substituting behaviors you want for those you wish to eliminate. A good example of this process would be Cyrus, who has been using incorrect fingers while typing but now wants to improve his speed. First, he needs to identify which keys he has been hitting with the wrong fingers and which keys he has been hitting correctly. Then he needs to identify the fingers he needs to practice. Finally, he practices exercises that emphasize the correct usage of the fingers he has been using improperly. With time and practice, the new patterns replace the old ones.

Changing the way you think is a similar process. First, you need to identify precisely when and how you think irrationally. Next, you develop rational self-talk that challenges the specific forms of distorted thinking you use. Finally, you practice the rational self-talk until it becomes automatic. At first, this practice usually is done after an incident has occurred. With time, however, the use of rational self-talk becomes more spontaneous. The Recommended Activities for this lesson include exercises that accomplish each of these steps in detail.

As a first step in this process, take a moment to examine the following summary of the forms of distorted thinking described in Lessons 4 and 5 listed below. Everyone uses all of them some of the time. However, a person usually uses some more than the others. Put a check by those you use most frequently.

- *Should/must thinking:* The transformation of personal choices, wants, or preferences into universal absolutes. This is usually done by using words and phrases such as "should," "must," "ought," and "have to." Should/must thinking can also be expressed indirectly through:

- *Circular questioning:* The repeated asking of questions that are irrelevant or have an answer you already know but are unwilling to accept. Common examples include "Why am I like this?" "Why can't I change?" "Why did this happen?" "How could he/she do that?" and "How could that happen?"
- *Can't thinking:* The use of the word "can't" to describe a need, want, decision, or choice.
- *All-or-nothing thinking:* The tendency to evaluate personal qualities and events in extreme, black-and-white categories. This is often expressed with the words "right," "wrong," "good," and "bad."
- *Overgeneralization:* The transformation of a single negative event into a never-ending pattern of defeat or misfortune. Often this is done by using words like "never," "always," and "every." A common variation is:
- *Labeling:* The use of simplistic and usually negative labels that exaggerate the importance of shortcomings or mistakes to define yourself or your behavior.
- *Magnification/minimization:* Magnification includes two types of exaggerations: catastrophizing, which is the exaggeration of personal flaws, small negative experiences, and mistakes; and the exaggeration of the abilities of others. Minimization, sometimes called discounting, also comes in two forms: the devaluing of personal strengths, abilities, or achievements; and the devaluing of mistakes and imperfections in others.
- *Personalization:* The act of assuming responsibility for a negative event when there is no basis for doing so.
- *Mind reading:* Assuming that you know what other people are thinking or feeling with little or no evidence to support the assumption and no attempt to confirm or deny the assumption.
- *Fortune-telling:* Making a prediction and then convincing yourself it is an already established fact.
- *Accepting questionable sources as authoritative:* Accepting as reliable an opinion or advice colored by personal interest, ignorance, lack of experience, or prejudice.

• *Emotional reasoning:* The use of emotions as the primary or only means for evaluating a situation, event, or belief.

Recommended Activities for Lesson 5

Continue Developing Your Relaxation Response

Continue practicing your relaxation response at least once a day. Also, continue to associate the cue you selected while doing Lesson 2 with the deep relaxation you are practicing. Continue this daily practice for the rest of the program.

Take Your Time with This Lesson

It is easy to feel overwhelmed when you first read this lesson. There is a lot of information in it. Applying it all to your life usually takes many weeks or months. Fortunately, you do not have to do everything during the week you are working on this lesson. Future lessons refer back to the various types of distorted thinking described in this one and provide you with additional opportunities to work on them. Concentrate on the forms of distorted thinking you use the most as you work with the lesson. If you are very busy, consider spending two weeks with this lesson. The extra time will be worth the effort.

Practice Identifying Distorted Thinking in People Around You

While you talk with others, watch television, listen to people talking on the radio, or listen to people talking around you, identify any of the various types of distorted thinking they might be using. Keep in mind that people tend to use distorted thinking more when they are excited or upset. It also helps to make a game out of it. However, do not tell others what you are doing as you do this exercise. Many people become either defensive or offended when their distorted thinking is pointed out.

This is a powerful and important exercise for two reasons. First, it's an excellent way to become skilled at identifying the different types of distorted thinking. If you are like most people, it is easier to see distorted thinking in others rather than yourself. Second, you soon come to realize that humans are terribly irrational. We pride ourselves on our ability to reason, and much of the time we do think in a fairly logical manner. However, whenever we are feeling strong emotions, we tend to use the various forms of distorted thinking described in this lesson. Seeing this distorted thinking in others enables you to see it as normal and avoid labeling yourself as crazy or weird because you often used distorted thinking. This, in turn, makes it easier to both accept and identify your own distorted thinking.

The Block Method

The Block Method applies the steps for changing behavior described in the lesson to the task of changing the way you think. The three steps are as follows:

Step 1: Record samples of self-talk during times when you are upset. Lesson 4 asked you to obtain a notebook or binder you can use to record your thoughts. If you have not done this, do so this week. Spend five to ten minutes every other day recalling times when you were anxious or upset or acting in a self-defeating manner. Take a moment to mentally place yourself back into the event and recall what you were thinking or saying to yourself. Then list as many of the thoughts you had at that time as you can recall. When possible, record your thoughts while you are still upset. Simply go someplace private, take a moment to monitor your self-talk, and list your thoughts on a piece of paper.

Step 2: Identify the forms of distorted thinking that are present and develop rational self-talk that challenges the distortions. After you have listed as much of your self-talk as you can recall, reread what you have written and identify any forms of distorted thinking that are present. When you identify a sentence or phrase that represents distorted thinking, rewrite the statement a little lower on the page. Label the statement by writing the name for the type of distorted thinking the statement represents after it. Then, just below the statement, write out a rational response.

Step 3: Rehearse the rational self-talk you have developed.
After you have analyzed your self-talk and completed your rational
responses, spend a few minutes rehearsing the rational responses
you developed. Mentally place yourself in the situation and practice
saying the responses. Rehearsing the rational self-talk responses you
develop in this manner is the quickest way to make this new way of
thinking a part of your automatic behavior. In time it will replace the
irrational, automatic self-talk that generates much of your anxiety.

Here is an example of how Elliot applied the Block Method to a
situation where he became anxious while waiting to meet his friend
Bob. The following sample of self-talk is condensed from a paragraph
Elliot wrote while he was waiting.

**Step 1: Record samples of self-talk during times when you
are upset.** "Where is Bob? I can't stand it when this happens.
Bob is going to forget and I'll be left standing here forever. Why
do I do this to myself?"
**Step 2: Identify the forms of distorted thinking that are
present and develop rational self-talk that challenges the
distortions.** (Note: The negative self-talk and corresponding
rational responses are labeled to make the example easy to follow.
You do not need to label everything you write when using this
method.)

Self-talk: "Where is Bob? (rational thought)."
Rational response: "This is a normal and rational thought. I was
uncomfortable not knowing where Bob was and wondering if
something had happened to him."

Self-talk: "I can't stand this (magnification)."
Rational response: "I can stand this. I may be anxious, but I am
functioning well."

Self-talk: "Bob is going to forget and I'll be left standing here
forever (fortune-telling and magnification)."
Rational response: "It's possible that Bob may forget. However,

he is very reliable and usually remembers appointments. As far as standing here forever goes, it was only a few minutes. I know I can always wait fifteen minutes, leave a note, and go. Fifteen minutes is really not that long."

Self-talk: "Why do I do this to myself? (should/must thinking in the form of circular questioning and magnification)."

Rational response: "I'm actually saying I shouldn't be this way and it's terrible that I am. While I want to change and don't like some of the things I do, given my background I am exactly who and what I 'should' be. Furthermore, I am in the process of learning how to think and act in new and more effective ways. This is a process that takes time. As for this being terrible, it is really only inconvenient."

Step 3: Rehearse the rational self-talk you have developed. Elliot rehearsed his rational responses several times then laid his work aside. He experienced more incidents like this over the next few weeks. For each one, he recorded his self-talk, analyzed, and developed rational responses. He then rehearsed the rational responses. Eventually, he found himself challenging his distorted thinking almost as fast as it occurred. As this began to take place, he found himself using less distorted thinking.

Continue to record your thoughts from times when you are anxious or upset and use the Block Method to challenge them throughout the rest of this program. If rational self-talk is difficult for you, select appropriate examples of rational self-talk from the lessons and copy them exactly as they appear. Then see if you can change the examples to fit both your personality and the situation more closely.

The Good-Day Rule

The Good-Day Rule is simple: Work hardest at developing the skills presented in this program when you are feeling your best—on your good days. People tend to work hardest when they are feeling their worst. Pain can provide strong motivation to take the actions required to change behavior. When you're feeling good, it's easy to discount the need to continue working. Since you do not complete the work needed to change the thinking and behavior patterns that generate anxiety, you set yourself up for a relapse into old patterns when you again encounter the right stressors.

Remind yourself periodically of this tendency to put off work when things are going well. Then commit yourself to the task of working with this program hardest when you are feeling good. If you do this, you will find that ideas and skills that seemed difficult to understand or use when you were having a bad day become much easier to understand and use on your good days. Following the Good-Day Rule is the fastest way to progress.

Indications Your Body Is Sick, Hungry, Tired, or Overstressed

Irrational thinking, self-defeating behaviors, and unpleasant physical symptoms increase whenever you are sick, hungry, tired, or overstressed. This is normal. Everyone experiences this to some degree. As pointed out in Lesson 3, the best way to minimize these reactions is to become skilled at identifying the early signs of stress and fatigue. Here are several common symptoms:

- Irritability.
- Tension or pain (common places are the head, neck, shoulders, stomach, arms, or legs).
- A change in the way you use language (often the increased use of profanity, put-downs, sarcasm, or other negative language you normally do not use).
- Increased emotionality (you become upset or excited more easily than normal).
- Inability to concentrate or think straight.
- Memory deficiency (you cannot remember things as well as you usually do and may forget important things).
- Unusual behavior or thoughts (weird or morbid thoughts).

Your specific signs may be one or more of the above, or they may be something not on the list. Review the symptoms you listed in

Lesson 3 on the Stress Symptom Inventory. Identify three to five specific symptoms you can use this week that indicate your body has
used its limited supply of energy and needs time to rest and rebuild
itself. Whenever you notice one of these symptoms, reduce your
activities and take care of your body's physical needs.

Two or Three Steps Forward, One Step Backward

Progress is rarely continuous. Often, you go two or three steps
forward then one step backward. There will be times when you slip
into old patterns or need to stop briefly to practice what you have
learned. Unfortunately, people with anxiety-related problems often
attach great significance to lapses into old behaviors or resting periods. The result is usually self-talk similar to the following:

- This experience proves that nothing works (all-or-nothing
  thinking).
- I will never get over this (fortune-telling).
- This experience is awful (magnification) and has undone all of
  the work I have done (overgeneralization/fortune-telling).
- Returning to past behaviors this time means I will always return
  to them (overgeneralization). I will never change or overcome
  this condition (fortune-telling).
- This is a major setback (magnification/labeling). I guess I
  haven't really changed anything (minimization).

Whenever you have a lapse into old behaviors or are in a resting
period, challenge this type of negative self-talk with rational self-talk.
Remind yourself that it is normal to slip into old behavior patterns
periodically. It is not a failure. Then examine the experience objectively by answering the following questions.

TROUBLESHOOTING CHECKLIST
- Was I tired, sick, or hungry? (This will be the primary cause of
  most lapses into old patterns.)
- Did I use the skills I have been learning?

- If so, how did I use them?
- Did I forget to use one or more important skills? (Refer to the summary at the end of this set of Recommended Activities.)
- How can I handle this type of situation more effectively in the future? (Answer this question in detail.)

Write the above questions on a card and put it where it is easy to find. Refer to it whenever you lapse into old patterns. This will help you turn lapses into valuable lessons that create a firm foundation for future growth. As you begin to accept these negative experiences as a natural part of the learning process, you will no longer view them with alarm. With time your lapses into old patterns will become fewer and further apart.

> The concepts and skills presented in this lesson form the foundation for much of the work presented in the following lessons. If your time is limited or if you are finding it difficult to develop rational self-talk skills, spend an extra week with this lesson.

LESSON 6

Learning to Enjoy Being Human

L esson 1 identified perfectionism as one of the personality traits that can contribute to anxiety. This lesson explores how perfectionistic tendencies can be either a positive or negative force in a person's life. While it often takes time to moderate perfectionistic tendencies that are contributing to anxiety, many find that learning to do so is an essential step in overcoming their anxiety-related problems.

Characteristics of Perfectionism

As with all human traits, perfectionism has both positive and negative sides. In its healthy form, perfectionism is characterized by setting demanding, but attainable goals for oneself. Healthy perfectionists also tend to enjoy working on tasks that require great attention to detail. This type of perfectionism leads to excellence in a chosen field and can help a person tremendously.

In its negative form, perfectionism has three primary characteristics. The first is the tendency to set unrealistically high standards and goals for oneself, and often for others as well. The second is the tendency to use all-or-nothing thinking when evaluating one's actions or achievements and to consider as a failure anything that does not meet the unrealistically high standards. The third characteristic is a selective point of view that focuses on small flaws and errors rather than on one's overall progress or achievement. Throughout the rest of this and the following lessons, the term *perfectionism* will refer to the negative type of perfectionism described above.

This negative type of perfectionism can be restricted to one or two areas of one's life or can dominate one's entire existence. When present, it can greatly increase the amount of anxiety a person experiences because accomplishments and experiences never measure up to the unrealistically high standards. Often this can lead to a very negative self-image and cause a person to avoid taking risks and trying new, unfamiliar activities.

People are often unaware of their perfectionistic tendencies because it has been the only way they have thought and acted all of their life. As you read through the rest of this lesson, put a check by any sections that describe you or address behaviors or tendencies that you would like to moderate.

Recognizing Perfectionistic Self-Talk

The place to begin when considering how much of a perfectionist you are is to look at your self-talk. Common examples of perfectionistic self-talk are listed below in the left column. The form of distorted thinking that each one represents is listed in the right column. Take a moment to read only the examples of self-talk in the left-hand column and place a check by any of the phrases that are similar to ones you use. Do not read the descriptions in the right-hand column until you have finished on the left. Be sure to record in your notebook any phrases you frequently use that are variations on the following examples.

PERFECTIONISTIC SELF-TALK	
Self-Talk	Form of Distorted Thinking
I should be able to (or have to) do this right.	Should/must thinking.
I shouldn't have made that mistake.	Should/must thinking.
Why can't I do this right?	Should/must thinking in the form of circular questioning: "I should always do things correctly."
Why didn't I see that mistake?	Should/must thinking in the form of circular questioning: "I should never make mistakes."

Self-Talk	Form of Distorted Thinking
How could I let something like that happen?	Should/must thinking in the form of circular questioning: "I should be able to prevent this."
This is all wrong.	Should/must thinking in the form of all-or-nothing thinking: "I should never make mistakes."
I just can't seem to find the right thing to do/ I just can't seem to find a good answer.	Should/must thinking in the form of all-or-nothing thinking: "I should always be able to find the perfect solution to problems."
Why do I act so stupid?	Should/must thinking in the form of circular questioning and overgeneralization/labeling: "I should always understand things."
I'm always so clumsy (thoughtless, etc.).	Overgeneralization/labeling with the underlying should/must rule: "I should always be graceful, witty, and never make mistakes."
I never seem to get this right.	Overgeneralization with the underlying should/must rule: "I should never make mistakes."
Every time I try to do this, it comes out all wrong.	Overgeneralization with the underlying should/must rule: "I should be able to do things without mistakes or problems."
No matter how hard I try, I always seem to come up short.	Overgeneralization with the underlying should/must rule: "I should always be skilled at everything I do."
This is awful (said in response to a small error).	Magnification with the underlying should/must rule: "I should never make mistakes."
I can't stand not knowing how to do this (or do this right).	Magnification with the underlying should/must rule: "I should know how to do this/I should never make mistakes."
Look at this error; it ruins everything I've done.	Magnification with the underlying should/must rule: "I should be able to do things perfectly."

Now go back through the above list and read the description in the right-hand column that identifies the type of distorted thinking that is being used with each phrase you checked.

Challenging Beliefs That Support Perfectionism

Negative perfectionism is usually maintained by a combination of irrational beliefs and learned habit patterns. Unfortunately, people with this trait often are unaware of their irrational beliefs because they are part of the mostly unconscious core beliefs developed during childhood, as discussed in Lesson 4.

Fortunately, most of the irrational beliefs and habitual thinking patterns from childhood are not that hard to identify. As an old saying goes, *If it looks like a duck, walks like a duck, and sounds like a duck, it's probably a duck.* In the same way, if you look like you believe an idea, act like you believe an idea, and sound like you believe an idea, that idea is part of your belief system and generating at least some of its behavior. Often these ideas are simply a set of conditioned response reactions. Still, it is useful to label them as beliefs because this allows you to both recognize the behavior more easily and challenge it more effectively with your self-talk.

Three basic irrational beliefs underlie most perfectionistic behavior. Whenever you act, think, or talk in ways similar to those described in the preceding section, you are basing your interpretation of events on one or more of them. Whenever you notice yourself acting or thinking in a perfectionistic manner, take a moment to identify and challenge the irrational belief generating your perfectionistic interpretation. With time, this helps to transform negative perfectionism into a positive asset.

The Irrational Belief That Perfection Is Possible

The first and most basic irrational, perfectionistic belief to challenge is the notion that perfection is possible. While most people, upon reflection, will agree that this idea is absurd, the idea that one can do things without any mistakes or problems underlies much of the thinking of a perfectionist. Here are several examples of statements that challenge this irrational belief.

- The goal of doing something perfectly is unattainable in the real world. There are always improvements that can be made in everything I see and do.
- I do not need to do things perfectly to be a success. Doing things well is all that is needed in most situations. Sometimes, even this is not necessary.
- Because it is impossible to do anything absolutely perfectly, if my goal is perfection, I've guaranteed that I'll fail.
- I need to accept that there will always be improvements that can be made and simply strive to do things as well as I am able. The next time, I will probably be able to do it better.

The Irrational Belief That a Person's Worth Is Determined by Achievement

Among the primary forces that shapes your thinking and behavior are the beliefs you have about yourself. People with perfectionistic tendencies often have the irrational belief that their worth is determined by their achievement. Such thinking creates a no-win situation in which you feel worthwhile only when you achieve, yet your achievements always fall short of your perfectionistic standards. The result is a feeling that you never do enough and are always falling short of what is required in any situation.

The irrational, perfectionistic belief that worth is determined by achievement can also generate the need to excel above others in order to feel important. When this occurs, it becomes a major source of anxiety. No matter how talented you are in a given area, there is usually someone more talented. Those who need to excel above others in order to feel important often feel glad or relieved when others fail or do poorly at an activity in which they feel competitive. Sometimes people like this may even resort to sabotage in order to ensure that others will do poorly.

There is a wide range of thinking about what makes a person valuable. People with a strong religious tradition often see this in terms of one's relationship to God. Take some time this week to talk with someone in your faith about what makes a person valuable and how this relates to a person's achievements. If you have no spiritual or religious leanings, you may find that a philosophical approach will work. Here are some ideas from this viewpoint that many have found useful when challenging the irrational belief that worth is determined by achievement:

- When older people look back on their lives, they usually find that the satisfaction they received from relationships and how they lived were far more important than what they did.
- As far as healthy, satisfying, long-term relationships are concerned, who you are as a person is far more important than what you achieve.
- Your value as a person is entirely separate from the value of the activities you do. Equating worth with achievement is an arbitrary value system for which there is no objective support. Technically you are only a human being who does various activities. You are not those activities. While your activities may or may not be valuable, they do not add or subtract from your value as a person.
- You probably treat others with respect because you believe people have value in and of themselves as a member of the human race. You have this same intrinsic value as others simply because you are human.
- If you have a spouse or children, you probably see them as valuable even when they fail at something. Their value as people is an entirely separate issue from the value of what they do. The same is true for you.
- You do not need to be especially talented to be happy and successful in life. Many very happy and successful people have very average talent and ability.
- People usually achieve more when they do things because they enjoy doing them rather because they are a source of self-worth and self-esteem.
- Overconcern with achievement creates anxiety that interferes with your ability to achieve. Setting realistic goals you can achieve helps you be more productive.

The Irrational Belief That All Mistakes Are Terrible

When a perfectionist makes a mistake, it is usually seen as one of the worst things that can happen. This is usually true even when the mistake is a minor one with no real negative consequences. This dread of making a mistake can come from many sources. Sometimes it is due to parents who train a child by constantly pointing out what the child is doing wrong but rarely state what the child is doing well. This is usually not done out of malice. These types of parents want the child to do well. Unfortunately, it often teaches the child to fear making mistakes and taking risks. It also can generate the tendency to focus on small flaws and errors and magnify the importance of mistakes.

The fear of making mistakes can also be learned by modeling after a parent who is a perfectionist. And it can come from experiences at school where a child is teased by other children or made to look stupid by a teacher. This trait is also common in children with learning disabilities who struggle with learning.

The best way to challenge the idea that mistakes are terrible is to become convinced that most mistakes are unimportant. Take a moment to recall all the mistakes you have made in the past twenty-four hours. Now, consider the effect each will have on your life one day, one week, or one year from now. Unless this is a very unusual day for you, you will probably agree that these mistakes will have no real lasting effect on your life. While mistakes sometimes have unfortunate consequences, most of the mistakes you make in daily life do not seriously affect you and are, at most, minor inconveniences. Most mistakes take on major importance only when magnified by the fear of failure and perfectionistic all-or-nothing thinking.

But mistakes are more than just nuisances having little lasting effect. Mistakes are an indispensable and natural part of the learning process. They offer wonderful opportunities to gain knowledge and develop skills. This process can be diagrammed as follows:

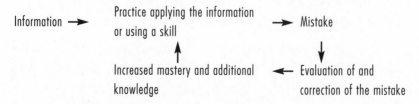

Every complex skill you have was gained through the above process. This includes everything from walking and talking to reading and writing. It is also the process you are now using to learn how to think and act in positive new ways. In this sense, mistakes are gifts of wisdom.

The following statements are examples of how you can use the above ideas to help put your mistakes in perspective.

- Is this mistake really all that terrible? Will this mistake really affect my life in a day, month, or year from now?
- Most mistakes are unimportant in the long run.
- Mistakes are a natural part of the learning process. Expect things like this to happen.
- It's okay to make mistakes. Everyone does. They are a natural part of being human.
- Instead of looking at what is wrong, focus on what is right with this: What did I do well?
- This mistake is a gift of wisdom. What have I learned?

Changing Perfectionistic Behavior

This section describes nine different ways in which you can replace behaviors associated with negative perfectionism with more positive and realistic behaviors. It usually takes many weeks or months to make all of these behaviors a natural part of your life. During the time you are working with this lesson, put most of your time and energy into the first three. If your situation allows you to work with additional approaches, do so. However, do not be concerned if you are only able to work with the first three. As you proceed through this program, there will be many opportunities to return to this lesson and work with those approaches you skip at this time.

Develop and Practice Rational Self-Talk That Challenges Perfectionistic Beliefs

The first step in changing perfectionistic tendencies is to develop rational self-talk that can be used to challenge the irrational beliefs associated with perfectionistic behavior. The following example shows how Steffany challenged her perfectionistic beliefs with ideas from the preceding section.

Example: Steffany was trying a new recipe. She misread the directions, causing the dish she was preparing to turn out poorly. Her first thought was, "This is terrible! Why can't I do anything right?"

Steffany's rational self-talk: "Here is that old perfectionistic self-talk again. I am really saying I should be able to do this perfectly and never make mistakes (identify the distortion). This is irrational because perfection by definition cannot be achieved. Mistakes are also not that bad (rational challenge). As for my never doing anything correctly, I am actually a pretty good cook. Most of what I make turns out well. As for this mistake, it's really no big deal. Besides, I now know how to make it come out the way I want it to next time (objective analysis and substitution). That's great (ego strengthener)."

Develop a Problem-Solving Approach to Mistakes

The previous section pointed out that mistakes are often a major source of anxiety. If you frequently dwell on mistakes, condemn yourself when you make mistakes, or avoid activities because you fear making mistakes, memorize the following three-step approach and begin applying it to every mistake you make.

Step 1: Identify why the mistake was made. This is often the most difficult step since perfectionists tend to be sidetracked by self-condemnation and negative self-labeling. When you notice this occurring, remind yourself that you are simply trying to identify the source of the mistake so you can take positive action, and that mistakes are expected—a natural part of the learning process. If it is difficult for you to remain objective during this step, review the previous sections and develop a few short phrases you can memorize to help you remain objective as you identify why the mistake was made.

Sometimes you will not be able to identify the cause of a mistake. When this occurs, go on to the next step.

Step 2: Identify any action that can be taken to correct the mistake and, if practical, take it. Your task at this step is to evaluate objectively whether or not an error can be corrected and whether you wish to take the action that would be required to correct it. Just as it is not always possible to identify the cause of a mistake, it is not always possible to correct a flaw or error. When errors can be corrected, take a moment to decide whether there is any real benefit in doing so. Sometimes it is simply not worth the time, energy, or money required to correct a flaw or error.

Step 3: Identify actions that can be taken to reduce the likelihood of repeating the mistake in the future and, if practical, take them. As with the previous steps, this is not always possible. Still, it is a step that many people with perfectionistic tendencies never even arrive at because they get stuck dwelling on the awfulness of the mistake or their personal inadequacy. When considering possible actions, remember that rehearsing new behaviors increases the likelihood of your using them in the future. Take time to identify exactly what you would say or do differently if you were in a similar situation again. Then rehearse those words or actions several times in your mind.

When you use this three-step approach, you transform mistakes into gifts of wisdom. With time, this process becomes as automatic as your old patterns.

Focus on Positives

Whenever you are trying to change a habit pattern, it is not enough to simply stop the old, negative pattern. You must also practice a new, positive pattern that will, with time, replace the old one. One of the common characteristics of perfectionism identified at the beginning of this lesson is the tendency to focus on small flaws and errors. The opposite positive tendency is the habit of focusing on positives. From this day on, make it a habit to take a moment during any activity, no matter how small, to find something positive about it.

Eliminate the "But" Habit

People with perfectionistic tendencies often use such words as "but" and "however" to cancel positives. Here are three examples of this type of self-talk:

- I had a fairly good week, but there was one afternoon when things didn't go very well.
- I did more yesterday than I have ever done, but I felt somewhat nervous the whole time.
- I finally completed the project, and, overall, it looks pretty good. However, one part isn't quite right.

Notice how the negative second half of each sentence cancels out the positive first half. One way to eliminate this habit is to begin reversing the order of your thoughts or statements and put the negative part first. This allows the positive to reduce or cancel out the negative part. Doing this with the three examples produces the following:

- There was one afternoon when things didn't go very well, but I had a fairly good week.
- I felt somewhat nervous the whole time, but I did more yesterday than I have ever done.
- One part isn't quite right. However, I finally completed the project, and, overall, it looks pretty good.

Another approach that is even better is to simply leave off the negative half. Doing this with the three examples produces the following:

- I had a fairly good week.
- I did more yesterday than I have ever done.
- I finally completed the project, and, overall, it looks pretty good.

If you are a hard-core perfectionist, the second approach may be difficult. You may feel as though you are not being completely honest. Just persist until it does become comfortable.

Set Realistic Goals

Setting realistic goals is often very difficult for perfectionists. A saying used by carpenters is, *This ain't a piano!*—meaning that the amount of precision and care needed to build a piano is far greater than that needed to frame a house. Perfectionists often approach every task as if they are doing a precision job.

The following approaches are designed to help you set more realistic and attainable goals. Place a check by those that you feel would be most useful for you.

- Consider what you would expect if you were setting the goal for someone else. Most perfectionists are more realistic when setting goals for others.
- Set goals in your normal fashion, then reduce them somewhat. For example, if you believe you "should" produce a hundred items an hour at work, set eighty items an hour as your goal.
- Be aware of any should/must thinking that creeps into your goal setting such as, "I have to get an A." When you discover this type of thinking, use the ideas presented in this lesson along with the rational self-talk tools presented in the previous lessons to challenge it.
- Give yourself permission to make errors and reevaluate your goal. Make the acceptance of some errors and flaws part of your goal.
- Aim to simply do or do well instead of doing perfectly.
- Aim to simply better your own performance rather than to be perfect or exceed the performance of others.
- Discuss your goal with an objective person you trust in order to get a reality check.

Use the strategies you checked whenever you set a goal for yourself—whether it involves a small daily task, such as how much you should clean around your home, or a major life goal, such as making a career choice.

Give Yourself Permission to Experience Pleasure

Perfectionists rarely give themselves permission to experience pleasure. Often this is because they are too busy seeking the impossible goal of perfection to be bothered with pleasure. People who believe that worth only comes from achievement may also believe that pleasure has little or no value. In addition, when perfectionism is accompanied by an excessive need for approval and low self-esteem, the perfectionist places the needs of others first and ignores personal needs.

The way to remedy this situation is simple and fun. Every day, do at least one thing for yourself that is fun and pleasurable. This may be an activity you do by yourself or with others; it can be simple or complex, short or long. The point is to choose an activity for the enjoyment it brings to you rather than for the benefits or pleasure it brings to others. Several examples are listed in Lesson 3 in the section on relaxation.

Develop a Process Orientation

Spend more time and energy focusing on the process of doing an activity than on the end product or achievement. One way to do this is to read this section at the beginning of the day and give yourself permission to enjoy the pleasurable aspects of what you do. You may even want to post cue cards that remind you to take time to enjoy what you are doing. Here are a few process-oriented sayings you can put on your cue cards:

- Enjoy the "doing."
- In life, the journey is far more important than the destination.
- Seek enjoyment rather than accomplishment (the two often go together).
- How I live is more important than what I do.
- Savor the present.
- Stop and smell the roses.
- Live now!

Another way to develop a process orientation is summarized by the joke that asks "How do you eat an elephant?" The answer: "One bite at a time." Because perfectionistic thinking is overly concerned with the end result, large projects often seem overwhelming. This usually generates unnecessary anxiety and a tendency to procrastinate.

Whenever you are faced with a large project, divide it into several small ones. Concentrate only on the part you are doing instead of the whole project. For example, if you are going to clean your house, divide it into many small projects, each of which can be done in a short amount of time—the dishes, floors, dusting, and so on. If you start with the dishes, concentrate only on that job. Pretend this is the only thing in the world you need to do. This "elephant" approach helps you become more productive, enjoy what you are doing, and become less concerned with the end results of large projects.

Many of the other approaches in this lesson can be combined with this one. For example, you may want to schedule how much time you want to spend with each task and then stick to your schedule whether you have completed the task or not. Another one that is especially useful is to note and compliment yourself on the positive aspects of each job as you complete it.

Use the Bottom-Line Technique to Eliminate Fears Underlying Perfectionistic Behavior

Perfectionistic behavior is often driven by one or more underlying fears. The Bottom-Line Technique is a variation of the Block Method described in Lesson 5. It provides a simple method for identifying these underlying fears as well as any forms of distorted thinking that might be involved. Use this approach whenever you are becoming upset because of a mistake or because your performance is not as good as you would like it to be.

Begin by describing the mistake you made or the goal for which you are striving. Next, list the worst possible thing that could happen as a result of this mistake or as a result of your unsatisfactory performance. After you list the negative outcome, ask yourself if there is anything worse than that. Continue until you find yourself unable to come up with any new responses. Here is an example that Maribeth wrote after wrapping a present for a friend:

> *Situation:* "I'm doing a terrible job of wrapping this present!"
> *And what would happen if it weren't wrapped well?* "My friend would think I didn't care."
> *So what if he thought that?* "My friend would not like me."
> *So what if he didn't like you?* "It would be terrible; I would feel alone and horrible."
> *So what if that happened?* "I couldn't stand it."
> *So what if that happened?* "I would feel alone and no one would like me."

At this point Maribeth could not think of anything worse and began repeating the previous responses. This indicated the fear of rejection and the mistaken idea that worth is determined by achievement were underlying this behavior. Here are the rational self-talk responses she developed:

> *Self-talk:* "I'm doing a terrible job of wrapping this present! (magnification)."
> *Rational response:* "I'm exaggerating the minor imperfection in my work. It's not as good as I'd like it to be, but it's okay."

> *Self-talk:* "My friend will think I don't care. (fortune-telling and mind reading)."
> *Rational response:* "I'm making a prediction and acting as if it were a fact. I'm also mind reading since I don't really know what my friend will think. However, it's most likely that he'll like the gift very much."

> *Self-talk:* "My friend will not like me (fortune-telling)."
> *Rational response:* "Now I'm really making a wild guess about what would happen and acting as if it were a fact. It's very unlikely that he'll react in this manner. Besides, what kind of friend would he be if he rejected me just because I'm not an expert at wrapping gifts?"

Self-talk: "It would be terrible; I would feel alone and horrible (magnification)."

Rational response: "Even if my friend did reject me over such a minor thing, I would survive and find new friends. While it would be unfortunate and I would not like it, it wouldn't really be horrible."

Self-talk: "I couldn't stand it (magnification)."

Rational response: "I would survive and find new friends. I would be able to 'stand it' even though I might not like it."

Self-talk: "I would feel alone and no one would like me (over-generalization)."

Rational response: "No one would like me? I have many friends and they really don't care how I wrap presents. They like me even though I have imperfections. I now see that along with the fear of rejection, the mistaken idea that I only have worth when I do things well is underlying this behavior. I know that worth is *not* determined by achievement."

Schedule Activities

People with perfectionistic tendencies often accomplish little in a day. When they have a list of things that need to be done, they often spend so much time trying to do the first task on their list perfectly that there is no time left for the others. One way to prevent this is to set strict time limits for all your activities. If you wish to change your schedule, do so only at the beginning of the day. Be sure to quit a given activity at the end of the time you have set aside for it whether you have completed it or not. Then go on to the next activity you have scheduled. People who use this approach find they achieve much during the day. Using this approach also has an added benefit: You learn to become comfortable with the imperfection of tasks that are not done completely.

If procrastination is a major problem for you, repeat this activity periodically. It is especially good to repeat it whenever you find yourself becoming too concerned with "getting things done" or faced with a complex or long-term project.

Recommended Activities for Lesson 6

Develop Rational Challenges for Perfectionistic Beliefs

This lesson discussed three irrational beliefs that are a common source of perfectionistic thoughts and behaviors: the belief that perfection is possible, the belief that a person's worth is determined by achievement, and the belief that all mistakes are terrible. Select ideas from the discussion of these beliefs that you feel are the most powerful rational challenges and summarize them on cards. Review these cards once a day until you have memorized them. Here are the cards Steffany made:

Challenges for the Irrational Belief That Perfection Is Possible

- Absolute perfection does not exist in the real world.
- Perfection is a direction, not a place.
- If my goal is perfection, I've guaranteed failure because perfection by definition is impossible to achieve.
- Strive to do things well, not perfectly.

Challenges for the Irrational Belief That My Worth Is Determined by Achievement

- Failing at a task doesn't make me a failure.
- I am valuable because every person is valuable.
- I can be average and still be happy and successful in life—I don't have to be perfect or above average.

Challenges for the Irrational Belief That All Mistakes Are Terrible

- It's okay to make mistakes—everyone does.
- Most mistakes are unimportant.

- Mistakes are gifts of wisdom.
- Mistakes are a natural part of the learning process.
- Use the Three-Step Approach when you make a mistake: What happened? Can I fix it? What will I do differently next time?

Continue Using the Block Method

If you have not yet begun taking five or ten minutes every other day to use the Block Method, begin this week. Review the directions in the Recommended Activities of Lesson 5 if you are not sure how to use the Block Method. When you analyze your thoughts, identify self-talk characteristic of the perfectionistic beliefs discussed in this lesson. Be sure to use the ideas discussed in this lesson to challenge any underlying perfectionistic beliefs you discover.

Work to Eliminate Perfectionism

Do as many of the activities described in this lesson as possible. If this is the first time you've worked through this lesson, focus on the first three. If you are returning to this lesson, select the three activities that are the most difficult for you. Remember, exercises that are easy probably focus on skills you have already mastered. Exercises that are difficult probably focus on skills you need to develop. If perfectionism is a problem for you, spend two weeks with this lesson.

Be Patient and Continue to Practice

The growth you achieve while working through this program is the result of a gradual process. It is usually only noticed after you have done something in a new and more effective way. There are two reasons for this. First, you are working on attitudes and skills that are acquired and polished over time. It is much like watching a child grow. As you watch from day to day, you do not notice any difference, but when you stand the child against a wall where past heights are marked, growth becomes obvious.

The second reason progress is usually noticed after the fact is that the attitudes and skills you are developing are most effective when they are fully internalized. At first, you have to spend a lot of time and energy thinking about the skills and information you are learning. With time, they become so much a part of you that you no longer have to consciously think about them. They become as automatic as the old patterns that generated anxiety. You only notice this internalization process when you look back at an incident and realize you used the new patterns of thinking and acting without even thinking about it. It was just a natural and comfortable thing to do. This is when you know you are making these new skills and this new approach to life part of you.

An old Chinese proverb says: *I heard and I forgot. I saw and I remembered. I did and now I understand.*

All the information, skills, and tools about which you have been reading will have little effect on your life if you do not practice using them. Knowledge alone is not enough to overcome self-defeating behaviors and thinking patterns. If you have not been following the lessons as recommended or are starting to spend less time with them, make a firm commitment now to spend as much time and energy as possible practicing the skills and using the information and knowledge you are learning. If you do not have a regular time when you study the lessons, pick one now.

Consider Massage

People suffering from anxiety or stress often suffer from chronic muscle tension. Massage helps relieve chronic muscle tension and is an excellent form of relaxation. It is also an experience that both is very pleasurable and only benefits you. This is especially important for people who have difficulty giving themselves permission to experience pleasure or who rarely do anything just for themselves. If you have never received a professional massage, these are two excellent reasons to do so now.

Therapeutic massage offers one additional benefit for people who grew up in dysfunctional families where they never experienced positive touching, received little physical affection, or failed to learn how to establish healthy boundaries between self and others: an important opportunity to learn how to receive appropriate, nonsexual, positive touching. If you come from a family like this, be sure to interview potential massage therapists prior to scheduling a massage. It is important that you begin with someone you feel comfortable with. It is also likely that it may take two or three massages before you begin to relax and get the full benefit of massage.

Consider Keeping a Journal

You may find it valuable to begin keeping a journal. Use your journal to do the written activities, list problems and concerns, record insights, and keep track of progress. When you keep a journal, privacy is essential. This makes it easier to write with honesty and openness. If you write for an unseen audience, you lose much of the benefit of keeping a journal. Use any kind of notebook for your journal. The main value of a journal is not the permanent record you create but the work required to create it. After several months you may decide to destroy your journal or keep it.

> The insights and behavior changes that result from the activities in this lesson form a foundation for the following lessons. Take your time and spend at least one week with this lesson.

LESSON 7

Becoming a Positive Realist

The tendency to worry and look at life from a negative point of view often plays a major role in both the development and maintaining of anxiety-related problems. This lesson focuses on how to develop the opposite tendency, to become what I call a positive realist. Being a positive realist does not mean that you look at the world through rose-colored glasses and ignore problems and danger. It means you face life realistically but focus on solutions and possibilities rather than on life's fearful or troublesome aspects. Developing this perspective reduces worry and forms of negativism commonly associated with anxiety-related problems. This, in turn, not only helps reduce anxiety, but also helps you deal with people and problems more effectively and experience a greater sense of joy in daily living.

Negative Anticipation: What If?

The term used by psychologists to describe worry is *negative anticipation,* defined as the tendency to dwell on unpleasant or fearsome events that might occur in the future. Because the self-talk generated by this type of worry often begins with "what if," it is also called what-if thinking. Negative anticipation is the core feature in generalized anxiety disorder. It also plays a major role in the other anxiety-related problems.

Consider Robert, who suffers from panic disorder. While preparing to visit a friend, he thinks: "What if I become anxious at my friend's house?" Instead of evaluating this possibility objectively, Robert leaps to the conclusion that he will *definitely* become anxious (fortune-telling), this will be the worst thing that can happen (catastrophizing), and it will make him an utter failure in life (should/must thinking in the form of all-or-nothing thinking: "I should be calm and poised at everything I do/I should be perfect and have no problems like this").

The following approaches provide six different ways to reduce worry. During the week that you work on this lesson, focus on the first one, the Four-Step Analysis. If you have time, work on as many of the others as you can. If worry is a major problem for you, spend an extra week on this lesson.

The Four-Step Analysis

Whenever you notice yourself worrying about an unpleasant or fearsome event that might occur, use the following Four-Step Analysis to objectively assess the situation.

Step 1: Determine the odds. Realistically determine the probability of the feared event actually occurring. State the odds of the event occurring as a percentage—for example, "There is a 50 percent chance of this occurring."

This first step can be difficult for many because they use emotional reasoning to determine the probability that something is going to occur. For example, people with panic disorder often fear that they will faint when they go to a place that is associated with anxiety. When asked how likely it is that they will faint, they often respond with odds of 50 to 100 percent. When then asked, "How many times have you fainted in the past?" they usually say, "Never." They overestimate the odds because it is based on the *feeling* that they might faint rather than on the *reality* of their past history.

Keep in mind that people with the tendency to worry are terrible fortune-tellers. The vast majority of their predictions do not come true. In order to reduce fortune-telling that transforms a possibility into a probability, recall your track record and consider how you have done in previous situations similar to this one. This helps you to be more realistic.

Step 2: Assess the consequences. In this step you assess the consequences if the thing you are worrying about were to occur. In essence, you are considering the "awfulness" of the feared event. The easiest way to do this is to ask yourself, "On a scale from one to ten where ten is the worst thing that could happen to me, how bad would this be?"

This is the second place where people who worry tend to have difficulty because of their habit of using magnification, a form of distorted thinking described in Lesson 5. Using the previous example, when people with panic disorder are asked to rate the awfulness of fainting in public, they usually rate it as a ten. But when it is then pointed out that the scale would include things such as having a painful terminal illness or losing a loved one in a tragic way, they usually reposition the awfulness of fainting to three or four.

As you assess the trauma of a situation, keep in mind that a ten is the worst thing you can think of. Comparing daily worries to things that are truly awful helps you avoid catastrophic magnification.

Step 3: Develop a plan for preventing the feared event. People who worry a lot usually never get to these last two steps. They tend to get stuck thinking that a fearful event is very likely to occur and it will be traumatizing when it does. When you watch people who do not worry excessively consider a negative possibility, you find two things. First, they tend to be skilled at making realistic assessments of the odds of something happening and how awful it would be if it did occur. Second, when considering a negative possibility, they spend most of their time with these last two steps: "How could I prevent this from happening?" and "How would I deal with it if it were to occur?"

Sometimes, there is little you can do to prevent fearful events. For example, there is little you could do to prevent a plane from crashing into your house while you are sleeping. When this is the case, remind yourself of how unlikely this type of event would be.

For most everyday worries, there are usually many practical steps you could take to reduce the chances that they would occur. For example, one way to prevent the possibility of getting into a car accident is to drive defensively. A student worrying about not passing a class might instead list things that could be done to study more effectively or get help.

Step 4: Develop a plan for coping with the feared event if it does occur. As mentioned above, worriers usually fail to think of the unthinkable: "What would I actually do if this were to occur?" It is important to concentrate on listing practical actions you could take. Be concrete and specific.

Let's consider the examples in the previous step. If you drive, it is likely that at some time you will probably get into an accident. Remind yourself that the odds are that it will not be serious. Then list the things you would do, such as exchange information, file a report, and so on. The student worrying about failing a class could remind him- or herself that it would not be the end of the world. It would simply mean that she or he would have to take the class over again. Most people pass a failed class on the second attempt. While both of these situations would require time, energy, and money, they are really not that important when looked at from the perspective of a lifetime.

After you have completed the above steps, summarize your analysis into two or three sentences. These become coping self-statements that deal with your specific fears. If you are dealing with a major concern, write them on a card you can carry with you. Then, after reading them, redirect your attention to something positive or neutral.

If you notice yourself thinking about the feared event again, recall your summary of the analysis by rereading your coping self-statements, then redirect your attention elsewhere. The following example shows how Robert, who suffered from social phobia, used these steps to resolve his concern about becoming anxious at his friend's house:

Step 1: Determine the odds. "I can recall many times when I have become anxious at the home of friends, so this might actually happen. However, since I have been learning these new skills, I have been doing very well. So while I might experience some anxiety, I don't think the probability of experiencing the major anxiety that I did in the past is very high. I will give the possibility of experiencing major anxiety a 20 percent chance of occurring."

Step 2: Assess the consequences. "How terrible would this actually be? It would be very uncomfortable and I would not like it, but I would be able to stand it. After all, am I actually going to be harmed or have something taken away from me? No. While becoming anxious is upsetting to me, it is really not all that horrible. Indeed, I have seen many times how my anxiety comes and goes during social events. If I just remind myself that I'm okay and then find something to do to distract myself, I'm usually fine."

Step 3: Develop a plan for preventing the feared event. "What really sets me off is when I begin mind reading and think that everyone is watching me and being critical of me. I can review my coping cards just before leaving for the event so my self-talk skills are fresh when I arrive. I also tend to be very critical of any mistakes I make. I can review the notes I've taken on perfectionism and be kind with myself before I go. It is especially important to remind myself that it's okay to have some anxiety. I have already proven to myself that I can be anxious and still function. Indeed, as the evening goes on, I can usually calm down and do well. I don't have to be totally calm to be effective and enjoy myself. I can also take along a couple of the cards that list my anxiety-reduction skills. Knowing that I have them usually helps me be less anxious."

Step 4: Develop a plan for coping with the feared event if it does occur. "If I become anxious, I can simply excuse myself for a moment and use the skills listed on the card. This is usually fairly effective. I remember how I became anxious at the work luncheon and excused myself. After calming down, I returned and did well. If I do become so anxious that I decide to leave, I can just tell my friend that I would like to stay but I am not feeling well. It would also be good to say I will call later."

After completing the above analysis, Robert distracted himself with household chores. After a short time, he again found himself thinking about becoming anxious at his friend's house. Since he had already worked through the above steps in detail, he now used positive self-talk in the form of a quick review of his plans and conclusions: "Now, wait a minute. I've already thought about this and know the probability of becoming overly anxious is very low. I also have a plan to deal with anxiety if it does become a problem so I'm all prepared and will do just fine. If not, so what? It's no big deal. Most of what I'm feeling now is just excitement, and that's okay. Now, what else do I need to do before leaving?"

Use the "So What If" Approach

What-if thoughts and statements characteristic of negative anticipation tend to generate adrenaline and increase the amount of anxiety a person feels. Many find it helpful to rethink or repeat the thought or statement, but change the *what if* into *so what if.* For example: "What if I start to breathe funny?" becomes "So what if I start to breathe funny?"

"What if I start to get anxious?" becomes "So what if I start to get anxious?"

"What if I have to leave?" becomes "So what if I have to leave?"

Just as what-if thoughts generate adrenaline and increase anxiety, so-what-if thoughts tend to calm you. This calming effect can be increased by following the so-what-if thought with coping self-statements that address the fear expressed in the what-if. If you have a particular what-if that you frequently become stuck on, use the Bottom-Line Technique discussed in Lesson 6 so you have clearly identified the underlying fear. Then develop rational self-talk that addresses this fear. These coping self-statements can be general ones such as those described in Lesson 3 or ones tailored to a specific fear as a result of a Four-Step Analysis.

Another what-if that frequently came up for Robert when he had a social event was the thought, "What if I have to leave?" When he used the Bottom-Line Technique, he found that the underlying fear was that people might think there was something wrong with him. As a result, he developed the following rational response:

> *Example:* "What if I have to leave?"
> *Rational self-talk:* "So what if I have to leave. People leave these types of events before they've ended all the time. I can then use my coping skills. If I decide to return, most of the people there won't even know I've been gone. Those who do notice won't think anything about it."

Increase Your Ability to Accept Uncertainty

Worry is frequently generated by a demand for a degree of certainty that is unattainable. Many people want a 100 percent assurance that what is feared will not happen. Unfortunately, the need for a 100 percent guarantee is reinforced by several forces in our modern technological world. This world is a relatively safe and comfortable one. Movies and television programs reinforce the illusion that all problems can be easily solved and life should be safe and wonderful. We don't like to look at the truth that uncertainty is a part of life. The electronic and print media are also quick to look for someone to blame when something goes wrong and imply that accidents "should not" occur. We demand that our medicines, transportation, food, and everything else be 100 percent safe. This is impossible.

Learning to accept the inevitable danger and risks that go with life is essential in order to live fully and creatively. Use positive self-talk to convince yourself that there is often a 1 to 10 percent uncertainty factor that everyone lives with and develop the attitude: "That's just the way it is." Using the Four-Step Analysis to face your fears realistically is one way to develop this attitude. It also helps to develop the habit of looking at the positive side of uncertainty. Remind yourself that a 1 percent chance of a fearful event occurring means there is a 99 percent chance that it will not. In addition, you may want to reexamine your religious or philosophical beliefs. Are you able to make some sense out of the unfortunate and unfair events that are part of living? If not, you may need to review your beliefs about life and the world that form the basis of your belief system. Having a strong spiritual rock to stand upon is often the real key to facing the uncertainties of life.

Develop Problem-Solving Skills

People with anxiety-related problems often spend much time and energy worrying when they need to make a decision. Sometimes this is due to perfectionistic thinking that causes a person to worry about making a wrong decision. Many of the ideas discussed in Lesson 6 can be used to challenge this type of perfectionistic thinking. Often, however, it is simply that the process of making a decision seems overwhelming. This is usually due to the fact that many people have never learned to see decisions as problems to be solved and work through them in a systematic way. The five basic steps to resolving a problem are as follows:

Step 1: **What is the problem?** As simple as it may sound, many people fail to stop and clearly define the problem they are facing. The simplest way to do this is to state the problem in a single statement—for example, "I need to decide whether or not to go on the trip with my friend."

Step 2: **What are my options (choices)?** This is where many people become sidetracked. Instead of listing possible options, they slip into negative self-talk or worry. It often helps to list possible options on a piece of paper. If you are finding it difficult to generate possible options, ask someone you trust who is knowledgeable about the problem you are facing to help you.

Step 3: **Gather information about the positive and negative aspects of each option.** This is the key to making a decision. This is also a step that is neglected by people who have difficulty making decisions. Seek as much information as possible so the consequences of each option you identified in Step 2 is clear. If this is a major decision, lists the pros and cons for each option on a piece of paper. Putting your choices on paper usually helps you think more objectively about them. Again, with complex problems you may need to consult with people you trust who are knowledgeable about the problem you are facing.

Step 4: Choose the option that generates the most positive or least negative feelings. If you have done your job well in Step 3, one option always generates more positive or less negative feelings than any of the others. If this does not occur, repeat the above steps. Once you reach this point, avoid procrastination and go ahead with that option since the anxiety generated by a prolonged conflict can be very debilitating. Use self-talk to counter the perfectionistic need for a "perfect" solution.

Step 5: Follow-up (optional). After you have experienced the consequences of your decision, take time to evaluate the actions you took. If things turned out poorly, use the problem-solving approach to mistakes discussed in Lesson 6. If things turned out well, be sure to congratulate yourself on a job well done!

Separate the Past from the Present

People often react to the present as if it were the past even though the two are very different. This is due, in part, to the reactions triggered by conditioned response learning as discussed in Lesson 2. When harmless everyday events have been associated with danger, they can trigger both anxiety and negative self-talk. When this occurs, use rational self-talk to remind yourself that while the threat you fear may have been real and important in the past, it now either no longer exists or is only a minor problem.

Anton provides a good example of how the past can distort the present. Anton was in a major car accident. Afterward, he began to experience very high anxiety while driving. Here is an example of the type of self-talk he used to calm himself while driving:

> I was injured in a bad accident. At that time, my brain associated danger with driving and now triggers my fight or flight response whenever I'm in a car. The accident is in the past. I survived it and the odds are that I will never be in another accident like that again. This is especially true because I'm a much more careful driver now. The anxiety I'm now feeling is simply my brain reacting to the past. It will slowly go away as I practice my driving. Now, let's find some music I can sing along to.

Here is another example from Barbara, who was recovering from panic disorder and, like many people with this problem, was very fearful of places where panic attacks had occurred in the past. Observe the self-talk she used to challenge these types of fears:

> The threat associated with this place was real and important when I did not understand why my panic attacks occurred and I had no skills to cope with them. However, I now understand why they occurred. I also have a wide range of skills for managing anxiety, which I have used successfully many times. The anxiety I am currently feeling is simply an old conditioned response habit pattern based on a threat that no longer exists. It's not dangerous. It's only an uncomfortable body sensation that will diminish with time.

Avoid Exaggerating the Importance of Special Items and Events

People with rigid thinking often exaggerate the importance of special objects or events such as a favorite cup, chair, or TV program. This can become the source of worry about what might happen if it is broken or negative self-talk if it is temporarily not available. If you have special items or events such as these, periodically use different items or enjoy different events other than your favorite ones. For example, if you use a cup other than your favorite, take time to enjoy its color, design, and feel.

Thinking and Acting Like a Victim

The tendency to think and act like a victim is very common. People with this trait experience themselves as powerless due to the mistaken belief that they have little or no ability to exert a positive influence on events. Victim thinking is often associated with worry and a negative worldview. While many people openly acknowledge they feel helpless and victimized, others think and act this way without even knowing it. The following examples of self-talk are common victim statements. Place a check by any that are similar to ones you use.

- If only . . . things would be different.

- It's his (her, their, its) fault.
- He (she, they, it) made me angry (anxious, sad, what have you).
- I've always been this way.
- I wish I could do it all over again. Then things would be different.
- That's just the way I am.
- You can't teach an old dog new tricks.
- I can't help myself.

Use the following two approaches to eliminate the tendency to think and act like a victim. This will help to increase your sense of personal power and strengthen your belief in yourself and your ability to influence events in a positive manner.

Develop a Strong Belief in Your Ability to Control and Change Your Emotions

Lesson 4 explained in detail that it is not people and events that generate emotions but the meaning you give to people and events. This is one of the most important ideas in these lessons and needs to become a firm part of your belief system. Whenever you notice yourself thinking or acting as if a person or event made you feel some way, remind yourself how emotions are generated. It is also useful to remind yourself that people and events can do nothing except, at worst, harm you physically or deprive you of something you want. In most cases this is very unlikely.

There are only two kinds of pain a person can experience, physical pain and emotional pain—the result of your wants and needs being frustrated or threatened. Your beliefs and attitudes about events generate emotional pain and cause you discomfort. Most of your misery about your discomfort is caused by your own distorted thinking and your constant repetition of it. As a popular saying goes, *In life, pain is inevitable; suffering is optional.*

Develop a Strong Belief in the Power of the Present

Many people mistakenly believe they are controlled by the past— that once something strongly influences their life, it continues to determine their feelings and behavior. This idea is a false overgeneralization. Just because something holds true in some circumstances hardly proves it equally true under all conditions. For example, just because you once felt weak doesn't mean you must always feel weak. Allowing yourself to remain too strongly influenced by past events causes you to cease trying. This causes the irrational belief that the past determines your future and becomes a self-fulfilling prophecy.

When you are strongly influenced by the past, feelings about people and things from the past are often transferred to the present. Going through life reacting to shadows from the past instead of current events usually results in self-defeating behavior.

For example, when Ryan was young he had an aunt whom he disliked intensely because she was very critical of everything he did. During his early adult life he found it very difficult to deal with people who resembled his aunt in appearance or speech. Ryan finally sought help to change this reaction when he was assigned a supervisor at work who was very good-natured but resembled his aunt. Here is an example of the type of self-talk Ryan used to let go of the past:

> My supervisor reminds me a lot of my aunt. That is why I tend to be so critical of her. My aunt was a mean, nasty old lady. This lady is not my aunt. She does not demean me like my aunt did. She is actually kind of nice. I need to treat her like I do my other co-workers.

Work at accepting the fact that while your past does influence you in some important ways, it has no magical, automatic effect on the present or future. Your present is tomorrow's past. Believing that today is your "point of power" helps you consider your past history more objectively and learn valuable lessons from it. This helps you avoid repeating mistakes you made in the past. Changing the present to create a better future also becomes easier.

Whenever you notice yourself doing something self-defeating and using phrases such as "If only . . . ," "I've always been this way," "I've always done it this way," or "I can't change" to justify the behavior, challenge your thinking with rational self-talk. Use the ideas in this lesson to challenge the idea that the past forces you to act in a certain manner. Then realistically assess your needs and wants and make a choice based on the present. Judy presents a good example of someone whose self-talk affected her negatively. Judy has social phobia and usually does not look at people where she works. One day she caught herself thinking, "If only I had more confidence, I could really make something out of myself." Here is the rational self-talk she used to challenge this thought:

> What do I mean "if only"? I'm acting and thinking as if it's impossible for me to change. Today is the point of power in my life. I cannot change the past. However, I can change tomorrow by acting differently today even though it may be difficult at first. I want to become more confident with people so I need to practice my social skills. I am going to smile, look directly at, and say "Hello" to at least two co-workers today.

Develop the Ability to Accept Frustration and Loss

Frustrations and irritations are a normal part of daily living. Usually, they do not create catastrophes. Develop rational self-talk that reinforces the belief that you can survive quite well despite them.

One way to do this is by becoming philosophical about loss and frustration. This helps you regard it as undesirable but not as unbearable or intolerable. This, in turn, helps you let go of past negative experiences. Another important strategy to use when faced with actual physical injury, deprivation, pain, or disease is distraction. While distraction does not affect the source of the problem, it does help you cope with difficult situations after you have done what is practical to eliminate or diminish your painful circumstances.

Blaming

Blaming has two parts. First, you shift the responsibility for some troublesome event to someone or something else. Then you condemn and criticize that person or circumstance for causing you problems. The person or circumstance that is seen as being responsible for your problems becomes a scapegoat. In essence, blaming is really just another form of living life as a victim and reflects a reluctance to take responsibility for your life and actions. The mistaken ideas that life should be fair and that achievements or actions determine worth are also frequently present.

Some blamers are very verbal and let everyone know who or what they think has caused their misfortune. Others remain silent and carry on long internal dialogues dwelling on who or what caused their misery. The following approaches are designed to help you eliminate this type of self-defeating behavior.

Take Responsibility for Your Life

When you look for scapegoats and blame others for your problems, you become powerless and lose the ability to change things for the better. It is only when you take ownership of problems that you regain the ability to take constructive action. In essence, every problem you have is *your* problem regardless of who's responsible. The solutions to your problems only come when you use your time and energy to choose effective actions instead of dwelling on whose fault or how horrible it is.

A good example of this would be when you are injured. It is important to know why you were injured so you can avoid doing this again in the future. It may also be important to identify anyone who contributed to your injury in case you need to take action against them for compensation. Your main focus, however, needs to be on what you need to do to heal. This is your sole responsibility whether anyone else tries to help you or not. You need to make sure you find proper treatment and do the things you need to do to recover. In a similar manner, any problem you face is your responsibility to solve regardless of how it came about.

Distinguish Between Responsibility and Blame

One of the uglier aspects of blaming is the tendency to condemn and criticize the person or thing that you see as being responsible for your problem. This usually occurs because you are confusing inappropriate or bad behavior with *being* bad. Use the ideas in Lesson 6 to challenge the idea that worth is determined by achievement or actions. As you learn to separate people's actions—your own and those of others—from their worth as humans, it becomes easier to look at behavior more objectively. In addition, use positive self-talk to keep yourself focused on objective problem solving instead of wasting your valuable time and energy condemning the person whom you believe is responsible. As you do this, remember that a particular event usually has many causes.

While often it is important to identify why something happened, learn to make assigning responsibility for a problem or misfortune an objective form of problem solving. Your goal is simply to decide what happened so you can identify if anything can be done differently in the future to prevent the recurrence of this type of misfortune.

If you habitually condemn and blame others, you also probably find that you sometimes focus your tendency to condemn and criticize on yourself. This results in self-loathing and feelings of worthlessness when you feel you have acted badly. Distinguishing between responsibility and blame becomes easier as you become more accepting of human weaknesses and shortcomings. Make allowances for the possibility— indeed, the practical certainty—that you and others will continue to make numerous errors and mistakes. When you notice that you are being hard on yourself, use self-talk to redirect your attention to problem-solving instead of blaming: "I definitely did act in an inappropriate way. Humans beings do this. Now, what exactly did I do and how can I correct it or at least not repeat it?"

Identify and Challenge Distorted Thinking That Reinforces Blaming

One of the primary forms of distorted thinking that reinforces blaming is should/must thinking, especially the mistaken idea that life should be fair. Whenever you find yourself saying or thinking that someone or some event is unfair, remind yourself that total fairness, like perfection, is impossible to achieve in the real world. Because people and events are complex, there is always something different about the way you treat each person you meet. Likewise, there is always something different about the way you behave in each situation no matter how similar situations seem. The belief that life should be fair magnifies these inequalities and makes them seem much more important than they really are.

Convince yourself that injustice and inequality are facts of life. Everyone will at times act in hurtful and unjust ways for either rational or irrational reasons. Actions done with good intentions sometimes turn out to be hurtful or unjust because of a lack of knowledge or understanding. The only rational approach to living in an unjust world is to focus on needs instead of fairness. Decide if something you really need or want is being frustrated or threatened. If it is, concentrate on developing a plan to improve the situation.

Overgeneralization and magnification are two other types of distorted thinking that reinforce blaming. Whenever you find yourself condemning or blaming someone for a problem instead of using a problem-solving approach to resolve it, reexamine your self-talk and look for should/must thinking (especially in the form of all-or-nothing thinking), overgeneralization, magnification and any other forms of distorted thinking you may have been using. If blaming is a major problem for you, use the Block Method described in Lesson 5 to analyze your thinking and practice rational self-talk. As your ability to identify and challenge distorted thinking increases, it becomes easier to stop blaming.

Learn to Deal with Negative Behaviors of Others Objectively

One sign of emotional maturity is the ability to avoid retaliating against people who act hatefully or harm you. Becoming upset interferes with your ability to reason and correct the situation. While you cannot control the thoughts or behaviors of others, you can control your own. Concentrate on identifying the most effective actions you can take to improve or at least cope with the situation.

Should/must thinking is the biggest obstacle to developing this ability. The need to punish and retaliate is often the result of focusing on how others "should" behave instead of concentrating on your main logical concern: planning actions you can take to protect yourself and, if possible, satisfy your needs. This becomes easier as your ability to identify and challenge should/must thinking increases.

Albert has a brother-in-law named Sam who acts like an emotional two-year-old. One day when Sam did something childish, Albert thought: "How can he act like this? He's thirty-five and should know better. I can't stand it. He shouldn't treat people like this." Here is how Albert challenged his negative self-talk:

Wait a minute. Here I am expecting Sam to be reasonable and fair and treat me with respect. I know he's self-centered, unreasonable, and often acts like a two-year-old. I can't do anything about that. I can, however, choose to respond in a way that protects me and fulfills my needs. I can also stop magnifying the awfulness of the situation. I would sure like everyone to be fair and kind, but they aren't. Now, what exactly would be the most effective way to deal with Sam's selfish and immature behavior and take care of myself?

Another way to stay more objective when faced with negative behaviors from others is to ask yourself the following four questions:

- Do I really care what this person does?
- Do this person's actions truly affect me?
- Is it likely that this person will change if I make the effort to help him or her do so?
- Do I actually have the time and energy required to help this person change?

Unless you can answer all the above with a resounding yes, stay somewhat aloof from the errors and shortcomings of others. When you do consider it worthwhile to become involved with helping someone change, do so in an unfrantic way. Adopt a permissive, uncritical attitude. Keep in mind how difficult it is for you to change.

Recommended Activities for Lesson 7
Develop the Beliefs of a Positive Realist

This lesson discussed many of the beliefs that enable a person to face the world as a positive realist. Reread the lesson and put a check by any ideas that you feel you need to use to challenge irrational beliefs that you hold. Then summarize them on cards. Review these cards once a day for at least a week. Here are samples of cards Robert, Judy, and Albert made:

Robert's Card: Dealing with What-Ifs

- Use the Four-Step Analysis to face your fears then redirect your attention elsewhere.
- Remember that uncertainty is a fact of life—a 1 percent chance of a negative outcome means a 99 percent chance of a positive outcome.
- Stop, look, and choose actions based on present realities, not on the past.

Judy's Card: Challenges for Victim Thinking

- People and events don't cause me to feel things; it is the interpretation I give to events that generates my emotions.
- Pain is inevitable, suffering is optional—my choice.
- Today is my point of power—make choices that bring what I want based on the realities present here and now.
- Humans can be very tough critters—I can, if I choose, tolerate frustration and loss. I don't have to let it defeat me.

Albert's Card: Challenges for Blaming and Scapegoating

- Take ownership of your life and problems.
- People frequently act in hurtful and irresponsible ways. That's life. When this happens, focus on your response, not on how bad or awful they are.
- Your parents were right—life isn't fair. That's just the way it is.
- Don't worry about other people's shortcomings unless it affects you directly.

Practice Using the Four-Step Analysis

Using paper and pencil, do a Four-Step Analysis with the two most important concerns you currently have. Create coping self-statements that summarize your analysis and record them on a card you can refer to in the future.

Increase Your Problem-Solving Skills

Think of a recent occasion when you had difficulty making a decision, resolving a conflict, or solving a problem. Then review the five steps to problem solving outlined in the lesson and identify the step or steps that were difficult or that you simply skipped. Next, list ways in which you could have completed the step or steps more effectively. Summarize your ideas in your journal or on a card where you can refer to them in the future when you are having difficulty with a decision.

Practice Becoming a Positive Realist

After you have done the preceding exercises, review the lesson again and identify any additional approaches not covered in the above exercises that would help you become more of a positive realist. List them on a card and practice them during the time you are working on this lesson. If negative anticipation, the tendency to think like a victim, or the tendency to blame or scapegoat either yourself or others is a problem for you, spend two weeks with this lesson.

A Note to People with Generalized Anxiety Disorder

While the ideas and skills presented in this lesson apply to all the anxiety-related problems, they are of special importance to people suffering from generalized anxiety disorder. If you have GAD, spend extra time with this lesson. It is especially important to become skilled with the Four-Step Analysis.

What's Happening? What's Real?

The idea of separating the past from the present has a special application for people who experienced trauma as children. When this is the case, emotions associated with people and events in the past will often be triggered by things in the present. For example, a teacher or supervisor might trigger anxiety or fear that was originally associated with an abusive parent. When this is the case, ask and answer the following two questions: "What's happening?" and "What's real?" Here is an example from Paula, who often found herself becoming very nervous around her supervisor:

> *What's happening?* "When my supervisor talks, she sounds a lot like my mother. She also is in a position of authority. Both of these things cause me to feel like I'm a little girl at home and that my mother is going to yell at me or hit me."
>
> *What's real?* "She is not my mother, she is just my supervisor. She has never yelled at me and she will never hit me. We are simply two professionals working together."

As Paula practiced using this technique, she found that after a few weeks she was much calmer around her supervisor.

> Be sure to spend at least one week with this lesson. The skills and concepts it presents are an essential part of the process you are using to become a positive realist.

LESSON 8

The Excessive Need for Approval

We are all born with the need for relationship—to have at least one other person in our lives who knows us, enjoys our company, and likes us. Like many of the other traits discussed in these lessons, this need for approval is neither good nor bad. Instead, it is a basic need that is essential for healthy relationships. It is only when this need has been suppressed or becomes exaggerated that it creates problems. Because the excessive need for approval is a common problem for people with anxiety-related problems, you will probably find yourself returning to this lesson many times. Each time you will find the rewards of working through the information and exercises systematically well worth the effort.

How the Excessive Need for Approval Is Expressed

People with an excessive need for approval usually view themselves as being flawed in some way and thus unacceptable to others. For some, the flaws that make them unacceptable are a part of their conscious belief system. They can easily identify personal shortcomings that make them inadequate and describe them in detail. For others, the idea that they are inferior to others is less obvious but still a basic part of their self-image. This belief in their inadequacy generates a selective point of view as described in Lesson 4. This selective point of view causes them to notice evidence of their inferiority in whatever situation they find themselves in and confirms the mistaken belief that they are inadequate and unacceptable.

As with most core beliefs, the mistaken belief that one is unacceptable or inferior in some way usually develops in childhood. All the childhood experiences described in Lesson 1 can contribute to the development of this trait. In addition to these experiences, the presence of a disability or being different because of economic, ethnic, or religious factors can be contributing elements. As children develop, the belief that they are inadequate, or inferior in some way can cause them to become overly focused on winning approval from others in an attempt to quiet the feelings of inadequacy churning inside.

As the excessive need for approval develops, it can make a person overly sensitive to criticism. Difficulty with saying no to the demands of others can also develop, since the refusal of requests might bring disapproval. For some, the fear of rejection and disapproval can also make it difficult to deal with authority figures such as supervisors or teachers.

Sometimes, an excessive need for approval can generate an excessive empathy for others. This is usually due to the mistaken belief that others are also supersensitive to criticism and rejection. Excessive empathy usually leads to the creation of a rigid rule that a person must always be considerate, kind, sensitive, and generous. It can also cause a person to become a "rescuer" and assume responsibility for keeping friends and relatives happy.

The self-esteem of a person with an excessive need for approval is fairly unstable and dependent upon the opinions of others. Acceptance by others generates confidence and improved performance. Rejection shatters confidence and severely interferes with a person's performance. This can cause a person to assume a child's role toward friends, relatives, or children and constantly check to see if decisions and actions meet the approval of others.

It is common for the excessive need for approval to cause a person to see rejection by others and attribute negative intentions to their actions even though there is no logical reason to do so. For example, Jim had not received a call from a friend for more than a week. Even though he knew his friend was busy remodeling part of his house, Jim believed that his friend either no longer cared for him or was angry about something he had done.

Occasionally, the excessive need for approval is expressed as a need to be treated as a favorite child. When this is the case, the lack of special treatment in social situations is viewed as a slight or rejection. In extreme cases, failure to be invited or considered for an event is seen as rejection.

The following examples of self-talk are characteristic of the excessive need for approval. Check any that are similar to thoughts you have had:

- If someone important to me expects me to do something, I should do it.
- How could I be so selfish?
- I'm not doing enough; I should do more.
- Why didn't I see what needed to be done?
- I should do what people expect me to do.
- I shouldn't be irritable or unpleasant.
- How could I be so unpleasant?
- I shouldn't make others angry at me.
- Why did I act that way (you caused someone to become angry)?
- I should keep people I love happy.
- Why can't I be nicer?
- It's my fault he/she is upset.
- Rejection is the worst thing that can happen.
- I can't stand it when others are upset with me.
- I can't be happy if others don't like me.
- Why don't people like me?
- I can't stand being alone.
- I'm nothing unless I'm loved.
- It's terrible when I'm not noticed.
- How can they be so insensitive/dense?
- I need to be understood.
- Why can't they be more appreciative?
- Others should show appreciation for what I do.

Eliminating the Excessive Need for Approval

Three approaches for eliminating an excessive need for approval are described below. While they may seem simple, each one takes time and practice to master. Additional activities that build on these are described later in the program when the complex issue of acceptance is discussed in relation to self-esteem and assertiveness.

Develop Rational and Realistic Views of Approval and Rejection

If you are going to include other people in your life, you will experience disapproval and rejection regularly. Sometimes this is because you have done something genuinely harmful or mean. But much, if not most, of the disapproval and rejection you encounter has little to do with you personally. If you analyze the last few times someone showed disapproval toward you or rejected you, you will probably find that the rejection had little to do with who you are or what you did. When someone reacts negatively toward you, it is often because this person is either thinking irrationally or directing emotions at you that were generated by an event that has nothing to do with you.

Consider Sharon, who came home after a difficult day and noticed that her roommate, Betty, had not started dinner. Because Sharon was tired, hungry, and frustrated, she became very angry. Betty had also had a difficult day and did not take time to analyze what was happening, so she took Sharon's attack personally and felt very rejected. This is what often happens in a situation like this. Later that day, however, Betty took a second look at what happened and realized that Sharon's actions and rejection were due more to Sharon's hunger, fatigue, and frustration with work than to her own actions.

The next time you feel rejected, take a moment to calm down and analyze whether the person acting negatively toward you is reacting mainly to something you did or more to something that has nothing to do with you. Keep in mind that illness, hunger, fatigue, and excessive stress can interfere with a person's ability to think in a logical and realistic manner. The negative behaviors that result from these temporary conditions often do not reflect a person's true beliefs or feelings toward you. In addition, people often have irrational beliefs or wounds from the past that make it difficult for them to see you as you actually are.

The perfectionistic beliefs that worth is determined by achievement and mistakes are terrible often play a role in exaggerating the need for approval. This is especially true when you are trying to live up to a model of a "perfect person" who is always pleasant, rational, and understanding. When this is the case, rejection is seen as a failure. This sense of failure is even greater if the rejection is due to inappropriate actions on your part.

When someone rejects you, remind yourself that it does not mean you are worthless. When you actually do something that is unpleasant or thoughtless, separate your actions from your worth as a person. Also be sure to challenge irrational beliefs you may have about mistakes. Then adopt a problem-solving approach to the situation and think about how you can either correct the error you made or prevent it from recurring in the future. Specific ideas that can be used to challenge the perfectionistic beliefs that worth is determined by achievement and all mistakes are terrible are found in Lesson 6.

When you are rejected, remember that emotions are transitory. An emotion can only be sustained if you work very hard to keep it alive. This is usually done by recalling and dwelling on memories of whatever originally triggered the emotion or by repeating self-talk that reinforces the emotion over and over. While disapproval and criticism are uncomfortable, the discomfort usually passes fairly quickly if you avoid distorted thinking and distract yourself with positive activities. So even though you may feel it's pointless to start, begin an activity you have enjoyed in the past. If you notice yourself recalling the hurtful event or negative thoughts about it, redirect your attention to more positive ones.

The excessive need for approval often generates the tendency to overgeneralize and homogenize—to see everyone's acceptance and approval as both essential and equally important. Remember that being rejected by one person does not automatically lead to a never-ending series of rejections. Everyone judges you differently no matter how well or how poorly you behave. Even when someone does reject you, there are still many people who will accept you.

Develop an understanding and acceptance of the fact that you do not need the approval of everyone you meet in order to live a happy and meaningful life. Acceptance by a mail carrier, salesperson, or stranger on the street is not as important as acceptance by people close to you. While it is more pleasant and often more efficient to do business with people who are friendly and accepting, in most cases you can still function well with people who don't like you. Only your thoughts can raise or lower your spirits. Another person's approval or disapproval has no ability to affect your mood unless you believe what was said is true. Seek out those who appreciate and accept you instead of wallowing in the rejection of one person.

In healthy relationships, disapproval is usually temporary. When you do something unpleasant or thoughtless, the other person responds in a positive way to your attempts at making amends. A relationship in which the other person is so negative, critical, rejecting, unreasonable, or unforgiving that you must behave in a demeaning or self-defeating way in order to win approval is not worth your time and energy. If you are in such a relationship, you may want to end it. If this is not possible because the other person is a relative or co-worker, consider ways in which you can protect yourself. Suggestions on how to protect yourself from negative people are given in Negative Friends, one of the Recommended Activities in Lesson 4. Suggestions on how to find positive emotional support are given in Emotional Support in Lesson 3.

Rejection and disapproval are very upsetting for a person who is a perfectionist and who finds it difficult to accept mistakes. Review the sections Challenging Beliefs That Support Perfectionism and Develop a Problem-Solving Approach to Mistakes in Lesson 6. If you still find it difficult to use the ideas and skills described in these two sections, work through them again along with this section.

Learn to Approach Criticism in an Objective, Problem-Solving Fashion

Criticism can be a positive force in your life. It does not need to intimidate, frustrate, or devastate you. The following four-step approach is an effective way to deal with criticism constructively. Place a check by any step you find difficult.

Step 1: Use coping self-statements to maintain objectivity and adopt a problem-solving attitude. There are two types of coping self-statements that are useful when faced with criticism. The first set includes redirecting statements that focus your attention and energy onto the next three steps–asking for details, evaluating the criticism, and choosing a response. Here are some examples of this first type of coping self-statement:

- Remember to ask for details and evaluate before choosing a response.
- Don't accept any of this criticism until you have looked at it objectively.
- Stop taking things so personally and use your brain to evaluate what is happening and being said.
- Don't respond until you take time to evaluate what was said.

The second set includes statements that identify and challenge any irrational ideas you have about criticism or forms of distorted thinking you commonly use when criticized. Most of the ideas in the three previous sections can be used in this fashion. Some examples:

- This criticism may be a good opportunity to learn something valuable.
- This criticism concerns only a few of my actions, not my entire being.
- While this may feel uncomfortable, it does not mean I am being totally rejected and disapproved of.
- My worth is not determined by actions or achievements.

Step 2: Ask for details. In order for criticism to be useful, you need details. Ask the person providing the criticism to specify the behaviors he or she finds offensive or undesirable. In addition, have this person specify actions that can be taken to correct the situation or new behaviors that can replace the old ones. If the other person is unwilling or unable to state specifics, the criticism is probably not valid and can be dismissed.

Step 3: Evaluate the critic and the criticism. Before you evaluate the criticism, consider the source of the criticism. Ask yourself the following questions:

- What are the qualifications of the person criticizing me?
- Does this person have experience or training that provides special insight?
- Have I been criticized for this particular issue before? If so, was it by several different people or by this same person on several different occasions?
- In what context was the present and past criticism given? (Keep in mind that criticism given during an argument or when the other person is stressed or not feeling well is often not valid.)
- Does this person have a bias or need that might reduce his or her objectivity?

After considering the above, you are ready to decide whether or not you feel the criticism is valid. As you do this, be aware of any tendency you might have to automatically consider others as better judges of your interests than you are, and remind yourself that you know more about yourself than any other person in the world. The opinion of others is simply information you need to evaluate for yourself before you accept or reject it.

If you do not feel a criticism is valid, dismiss it and get on with your life. If you feel a criticism is valid, go on to the final step.

Step 4: Choose a response. When you feel a criticism is valid, the following questions can help you decide what action, if any, would be appropriate:

- How important is the behavior specified by the criticism both to the person offering the criticism and to me?
- How satisfied am I with things as they are now?
- How hard will it be to make the changes the person specified?
- What benefits will I gain if I take the time and trouble to change my behavior?

- Will it really improve the situation if I make these changes?
- What are my chances of succeeding if I spend the time and energy required to make these changes?

If you decide that responding to the criticism is not worth your time and energy, use positive self-talk to help you accept this aspect of yourself. If you have several possible courses of action that can be taken, use the above series of questions to evaluate each alternative separately.

Strive to Do What You Want Instead of What Others Think You Should Do

Have you ever agreed to do something and then later realized it was either something you really did not want to do or something that was not good for you to do? Many people with an excessive need for approval find this a frequent experience. The fear of disapproval and rejection often makes it difficult to say no to the demands of others. If you spend your life pleasing others, you may also lose the ability to know what it is you want in a given situation. Ignoring personal needs and wants becomes an automatic habit pattern.

There are two ways to reestablish the ability of knowing what you want. First, avoid making decisions on the spur of the moment. Postpone decisions by responding to requests with statements like, "I need to think about it," or "I'll let you know later." Second, when considering the request, ask yourself the following two questions: "What do I really want to do in this situation?" and "What would be best for me to do in this situation?" Most people find that simply asking these questions makes them aware of what it is they want and what would be best for them to do. Some, however, find that it takes time to answer these questions honestly. Practice delaying decisions and asking yourself these two questions until it is easy for you to determine what you want and what would be best for you in most everyday situations. Some people find that this takes only a week, while others find it takes several months.

In order to identify what you want, you need to be able to identify your emotions accurately. Lesson 4 described in detail how positive emotions are simply a message that a need or want has or will be met while negative emotions mean that you believe a threat exists or a loss has or may occur. Practice identifying your emotional reactions with simple language such as *happy, excited, anxious, afraid, angry,* or *sad.* Once you've identified the emotion you're experiencing, you can identify whether a need or want is being met or threatened or a loss might occur. This information is essential to making a good decision.

Betty, who was discussed earlier, had an experience that illustrates this process. While at work, a co-worker asked her if she wanted to go to lunch. Betty's usual response would have been to immediately say yes. Because she was working on this lesson, however, she said, "Let me check my schedule and get back to you in a few minutes." Betty then asked herself, "Do I really want to go to lunch with this person today, and do I have the time to do this?" As she asked herself these questions, she noticed she was both anxious and a little irritated. She knew this meant that she must be perceiving a threat, so she asked herself, "Where is the threat in going to lunch?" Betty recalled that this person was a chronic complainer. She also became aware of negative feelings she'd had in the past when she went to lunch and this person spent the entire time complaining about her boss and the company. Betty decided that she really did not want to go to lunch with this person and told her, "I'm sorry, I just realized I have other plans."

Recommended Activities for Lesson 8
Develop Rational and Realistic Beliefs About Approval and Rejection

This lesson identified many common irrational beliefs people hold about approval and rejection along with ideas that can be used to challenge these irrational beliefs. As you review the lesson, select those ideas that you feel are the most powerful rational challenges for irrational beliefs you hold and summarize them on cards. Review these cards once a day until you have memorized them. Here is the card that Betty made:

Betty's Card: Rational Challenges for Irrational Beliefs

- Rejection is a part of life.
- While I would like everyone's approval, there will always be a few people who won't like me no matter what I do.
- Rejection doesn't have to defeat me.
- Most of the rejection and disapproval I encounter has little to do with me—often it is due to illness, hunger, fatigue, or stress in the other person.
- People may also reject or disapprove of me for irrational reasons—they are really angry at someone or something else; or they have irrational beliefs or wounds from the past that are distorting their view of me and the present.
- Remember that disapproval is usually temporary in healthy relationships.
- If someone is so demanding that I have to act in a demeaning way to win approval, this person is not worth my time and effort.
- Don't try to be so perfect—I'm human and will sometimes make mistakes and act inappropriately. I will forgive myself when this occurs and challenge the irrational need to be perfect.

Continue to Work with the Block Method

Continue taking five to ten minutes every other day to use the Block Method. As you analyze your thoughts, look for irrational self-talk that is generated by irrational beliefs about rejection or approval. Challenge any irrational beliefs you find with the ideas in this lesson. Review the directions in the Recommended Activities of Lesson 5 if you are still having difficulty with the Block Method.

Learn to Approach Criticism in an Objective, Problem-Solving Fashion

Develop a list of coping self-statements you can use to stay more objective when faced with criticism. Write them down and practice reciting them until you can easily recall them from memory. Then

178 / ANXIETY, PHOBIAS, AND PANIC

review the four steps for responding to criticism described in the lesson until you can recall them using your own words. Spend extra time with steps that are difficult for you. Whenever you find yourself dwelling on a criticism, return to this section and work through the four steps in a systematic manner.

Strive to Do What You Want Instead of What Others Think You Should Do

The lesson listed two different ways to reestablish the ability of knowing what you want—postponing decisions and taking time to ask yourself two questions, "What do I really want to do in this situation?" and "What would be best for me to do in this situation?" If it is often difficult for you to know what you want or what would be best for you to do, practice these two techniques for at least one week. Be sure to also practice identifying your emotions with simple language as you do this. If this is difficult for you, review the discussion on the healthy management of emotions in Lesson 5's section, Emotional Reasoning.

Take a Second Look at Nutrition and Exercise

Lesson 2 stressed the importance of proper nutrition and exercise. Examine your diet to make sure it is providing your body with the nutrition it needs. A healthy body makes the work of changing behavior much easier.

If you are not involved in any type of regular physical exercise, consider ways you could do something in this area as well. Remember that a minimum of twenty minutes of light exercise such as walking three times a week not only works wonders for your physical stamina and health, but also creates a more positive mental outlook. If your ability to travel or finances are limited, there are many programs on television or in books that offer a sensible approach to exercise. If you decide to join a health spa or exercise class, remember to join one that is close to where you live or work. Having a convenient program and location helps maintain momentum in a physical exercise program.

If you have not exercised regularly for a long time, remember to begin with an easy routine and increase the level of difficulty slowly. Consistency and moderation are the keys to success. Before starting a new exercise program or drastically changing your current program, it is always best to check with your doctor.

Avoid Trying to Do Too Much

Considering your body a machine with a limited supply of energy is one of the key concepts presented in these lessons. In the weeks and months ahead, there will be many times when you will experience extra stress. Some of these times are predictable, such as holidays or regular periods of stress at work. Others are not, such as when someone close to you is injured or ill. Keep in mind that joyful experiences, like winning money, gaining a promotion, or the birth of a child, can be just as stressful as negative ones. Whenever you encounter a period of high stress, set priorities and do less than you normally do. Doing less gives you the extra energy you need to handle the additional stress during these periods. Review the section titled Indications Your Body Is Sick, Hungry, Tired, or Overstressed in the Recommended Activities in Lesson 5. Also, review Three Guidelines for Periods of High Stress in Lesson 3.

Spend at least one week with this lesson and do it as thoroughly as possible. If an excessive need for approval is a major problem for you, spend two weeks with it.

LESSON 9

Eliminating the Self-Defeating Behaviors Commonly Associated with Anxiety

Overcoming anxiety is much like working on a puzzle. Just as each piece of a puzzle gives meaning to the pieces with which it joins, each concept and skill you learn reinforces those you have already mastered. By now you are probably beginning to see how many of the pieces of the puzzle that make up your anxiety-related problems fit together. You are now ready to explore a new part of this puzzle and begin working to overcome the self-defeating behaviors associated with your anxiety.

Behavioral Therapy

The previous lessons have mainly used what is commonly called a cognitive approach, where thoughts and beliefs that generate anxiety-related problems are identified and challenged. This lesson focuses on what is commonly called behavioral therapy, an approach that is concerned only with changing the behaviors associated with anxiety. Together these two approaches are referred to as a cognitive–behavioral approach. Because these lessons deal with a wide range of anxiety-related problems, some of the material in each of the following sections may not apply directly to your specific anxiety-related problems. However, it is important to first read through each section in its entirety so you understand the principles it is presenting. Then focus on the parts that address your specific behavioral symptoms.

Identifying Problem Behaviors

The first step in eliminating unwanted behaviors is to identify problem behaviors you want to eliminate. The most common problem behavior associated with anxiety is the avoidance of specific situations, places, or objects that trigger anxiety. Make a list of situations, places, or objects that you avoid for this reason. Using the following scale, rate each item on your list with respect to the level of discomfort it causes and the amount of avoidance behavior associated with it.

RATING PROBLEM BEHAVIORS	
Level of Discomfort	**Amount of Avoidance Behavior**
1. Comfortable	1. Never avoid
2. Slightly uncomfortable	2. Seldom avoid
3. Uncomfortable	3. Sometimes avoid
4. Very uncomfortable	4. Often avoid
5. Panicky	5. Always avoid

Here are two examples made by a person who had panic disorder with agoraphobia and a person with severe social phobia.

AN AGORAPHOBIC'S AVOIDANCE PATTERNS		
Situation	**Level of Discomfort**	**Amount of Avoidance**
Talking on the phone to an answering device	Slightly uncomfortable	Seldom avoid
Meeting new people	Uncomfortable	Sometimes avoid
Waiting in lines	Uncomfortable	Sometimes avoid
Being in a dentist or doctor's waiting room	Very uncomfortable	Sometimes avoid
Being in a restaurant or theater alone	Panicky	Always avoid
Being in a restaurant or theater with friend or spouse	Uncomfortable	Often avoid
Driving on freeways	Panicky	Always avoid
Walking down the street by my house alone	Very uncomfortable	Always avoid

Situation	Level of Discomfort	Amount of Avoidance
Going more than two miles from my house alone	Panicky	Always avoid

A SOCIAL PHOBIC'S AVOIDANCE PATTERNS		
Situation	Level of Discomfort	Amount of Avoidance
Going to a theater or restaurant	Uncomfortable	Often avoid
Maintaining eye contact when talking to someone	Very uncomfortable	Always avoid
Standing in lines	Slightly uncomfortable	Sometimes avoid
Dating	Panicky	Always avoid
Meeting new people	Very uncomfortable	Often avoid
Parties or social situations with more than three people	Panicky	Always avoid

The primary problem behaviors for people suffering from obsessive-compulsive disorder involve compulsions. (If you do not have compulsions, you can skip to the last two paragraphs of this section.) These compulsions usually accompany and are triggered by obsessions—persistent ideas, thoughts, images, or impulses that are senseless or repulsive and seem to intrude upon one's consciousness. Common examples of obsessions include thoughts of harming others, violating social norms, contaminating or infecting oneself or others, and doubt about whether some action has been or will be performed. The compulsions that accompany these types of obsessions fall into two general categories. The first includes actions intended to produce or prevent a future event or situation even though the compulsion has no realistic bearing on the event it is meant to affect. The second includes normal, rational activities performed in a clearly excessive manner. Both of these types of compulsions are also called rituals. Common examples include hand washing, counting, checking, and touching.

When listing compulsions you wish to eliminate, specify the number of times you perform each one. If your compulsions also cause you to avoid things, list the specific situations or places you avoid along with the level of discomfort and amount of avoidance associated with each one. The following list was made by a person obsessed with germs and becoming infected:

An Obsessive-Compulsive's Compulsions

- I wash my hands at least two times whenever I touch a contaminated object, often more.
- I change my clothes after being in crowds.
- I shower or bathe at least twice a day, sometimes several times.

AN OBSESSIVE-COMPULSIVE'S AVOIDANCE PATTERNS		
Situation	**Level of Discomfort**	**Amount of Avoidance**
Shaking hands	Very uncomfortable	Always avoid
Touching things I consider "dirty" such as the floor, trash, or things outside	Very uncomfortable	Often avoid unless I have to do it (such as taking out trash)
Parties or social situations	Uncomfortable	Often avoid unless I can bathe soon afterward
Crowded public places	Very uncomfortable	Same as the above
Public transportation	Very uncomfortable	Same as the above

If your anxiety trigger involves only a compulsion, with no avoidance patterns, simply list the frequency of the behavior. Here are some examples:

- I mentally or verbally say a person's name three times whenever I think of him or her.
- I check electrical appliances at least five times after use to make sure they are switched off.
- I wash my hands three to five times each hour.

Most people working through these lessons are painfully aware of the behaviors associated with their anxiety and can easily list specific situations they avoid or rituals they perform. If it is difficult for you to be specific about your avoidance patterns or rituals, however, spend a few days observing when and where you become anxious. Carry a small notebook, and whenever you become anxious, record any thoughts or events that triggered the anxiety. If you cannot identify a specific trigger, simply describe where you are and what you were doing just before becoming anxious. With each entry, be sure to also rate the level of your anxiety using the scale at the beginning of this section.

Taking time to observe and record when and where you become anxious helps you identify patterns you may be unaware of. While you are doing this exercise, read through the rest of the lesson. Some of the examples may alert you to currently unknown patterns. After one week, if you cannot identify any event that repeatedly triggers anxiety, go on to the next lesson.

Developing Well-Defined Goals

Once you have identified the specific situations or rituals you want to eliminate, the second step in the behavioral approach is to develop specific, well-defined goals. The importance of this second step is summarized by the popular maxim *If you don't have a goal, you'll never get anywhere.*

Begin by reviewing the list you created of situations you avoid or rituals you perform. For each one, list a goal you would like to achieve. These goals need to describe a specific, well-defined behavior or skill you want to develop. The approaches described in this lesson do not work well with goals stated in vague, general terms. The following examples illustrate the difference between vague, general goals and specific, well-defined goals.

DEFINING GOALS	
General Goal	Specific, Well-Defined Goal
I want to be able to go out by myself.	I want to be able to walk around my block alone. *or*
	I want to drive to the mall three miles away and spend at least one hour shopping alone.
I want to be able to socialize.	I want to be able to go on a date to a movie. *or*
	I want to go to a party or club meeting and stay at least two hours.
I want to spend less time thinking about germs and infection.	I want to go to crowded places such as a store without bathing afterward. *or* I want to shake hands and touch door handles without feeling that I need to wash my hands immediately afterward.

After you have completed your list of goals you want to achieve, make another list of the benefits you will receive when your goals are achieved. Here are several benefits for the people in the previous examples:

DEFINING BENEFITS	
I will be able to:	Go on vacations with my family.
	Go to dinner parties and social events.
	Drive wherever I want and get to places faster.
	Attend to my personal health needs, which have been neglected.
I will be able to:	Go out on dates and attend parties.
	Dine out and have more friends.
I will be able to:	Hold hands and be physically affectionate with my spouse.
	Be more effective at work.
	Go places more freely since there will be no need to bathe immediately afterward.
	Accomplish much more each day because I won't be spending so much time with my rituals.

Eliminating problem behaviors is a lot of work. On the other hand, thinking about the benefits you will receive by doing this work is a powerful motivator that will help you continue to practice and reach your goals. If you cannot think of any benefits that are important to you, the goals you listed may not be worth the time and energy needed to reach them. This second point is especially important for people with anxiety-related problems since they often view every limitation or unusual personal characteristic as a problem. Everyone has some minor limitations and personal quirks. These only become a problem when they interfere with your life goals or deprive you of something you strongly desire.

Consider Alice, who has never driven a car. She has no real desire to drive and would gain no benefit from learning. During a period of severe anxiety it would be easy for Alice to consider her inability to drive a problem. This would especially be true if most of her friends could drive. Alice might view her lack of skill in this area as more proof of her inadequacy and failure as a person.

Problems on your list that do not interfere with your life and that would offer no real benefits if they were eliminated are not really problems. Cross them off your list and concentrate on goals that will bring real benefits.

Exposure Therapy

Lesson 2 discussed how I. P. Pavlov presented a neutral stimulus to hungry dogs, such as ringing a bell, then followed it by giving them food. The food caused the dogs to salivate. With repetition, the neutral stimulus (the ringing bell) eventually would trigger salivation. Most of the anxiety behind avoidance behaviors associated with anxiety-related problems is due to this type of conditioned response learning. The good news is that you can reverse this type of conditioning. If you take dogs that have been conditioned to salivate when they hear a bell, and sound the bell repeatedly over several days without giving them food after they hear it, the conditioned response of salivating to the bell will eventually fade. When this happens, the response is said to be extinct. The process used to cause the response to become extinct is called desensitization.

When used with people, the process of gradually exposing a person to a fearful situation or object is called *exposure therapy*. Exposure therapy can be done in three basic ways. The first, referred to as in vivo exposure, exposes a person to the feared situation or object in real life. A second type, called imaginal exposure, involves imagining anxiety-provoking situations. A more recent form of exposure, called virtual reality exposure, has a person enter a computer-generated three-dimensional virtual world that re-creates anxiety-producing situations such as riding an elevator, crossing a bridge, or flying on a plane. Within the computer program, a person has control over the exact nature of the fearful stimulus being experienced as well as how long it is experienced.

Of the three types of exposure therapy, in vivo exposure is the most widely used and usually the most effective form of exposure for overcoming avoidance behaviors. The four basic steps used with gradual in vivo exposure are described below.

Step 1: Select a Goal and Break It into Small Steps. Look at the list of goals you made earlier in this lesson and number them beginning with the one you feel is easiest to attain and ending with the most difficult. With gradual exposure, you always start with the easiest goal and slowly work your way up toward your most difficult goal. The success you achieve with the easier goals provides skills and confidence that are essential for success with the more difficult goals.

If the first goal on your list seems very difficult, divide it into several easy-to-reach steps. Mike had panic disorder with agoraphobia and refused to leave the house alone. He set as his first goal the ability to go to the mailbox, about twenty steps from his front door. Since this seemed very difficult, he divided it into the following steps:

1. Stand on the front porch with the door open.
2. Stand on the front porch with the door closed.
3. Step off the front porch.
4. Walk halfway to the mailbox and back.
5. Walk to the mailbox and back.

Kathy had post-traumatic stress disorder due to a bad car accident. The only avoidance pattern she considered a problem involved driving alone. Since she was now becoming skilled at controlling anxiety, she decided to work toward the goal of being able to drive alone across town on the freeway. Kathy's first goal was to drive to a local store alone. Since even this seemed quite frightening, she divided this goal into the following steps:

1. Sit behind the wheel alone for fifteen minutes.
2. Back the car to the end of the driveway and return.
3. Back the car into the street and return.
4. Drive to the end of the block and return.
5. Drive around the block.
6. Drive two blocks away and return.
7. Drive to the local store four blocks away and return.

As you reach each goal on your list, decide if the next goal needs to be broken into small steps before proceeding. The more difficult a goal seems, the more important it is to break the goal into several small steps. If you become stuck while working on a particular goal, it simply means you have not broken the goal into small enough steps.

Step 2: Identify Sensations and Thoughts That Create Anxiety or Fear. Recall several times when you have been in a situation similar to the one you plan to practice. Make a list of the unpleasant physical sensations you felt at those times. Then make a list of as many of your anxiety-producing thoughts as you can recall. Your goal is to develop a list of both the anxiety symptoms and frightening thoughts you might encounter so you can develop a plan for coping with them. Mike, mentioned earlier in the lesson, developed the following lists:

MIKE'S LISTS OF SYMPTOMS AND THOUGHTS	
Physical Symptoms	**Thoughts**
Light-headedness	I'm going to go crazy.
Pounding heart	This is awful, I can't stand it.
Sweating	They may come and lock me up.
Sometimes a feeling that I'm going to faint	People are going to see me like this and think I'm crazy. If I faint, I'll fall down and hurt myself. If I faint, I won't know what people are doing or saying.

As you practice, add any new symptoms or thoughts that cause a problem to your list. Be sure to take time to develop a plan for coping with these new additions as outlined in the following step before your next practice.

Step 3: Develop a List of Coping Skills. Once you identify the symptoms and thoughts that cause you problems, you are ready to develop a plan for coping with them. The main coping skills presented in the first half of the book include the following:

- *Relaxation response methods:* If you have not yet begun developing cue-controlled relaxation using the supplemental cassettes or the scripts in Appendix 2, begin now. Cue-controlled relaxation is usually the most practical type of relaxation response to use while practicing. Sometimes, however, it is possible to find a quiet place to sit or stand where you can go through a more formal method for developing a relaxation response. The muscle tensing and relaxing described in this lesson's Recommended Activities is also useful.
- *Diaphragmatic breathing:* This is a primary symptom-reducing skill for many people. You may want to review Lesson 2 if you have not been using it.
- *Coping self-statements:* If you have not been using coping self-statements, review the section in Lesson 2 that describes them and develop a list. If you have been using coping self-statements but do not yet feel skillful with them, take time to review and update your list.
- *Rational self-talk:* Of the skills listed in this step, rational self-talk is the most difficult to learn and the most difficult to apply to anxiety-producing situations. It is, however, an extremely effective skill once it is mastered. Review the basic principles given in Lessons 4 and 5 periodically.
- *Distraction:* Distraction methods are described in Lesson 2. These skills are especially useful for coping with the intense, short-term anxiety that sometimes occurs when you first encounter a frightening situation.

When you practice, carry with you a small card that lists those specific skills you find most useful. This helps you remember to

use them while you are practicing. Here is a list that Mike carried
with him:

- Use relaxed diaphragmatic breathing.
- Take a moment to tense and relax.
- Use coping self-statements.
- Externalize—observe carefully or talk to someone.
- Minimize negative self-talk.
- Watch out for magnification, catastrophizing, fortune-telling, and labeling.

It is especially important to develop skill in combating the anxiety-producing thoughts you listed in the previous step. One way
to do this is to substitute coping self-statements whenever you
notice yourself thinking or saying anxiety-producing statements.
Mike found it difficult to think of coping self-statements when he
first began practicing, so he carried the following list:

- Anxiety is *not* dangerous—only uncomfortable. I can be anxious and still function effectively.
- Just take things one step at a time. There's no need to rush.
- This will only last a short time. I can handle it.
- My symptoms are usually caused by hyperventilation—they won't hurt me and will soon subside if I use diaphragmatic breathing.
- I don't have to do this perfectly. It's okay to be anxious.
- Practice will make this easier. It has already become easier for me to do many things.
- There is no need to fight anxiety. It is just adrenaline triggered by old conditioned response habit patterns. These feelings will go away after a while.

In addition to having general coping self-statements that calm you, it is
very important that you develop coping self-statements addressing the
specific problem thoughts you listed in the previous step. As you review
these thoughts, identify the type of distorted thinking each represents
and write out a rational response. You may need to use the Four-Step

Analysis described in Lesson 7 for some of your concerns. Once you have developed your rational responses, write them on cards you can take with you. Review your cards at the start of your practice session so your rational challenges are fresh in your mind. These rational responses are powerful coping self-statements you can use to challenge your specific concerns when they arise during the practice session. Whenever new fearful thoughts come up, create new rational responses that challenge them. It also helps to update your rational responses periodically so they remain fresh. When Mike did this, he developed the following rational responses for his list of anxiety-producing thoughts:

Self-talk: "I'm going crazy (labeling)."
Rational response: "I am not going crazy. I am only experiencing adrenaline in my system and misinterpreting what it means. I am perfectly sane and able to cope with this situation even though I may feel uncomfortable. Feelings are not facts. I can feel anxious and still do whatever I want to do."

Self-talk: "This is awful; I can't stand it (magnification)."
Rational response: "This is not awful. The Holocaust was awful. This is only unpleasant. I can stand it. I am alive and will continue to live."

Self-talk: "People are going to see me like this and think I'm crazy (mind reading and fortune-telling)."
Rational response: "First of all, most of the people I meet won't even be aware of what I am doing or how I am feeling. Second, most don't care. Even if someone notices I am uncomfortable, he or she will probably have forgotten about it within five minutes. Besides, what people think is not really important. It is what I think that is important."

Self-talk: "They may come and lock me up (fortune-telling and catastrophizing)."
Rational response: "Now, this is a real fantasy. The worst that could happen is I might be taken to an emergency room if I fainted. That would probably be the safest place I could be."

Self-talk: "If I faint, I'll fall down and hurt myself (fortune-telling and catastrophizing)."

Rational response: "I have never fainted so it is very unlikely that I will faint when I practice. If I use my diaphragmatic breathing, it makes it even more unlikely that I will faint. If for some reason I do feel faint, I can simply sit down wherever I am. People around me will either ignore me or help me. After I breathe with my diaphragm for a few minutes, I will then feel fine. I might feel embarrassed, but I can handle that. No one ever died from embarrassment. It might be unpleasant but it is not really that big a deal."

Self-talk: "If I faint, I won't know what people are doing or saying (magnification and catastrophizing)."

Rational response: "This is a true statement that I am reacting to as if it were a catastrophe. There are two basic fears that are magnifying the importance of this possibility and transforming it into a catastrophe. One is my fear of losing control, which causes me to want total control of both myself and everything around me. There is always the 1 to 10 percent chance of something negative occurring. Actually, the possibility of my fainting is far less than 1 percent because I now know how to use diaphragmatic breathing. This means I have better than a 99 percent chance of being fine. Even if I did faint, nothing terrible would happen.

"The other fear underlying this concern is my excessive need for approval, which causes me to believe that people won't like me if I faint. This is simply not true. Most people would be concerned and help me. Even if my fainting did cause some people to reject me, I can handle that. I don't need everyone's approval. I have many good friends who like me despite my faults. What's even more important is my own self-approval.

Step 4: Practice Exposing Yourself to the Feared Situation. Once you have completed the first three steps, you are ready to begin practicing. If you have many limitations, keep a record of your practice sessions. This allows you to see your progress and identify coping skills you may need to perfect. There are many formats you can use when making a record of your practice sessions. Use any that you find useful. The following format was used by Mike. The portion shown describes practice sessions he had while working on the goal of walking to the mailbox and back.

Activity: Walk to the mailbox and back.

Wed. 8/11, 2:00–3:00 P.M.
At first I only got halfway, panicked, and returned. I practiced a relaxation response exercise (progressive relaxation), reviewed my coping skills, and tried again. I was panicky but I made it three times.

Thurs. 8/12, 2:15–3:00 P.M.
This time I walked to the mailbox and back eight times. I was very nervous the first few times but it didn't seem as bad as yesterday. I was only moderately uncomfortable the last few times. I remembered to use my diaphragmatic breathing and coping self-statements and did simple tensing and relaxing in between.

Fri. 8/13, 1:30–2:15 P.M.
Completed the task ten times. My coping self-statements seem to be coming more naturally now and feel more real when I repeat them. I was only moderately anxious so I spent a few minutes standing by the mailbox on each trip. Tensing and relaxing and diaphragmatic breathing in between trips really helped.

Sat. 8/14, 1:00–2:00 P.M.
Had much difficulty when I first started and stopped after getting about a third of the way. There were several people out as it was a nice day and I felt as though everyone was watching me. I took time to tense and relax and reviewed rational self-talk on mind reading and the excessive need for approval and tried again. I made it seven times. My anxiety dropped from a high to moderate level.

Sun. 8/15, 2:00–3:00 P.M.
I walked down and back with no problem. I felt so good that after completing the task eight times I walked to the edge of my property and chatted for a few minutes with my neighbor. I didn't even need to use my rational self-talk or coping self-statements. My anxiety level ranged from moderate to very low.

If you have a medical condition that limits the amount of anxiety your doctor thinks you can safely experience, review your plans with your doctor. Then proceed at a speed the two of you determine is safe. You may even want to practice exposure under the supervision of someone who is familiar with your condition and trained in this technique. Fortunately, for most people anxiety is *not* dangerous; it is only unpleasant.

Guidelines for Practicing

The following guidelines are designed to ensure your success while practicing gradual in vivo exposure. Review them often while you are working to reach your goals.

Practice Regularly

The only way you can convince yourself that you can face the situations you fear is to practice facing them. You need to demonstrate to yourself that you can function in the feared situation no matter how you feel. In addition, it takes time to desensitize and eliminate anxiety triggered by conditioned response learning. For these reasons you need to practice as much as possible, and practice regularly. Do not wait until you are "feeling up to it." While there are times when illness, work, or family problems prevent you from practicing, do not look for excuses to avoid it. Instead, make practicing one of your highest priorities.

A good general rule is to practice for at least an hour each day. If you have extensive limitations, you may need to practice more than one hour. If you have few limitations and a busy life, two or three practice sessions a week may be enough. When using fewer practice sessions, extend them to two or more hours. You cannot practice too much. Practice as much as your time and energy allow.

Learn to Tolerate Distress

Anxiety is something you can tolerate, so beware of magnifying the sensations you experience when anxious. While extreme anxiety and panic are uncomfortable, they cannot hurt you. They will not drive you mad or cause any harm to your body. In fact, you have probably already experienced the worst anxiety you will ever experience.

To prove this to yourself, recall the worst episode of anxiety you have had. At that time you most likely did not understand what was occurring and did not have the skills you have been developing while working through these lessons. It was the lack of knowledge and skills that allowed your anxiety to become so intense during this episode. You now understand why this occurred and have a wide range of skills for managing anxiety effectively. As a result, it is unlikely that future anxiety will approach the level you experienced during this past episode. But even if it did, so what? You now know you can stand it and function because you have already done so in the past. You also know that it would last for only a limited period of time.

Remind Yourself That You Are Dealing with an Unconscious Conditioned Response

One of the biggest stumbling blocks people face when confronting anxiety-provoking situations is the false belief that once they understand what is causing their anxiety, it should get better. Remember that much of the anxiety you are experiencing is being triggered by an unconscious, conditioned response stored in your amygdala. At this time, normal everyday events and sensations have been associated with danger at an unconscious level. Understanding this will not prevent them from triggering anxiety. While the anxiety can make a situation feel dangerous, it is only a false triggering of your fight or flight response by a faulty conditioned response. The only way to quiet these responses is to expose yourself to frightening situations in a systematic manner while using your anxiety-reduction skills to control your anxiety. As you do this, you will desensitize and these conditioned responses will eventually become extinct. There is no magic involved. It is a very mechanical process that has been proven to work by many people with symptoms just like yours.

Expect Anxiety to Accompany New Activities

When you first begin a new activity, you will probably feel anxious. You may even feel panicky. This is normal and passes with time.

Train yourself to expect and accept these feelings. Sometimes anxiety may even increase before it decreases. Fortunately, practicing as described in this lesson usually reduces anxiety to a tolerable level fairly quickly. Remember, much of this anxiety is simply a conditioned response. As you practice, you become more and more desensitized and the skills you are learning become more reliable and more effective. Approaches that work poorly at first and reduce anxiety only slightly eventually are able to reduce even extreme anxiety quickly.

Relabel Anxiety as Excitement

The way your body reacts when you are anxious is exactly the same as the way it reacts when you are excited. The only difference is in how you interpret the feelings inside your body. An excellent example of this is the way a musician or actor feels just before going on stage. New and inexperienced performers tend to identify their feelings as anxiety, while more seasoned performers delight in the excitement they are feeling. They all are feeling the same adrenaline response; the first group is interpreting it as anxiety, the second as excitement.

Identifying this extra energy in the body as anxiety causes it to interfere with your performance. When you start to identify it as excitement, though, it becomes a resource that makes for an even better performance. As a result, many people find it helps to label the physical sensations they experience while practicing as excitement.

This is more than just a mental game. Whenever you do something that you either have never done or have not done for a long time, there is an element of excitement. In order to get in touch with this, take a moment to recall the excitement you felt as a child during your first trip to the zoo, the circus, or some other fun place. Recall also how it felt in your body. A person with anxiety-related problems tends to misinterpret this type of normal excitement as anxiety. Considering the feelings you experience as you go on the adventure of a practice session as exciting or even thrilling helps transform them into friends and allies.

Expect Progress to Be Two or Three Steps Forward and One Step Backward

Expect occasional days when you slip back into old behaviors and find situations you thought you had conquered to be difficult. This is a normal and natural part of the learning process. When it occurs, use the Troubleshooting Checklist in Lesson 5 to identify what caused the temporary lapse into old patterns and what you can learn from it. Then resume practicing. Illness, fatigue, or stress often plays a major role in these periodic lapses into old behaviors, so remember the concept of the body as a machine with a limited supply of energy.

When old behavior patterns resurface because you are very tired, you're ill, or there has been a stressful event in your life, do not become alarmed. Just view the old patterns as a message that you need to take care of your body's physical needs and apply your stress management skills more diligently. If you are working on an especially difficult limitation during one of these periods, break it into a series of smaller, easier activities. Keep in mind that every complex skill you have learned, from walking to memorizing the multiplication tables, took time. You frequently had to go through a process of relearning skills you forgot or learned poorly before you mastered the skill.

Challenge Perfectionism

Sometimes people feel defeated after practice sessions because they have not done everything they set out to do. If they were especially anxious, they may even interpret the anxiety as a sign that they are getting worse. These reactions are the result of perfectionistic expectations.

There is no way for you or anyone else to know how fast you should proceed with your goals or what is best for you before you actually begin practicing. Learning the correct rate at which to pace yourself is a process of trial and error. You learn what is too much by doing too much. Fortunately, even when you do not accomplish all you want to, a practice session is still beneficial. Even when you only complete a small part of an activity, it is still a success.

Identify and challenge your perfectionistic tendencies whenever you find yourself pushing yourself too hard and putting yourself down with statements like, "I should have known better," or "It's terrible that I can't do what I planned." Instead, tell yourself that you have successfully found your current limit and start making plans to overcome it using the methods described in this lesson. It also helps to ask yourself "What do I want to do today?" and "What would be good for me to do today?" instead of assuming you should be able to do more than is reasonably comfortable. If perfectionism becomes a major problem, spend a week reviewing Lesson 6.

Practice with as Many Factors in Your Favor as Possible

When you begin practicing new activities, arrange as many factors in your favor as possible. For example, a person practicing driving on the freeway would select a time and a section of highway where there is little traffic as a first step. It would be unwise to begin during the commuter rush hour. Only after mastering easy stretches of highway during times of light traffic would it be appropriate to begin practicing in more difficult situations.

Another important factor to consider when practicing is your physical and emotional state. Remember that you have only a limited supply of energy. If you are spending most of it coping with a cold, a family problem, or some other stress, you have less energy left for practicing than during times when you feel healthy and relatively free from outside sources of stress. Go ahead and practice during times like these, but lower your expectations and plan easier activities for your practice sessions. If you are very sick or stressed, it may be wise to delay practicing for a few days in order to rebuild your strength.

In addition to the above, avoid combining your practice sessions with errands or work. Practice just for the sake of practicing. This avoids the problem of pressure that results from thinking about all of the things you "should" or "have to" do in relation to the errand or job.

Use Your Coping Skills at the First Sign of Anxiety

Lesson 2 pointed out that coping skills are most effective when used at the first sign of anxiety. Review the card on which you listed those skills that work best for you at the beginning of each practice session so you will be sure to use them. Whenever you begin to feel anxiety rising, become aware of what you are thinking and use the rational self-talk skills to challenge any distorted thinking you identify.

Keep Pushing Yourself a Little Bit Further

Do not repeat the same activity day after day because you are waiting to be completely at ease with it before going on to the next one. Once you can do an activity with only a low level of anxiety, go on to the next one. It may take a while before you are completely at ease in a given situation. Usually, this happens after you have progressed through several goals beyond it.

Since your goal is to be able to function whether you are anxious or not, proceed toward your goals at a pace that generates a moderate level of anxiety during at least some of your practice sessions. Keep pushing yourself a little bit further. Whenever a practice session is accomplished easily, either extend the time you spend on the activity or do just a little more than you had planned. If day after day you are repeating activities that generate little or no anxiety, you are not really practicing. At the same time, if day after day you are experiencing very high levels of anxiety or panic, you are probably going too fast and trying to do too much. When this occurs, reexamine your goal and break it into smaller, easier steps.

Response Prevention

Response prevention used in conjunction with in vivo exposure is usually the most effective approach to use with OCD. With response prevention you refuse to act upon the obsessive and compulsive urges you are feeling. Response prevention is used two different ways: to manage spontaneous occurrences of obsessions and compulsions, and as part of a planned practice period (as described in the previous section Exposure Therapy).

Response prevention is the heart of the third step in the four-step process for combating OCD developed by Jeffrey M. Schwartz. These four steps are described in Lesson 2's section Coping Self-Statements. As detailed there, refocusing involves refraining from acting upon the urges generated by an obsession or compulsion for a period of time by choosing to focus on some other, unrelated activity. As previously discussed, obsessions and compulsions cannot be willed away, because they are being generated by a malfunctioning of the brain. You can, however, control your *response*. When you refuse to do the compulsive behavior associated with the obsessive thought, research has shown that you actually begin to change the biochemistry, and perhaps even the structure, of your brain so it becomes less sensitive to obsessions and compulsions. While this may take several weeks or months, it does work.

As discussed in Lesson 2, whenever obsessions and compulsions are triggered, you need to delay acting upon them—to practice response prevention, even if for only a few minutes. Responding to the spontaneous occurrences of your obsessions and compulsions in this manner, combined with regular practice periods that couple exposure and response prevention, gradually reduces the urge to perform rituals generated by obsessions.

Stewart, who suffered from OCD, combined response prevention with in vivo exposure in the following way. After listing several specific goals he wanted to achieve, he decided that his compulsion to wash after touching doorknobs would be the easiest problem behavior to work on. At the time that he set this goal, he was washing his hands two to five times after coming into his house and going through an elaborate ritual when he left where he would open the door, wash his hands, then close the door with his foot as he left.

He began by listing benefits he would receive by accomplishing his goal of not washing after touching a door. Here is what he wrote:

STEWART'S LIST OF BENEFITS	
I will be able to:	Save time when I both leave for and come home from work.
	Save time when I use doors in public, because I usually look for a restroom after entering a building and use baby wipes when I leave.
	Go in and out of buildings with people without the need to make excuses so I can be by myself to perform my rituals.
	Feel better about myself.
	Accomplish more at work.
	Go more places; I currently restrict my movements because of my obsession with germs and need to wash after touching a doorknob.

Stewart then reviewed the four steps developed by Schwartz in Lesson 2 along with the guidelines given in this chapter. Since Stewart usually arrived home around six thirty in the evening, he decided to practice from six thirty to eight.

During the first few days of practice, Stewart found that he would give in to his compulsion to wash fairly quickly. After washing, he would take several minutes to calm down. During this time he would use his coping self-statements (as described in Lesson 2 and this one), then find something to refocus on. After he felt relatively calm, he would touch the doorknob again and resist the urge to wash for as long as he could. He initially found that waiting ten minutes was manageable. By the end of a week he was waiting twenty minutes before washing. By the end of three weeks he could wait for the entire period without washing.

Stewart, like most others who use this approach, found that as his ability to resist washing his hands increased, it became easier to resist several of his other compulsions. It took Stewart four months to work through his list and arrive at a point where he was again doing the things he once did without the obsessions and compulsions that had plagued him for many years as they gradually become stronger and stronger. If you suffer from obsessions and compulsions, the time it takes for you to reduce the intensity of them may be quite different from the four months it took Stewart, depending upon the nature of your obsessions and compulsions, how long you have had them, and how strong they are.

Two things that can help when you are practicing response stopping are, first, slowing down; and second, changing some aspect of your ritual. Slowing down involves both your thinking and your physical movements. One way to slow down your thinking is to take three or four relaxed diaphragmatic breaths as discussed in Lesson 2 while repeating a few coping self-statements. Slowing down your physical movements means you carry out your ritual in a slow and deliberate manner. This is especially helpful with checking rituals since it helps to reduce doubt about your actions.

Changing some aspect of your ritual involves altering some element in it. For example, Stewart always used a particular brand of soap when he washed. He began to use different types of soap. A person who checks the lights in the house in a particular order may want to reverse the order. A person who counts in a particular order may want to change the order in some way. Changing some aspect of a ritual may also involve changing some aspect of where the ritual is done or changing from sitting to standing while you do it.

There are three benefits from changing some aspect of your ritual. First, while changing a ritual will cause anxiety, it is usually easier to change a ritual than it is to stop it entirely. Second, it gives you a measure of control over the ritual. Creating a new habit interferes with the tendency to keep rituals unchanged. In essence, it is impossible to maintain rigid rituals when you constantly change them. Third, it helps you to become more aware of when and how you perform your rituals. This helps you recognize the first signs of your urge to ritualize. It is usually easier to use the four steps developed by Schwartz earlier in the cycle of obsessions and compulsions rather than later.

People with very strong obsessions and compulsions sometimes find that it helps to take medication to reduce the pressure of the obsessions and compulsions. The main type of medication that is being used at this writing is serotonin reuptake inhibitors. If you feel this would be beneficial for you, be sure to consult with a psychiatrist who specializes in OCD and who keeps up on the latest research on OCD medications.

Rapid In Vivo Exposure or Flooding

While it is not recommended for use in a self-help program like this, a rapid form of in vivo exposure called flooding is sometimes used by therapists. With flooding, you place yourself into a frightening situation or come into contact with a frightening object and allow yourself to experience the maximum amount of fear possible.

Alexa provides a good example of how flooding is done. Alexa was afraid of taking buses. Since she could not afford a car and needed to get to work to provide for her children, this was a major problem. She overcame this fear by spending several days taking buses around town. When she got on the bus for the first time, she was terrified. As the bus pulled away from the bus stop, her fear increased. After about thirty minutes her fear peaked and started to decrease. By the end of three hours, she was still anxious but no longer panicky. The next day she again felt a high level of anxiety when she first boarded the bus to practice. However, it was greatly reduced and decreased more quickly than on the first day. By the third day, she experienced very little anxiety. She then started using buses regularly with only occasional anxiety that would quickly dissipate as she used her self-talk and distraction skills.

At first rapid exposure might seem horrible. However, it is similar to removing a Band-Aid from a hairy part of your body. You can yank it off quickly and be done, or you can remove it slowly, one hair at a time. While some people who are highly motivated, like Alexa, are willing to experience this high level of anxiety and do well with flooding, most prefer the gradual approach.

Imaginal Exposure

Imaginal exposure was originally developed by Joseph Wolpe, who called it systematic desensitization. When used with limitations or feared situations associated with anxiety, it involves the following five steps.

Step 1: Select a goal on which to work. Begin with the first one on your list. After you can work comfortably with it, proceed to the next.

Step 2: Allow yourself to become relaxed. Once you've selected the goal you want to work on, use the relaxation response method you have been practicing to develop a state of relaxation. If you haven't been practicing a method, take one to two weeks to develop the ability to produce a relaxation response. Use any of the methods in appendix 2 that work well for you, or consider purchasing a commercially available CD such as the ones listed in the back of the book.

Step 3: Imagine yourself in the situation or activity. Imagine the situation or activity as vividly and with as many of your senses as you can. Create as much detail as is necessary to make it seem real to you. Then imagine yourself in the situation feeling calm and behaving in the way you want to behave. As you do this, it helps to remind yourself occasionally that while you are trying to imagine the situation as vividly as possible, it is still only occurring in your mind. That means you have total control over it and can make it take place however you want it to.

Step 4: Stop whenever you feel anxious. If you begin to feel anxious while doing Step 3, stop for a moment and spend a few minutes calming yourself. Often just thinking about something relaxing and reminding yourself that you are simply imagining things is all that is needed to calm down. If you become very anxious, however, take several minutes to use your relaxation response procedure to return to a relaxed state. It also helps to repeat a few coping self-statements and use rational self-talk to challenge any negative thoughts that have occurred.

Step 5: Repeat the above steps. Repeat the above steps until you can comfortably imagine yourself in the situation you selected for at least three minutes.

Sometimes a particular goal makes the third step difficult to do. When this is the case, do the following.

- *Remove yourself:* Spend several sessions simply imagining the situation or activity without being in it. After you can do this comfortably, practice imagining yourself in the situation or doing the activity.
- *Create an imaginary model to take your place:* Imagine someone of the same sex who is very similar to you in the situation or doing the activity on which you are working. Imagine this person acting in the calm and controlled manner that you would like to act and feel. When you can do this comfortably, substitute yourself for the person you have created.
- *Start with a short period of time and gradually increase it:* Imagine yourself in the situation or doing the activity for only a few seconds, then use your relaxation response method. After you can do this comfortably, gradually increase the amount of time you spend in the situation to three minutes.
- *Select an easier situation:* If the above suggestions do not help, work on an easier situation. Reexamine your goal and divide it into several steps.

When imaginal exposure is the only approach used, progress is usually very slow. Because of this, it is best to combine imaginal exposure with in vivo exposure. Imaginal exposure can be especially useful as a prelude to in vivo exposure when dealing with a particularly frightening situation.

Harold, who had a dog phobia, provides a good example of how imaginal exposure can be combined with in vivo exposure. Harold spent thirty minutes using imaginal exposure to imagine various situations involving dogs. He began by imagining dogs walking, eating, or sleeping. Next, he imagined situations where a dog was a short distance away from him. Then he imagined a dog rubbing against him. Finally, he imagined a dog putting its head in his lap. At the end of thirty minutes he was able to imagine all these situations comfortably. At this time a real dog was brought into the room. At first the dog was kept at the opposite end of the room. Slowly, over the course of another thirty minutes, the dog was brought closer until it was placed in Harold's lap. By the end of this practice session Harold was able to pet the dog without feeling anxious.

If you decide to try this combination approach, the amount of time it takes for your anxiety to decrease may be different from the above example. Some people spend several practice sessions with imaginal exposure before moving on to in vivo exposure.

Social Role-Playing

Social role-playing is a specialized form of exposure used to help people with social phobia who either lack basic social skills or lack the confidence to use the social skills they do have. As a person develops social skills, it is equally important to learn the skills described in Lesson 8 for dealing with criticism and disapproval from others and to work with the techniques for increasing self-esteem and self-acceptance described in Lesson 11.

Social role-playing usually involves practicing social skills with someone who is trusted until the skills become comfortable. This person can be a trusted friend, a study partner, or a therapist who specializes in social phobia. While this is the most effective way to develop these skills, most of the social skills in this section can also be practiced when you are alone. Then, later, you can practice them in everyday situations when you are with others. When practicing them by yourself, it can be especially effective to practice in front of a mirror. You can also practice them when you are alone and doing routine activities such as driving. Using imaginal exposure to rehearse social skills can also be effective. Eventually, however, social skills need to be applied to real-life situations that involve other people. Practicing with another person you are comfortable with makes it easier to use them when you begin practicing in real-life situations. When you do begin to use your skills in real-life situations, be sure to follow the suggestions given in Guidelines for Practicing. People with social phobia tend to be overly critical of themselves.

The basic social skills practiced in social role-playing include the following:

- *Greetings:* Greetings range from a simple smile to standard words and phrases such as "Hello" and "How are you doing?"
- *Comments on shared experiences:* Comments on shared experiences can be used to set yourself and others at ease and begin interaction in a wide variety of social situations. These experiences might include the weather, the temperature of the room, a long wait in a line, the decorations of the room you are in, or the surrounding scenery if you are outside.
- *Expressing an opinion:* Begin reading the papers or watching the news. Select one event each day and practice expressing an opinion about it. Listen to the conversations of others to gain ideas about how other people express their ideas. Rehearse those styles of expressing an opinion that appeal to you.
- *Telling a story:* People in social situations often tell stories about themselves or others. Select two or three incidents involving yourself and practice telling about them. These stories can either be something that happened recently or something that happened long ago.
- *Active listening skills:* Active listening is a powerful social skill. It is also a skill that most people have not learned. You can use active listening skills to encourage the other person to talk about him- or herself without the need to say much. At the end

of the conversation, the other person is usually delighted with the conversation. Several basic active listening skills are described in Appendix 5.

• *Body language and voice:* Practice standing and sitting with a more forceful posture. Speak a little louder and more forcefully.

Recommended Activities for Lesson 9
Begin Eliminating Self-Defeating Behaviors

Begin using the approaches described in this lesson to eliminate self-defeating behaviors associated with your anxiety. If you have many self-defeating behaviors, this work may take many weeks, possibly many months. The basic principles, however, can be mastered within one or two weeks. As you proceed through the following lessons, continue to practice regularly and review the Guidelines for Practicing periodically. If you encounter difficulty with your practice sessions, review the entire lesson to make sure you are following all the recommendations. If, after completing all the lessons, you feel you need further help in applying the behavioral techniques described in this lesson, seek help from a qualified professional.

While working with this lesson, be sure to do all of the paper-and-pencil work that is recommended. The more severe your self-defeating behaviors, the more important it is to actually write down your goals, symptoms, and coping strategies. The written work is your plan of attack for eliminating these unwanted behaviors. The more detailed and precise it is, the more successful you will be.

Reducing Anxiety by Tensing and Relaxing Muscles

Muscle tension is one of the main symptoms people use to determine how anxious they are. When you become anxious, the fight or flight response tenses your muscles as it prepares you for action. In contrast, the more relaxed you are, the less anxious you feel. This is why people who have become skilled at producing a relaxation response find it an effective way to reduce anxiety. This simple exercise can be used to reduce anxiety in a real-life situation where you are not able to do a formal relaxation response exercise:

1. Breathe in and hold your breath.
2. As you hold your breath, tense your muscles.
3. As you breathe out, let go of the muscle tension all at once.
4. Take two relaxed diaphragmatic breaths. As you breathe out, make a conscious effort to let your shoulders drop a little and feel your muscles relax a little more than they were when you breathed in.

This simple procedure can be done almost anywhere. If a particular part of your body is especially tense, you may want to just tense and relax that part. When you have the time and when it is practical, you can also go through the various parts of your body, tensing and relaxing them separately as described in the progressive relaxation method detailed in Appendix 2. Simply massaging the tensed area can also help.

Guidelines for Support People Assisting You in Your Practice Sessions

The following guidelines describe how a support person can be helpful during practice sessions. If someone is helping you with your desensitization work, ask this person to read them. Then discuss the guidelines so he or she knows which ones are especially important to you.

What to Do Before You Begin Assisting in Practice Sessions
- Read this lesson thoroughly so you understand the behavioral approaches being used.
- Discuss what you can do to help. Review the goals and coping strategies your friend or relative has identified so you understand what is being attempted and what skills are most helpful in reducing anxiety.
- Be realistic and fair to yourself. Do not promise more than you

can deliver as far as how much time you can commit to practice sessions. If you feel overburdened, you may give up or become resentful and interfere with practice sessions without realizing it.

- Be reliable. These practice sessions are very important to the person you are assisting. Do what you say you are going to do. If you don't, it will probably cause much hurt and resentment in your friend.
- If it is agreeable to the person you are helping, assist in planning practice sessions. Your objectivity can be very useful.

What to Do During a Practice Session

- Remember that the person you are helping is always the best judge of what he or she can or cannot do. Your role is to assist and encourage.
- Do not pretend to know more than you do. People suffering from anxiety are highly suggestible and often make connections where none exist. Do not offer advice on food additives, vitamins, or other things you may have heard about that are reported to be important. Stick to the principles given in these lessons or by the therapist your friend is working with.
- Try to remain as calm as possible. Your calmness can be a powerful force for reducing your friend's anxiety.
- Avoid being critical. A person suffering from severe anxiety is supersensitive to criticism, especially during a practice session. Encourage each attempt and step toward the goal.
- Remind your friend to use the coping skills you have discussed whenever you notice him or her becoming anxious.
- If your friend becomes angry during a practice session, do not take it personally. Remember that anxiety and tension causes a person to think less rationally than usual. If this is a recurring problem, read Lesson 12 for suggestions on how to deal with anger constructively.
- Expect ups and downs and the unexpected. One practice session may go very smoothly, then the next one very poorly. This is normal. After a difficult practice session, review the Troubleshooting Checklist in Lesson 5 with your friend. Encourage the view that the difficult period is only temporary.
- Encourage repeated practice of a newfound ability.

What to Do if the Person You Are Assisting Experiences Panic During a Practice Session

- Remain calm and speak in a confident, friendly manner. Your calm presence is a powerful form of support.
- If you are practicing away from home, help your friend make a graceful exit and find a relatively quiet place to sit or stand where the panic can subside. Choose a location that is as near to the scene that provoked the panic as possible.
- Offer reassurance that your friend does *not* have to finish the activity to be successful. Even partial completion of the activity is a success.
- Do not discuss the anxiety symptoms being experienced at this time. This tends to make them worse.
- Remind your friend to use coping skills. Name specific skills, since it is difficult for him or her to think when panicky. Then talk about some neutral topic until the panic subsides.
- When the panic subsides, suggest a return visit to the place in which the panic occurred. Do not force your friend to go, but encourage him or her as strongly as possible while remaining positive and encouraging. Immediate reexposure helps decrease the tendency for future avoidance.

Other Ways You Can Help

- Help your friend get past "stuck points" by finding in-between steps that can be taken. This is easier for you since you can view the activity more objectively.
- If you notice the return of an old negative behavior that had subsided, encourage the person you are helping to practice exposure or response prevention practice focusing on the old behavior that has come back.
- If progress is not being made after several weeks, suggest seeking professional help.

This is a very important lesson. If limitations or self-defeating behaviors seriously interfere with your life, spend two weeks with this lesson.

LESSON 10

The Process of Change

C hange is difficult. This is true even when change produces a more enjoyable and successful life. This lesson explores some of the factors that make change difficult along with ways to overcome the natural human tendency to avoid doing the things necessary to bring about change.

Learned Helplessness, Self-Efficacy, and Change

In the late 1960s a now classic experiment was performed in which dogs were given random electric shocks from which they could not escape. The dogs developed what is called learned helplessness. Once they learned that nothing they did made any difference, they became passive and gave up trying to escape. When they were subsequently placed in another situation in which they could easily escape the shocks, they hardly tried.

Later experiments involving humans led Albert Bandura, a psychologist at Stanford University and a leader in his field, to develop a concept he calls self-efficacy. The word *efficacy* refers to the power or capacity to produce a desired result: the ability to achieve results. The term *self-efficacy* refers to your belief in your ability to manage a specific situation and get the results you want. If you are confident that you will be able to manage the situation and do well, you have a strong sense of self-efficacy.

A person can have a strong sense of self-efficacy about one type of activity and lack this sense about another. For example, a skilled musician can be confident of performing well during a concert but doubt his or her ability to deliver a simple speech at a banquet. Your belief about your self-efficacy affects your behavior in a variety of ways. It helps determine what activities you attempt and is directly related to the level of anxiety you feel in various situations.

The concepts of learned helplessness and self-efficacy help explain more fully how many of the self-defeating behaviors associated with anxiety develop and how they can be overcome. For example, Gail suffered from panic disorder that had begun when she experienced a panic attack while driving. She did not understand what had happened and did not understand how the various factors described in Lesson 1 had generated the anxiety/panic cycle and were now maintaining it. As she found herself unable to escape the panic attacks, she gave up trying to drive. Gail lost her sense of self-efficacy and was in a state of learned helplessness.

As Gail worked through these lessons, she learned how to manage anxiety and prevent panic attacks by developing rational self-talk skills and using effective coping strategies. This began to increase her sense of self-efficacy. As she practiced driving using in vivo exposure, she became more and more confident of her ability to manage anxiety while driving. In essence, Gail had regenerated her sense of self-efficacy and overcame her state of learned helplessness.

Objects and situations are not intrinsically frightening. They only trigger fear and stress if you doubt your ability to manage them effectively. This is the result of a learning process. While it takes time, energy, and an effective method, new learning can replace old learning. As you learn how to think and act in new, more effective ways, your sense of self-efficacy in various situations increases and your level of anxiety decreases.

Rationalization and Denial

Defense mechanisms are habit patterns that help reduce your awareness of internal or external stress, pain, or danger. They are often unconscious and are usually learned during childhood. A child who is experiencing stress or anxiety does something, such as become angry or eat a treat, to feel a little better. Over time this becomes an unconscious habit pattern. While several different defense mechanisms have been identified, two that can hinder your recovery are rationalization and denial. Both of these defense mechanisms can cause you to avoid the work you need to do in order to bring about constructive change. An example of this is a person who talks about changing but channels energy into watching television, puttering around the house, working crossword puzzles, doing nonessential chores, and other nonproductive activities. This leaves little time and energy for the work of learning new skills and applying them.

When considering how you might be avoiding the work needed to change, remember the need for balance and moderation in your life. It is unreasonable to believe that you should jump at every opportunity and practice using new skills every day without fail. On days when illness or excessive stress are draining your energy, it is wise to reduce activities and concentrate on important tasks. You also need to schedule time for play and relaxation. When there is a recurring pattern of avoiding opportunities to learn or practice skills needed to overcome your problems, however, it usually indicates you are avoiding the work needed to change.

The defense mechanisms of rationalization and denial help you to do this without being aware of what you are doing. As with the various forms of distorted thinking, understanding these two defense mechanisms helps you become more aware of times when you are turning to them to avoid the anxiety associated with the work required to change. When you recognize what you are doing, you have the opportunity to make a conscious choice: "Do I choose to avoid the anxiety associated with change, or do I choose to practice my new skills?"

Rationalization is the use of seemingly rational and socially acceptable explanations to "justify" the lack of real effort when, in reality, they are not true. For example, a person with many anxiety-related problems skims through the lessons, pausing only to do a few of the Recommended Activities in a hasty, haphazard manner. This is justified by saying, "I already understand all of this, and besides, none of it really applies to me." These rationalizations allow this person to avoid spending the time and energy required to overcome the anxiety-related problems, yet still feel that some effort is being put forth.

Denial is the refusal to acknowledge some painful aspect of reality that would be apparent to those around you. A person using denial to avoid the work needed to change will use rationalizations, humor, sarcasm, or put-downs to characterize the actions needed to bring about constructive change as unimportant, ineffective, counterproductive, or even dangerous.

The key to minimizing the effects of these two defense mechanisms is to recognize that rationalization and denial are normal parts of human nature. As with every other human characteristic, rationalization and denial are sometimes important for survival. They can be very effective coping skills when faced with inescapable pain. Two examples would be a person in a concentration camp or a child in a dysfunctional family.

At one time or another, all of us refuse to acknowledge a problem or avoid working to overcome a self-defeating behavior either because we are busy with more important life issues or because the problem is too frightening to deal with. Once you acknowledge and accept this fact, it becomes easier to examine your behavior more objectively and notice those times when you are doing this. When you are, do not condemn yourself or view it with alarm. Instead, accept this as a common occurrence. Then make a firm commitment to use the information in the next section to overcome this common tendency.

Six Roadblocks to Change

There are six roadblocks that can prevent you from being successful. Each is described below along with methods for overcoming it. Whenever you notice that you are avoiding constructive change, read through this section and identify the specific roadblock or combination of roadblocks generating this tendency. Then use the suggestions given to overcome it.

Change Is Often Uncomfortable

At first, new thinking patterns and behaviors feel uncomfortable and strange. While this is less true for small changes, it can be a major roadblock for big changes. It is like buying a new pair of shoes. At first the new thoughts and actions do not feel right. They seem foreign and do not mold comfortably to your personality.

Fortunately, you can overcome this roadblock by reminding yourself to expect new behaviors to feel uncomfortable at first. A person usually expects to feel awkward when learning a new skill such as skiing, sewing, or playing a musical instrument. Learning the skills in these lessons is no different. Expect the same feelings of awkwardness. It takes time and practice to internalize new behaviors and thinking patterns. After a period of time, however, the new behaviors and thinking patterns become a part of you and feel as comfortable as a favorite pair of shoes. In fact, even behaviors that seem very strange and uncomfortable at first can soon feel very natural.

The Consequences of New Thoughts and Behaviors Are Unknown and Unpredictable

When you use old, familiar ways of thinking and behaving, you are fairly certain about what will happen. Even though this may cause pain, people and events are predictable. When you start to use new thinking patterns and behaviors, you begin to feel new and different feelings. People around you react differently, and events may occur in ways quite different from the past. At first, this may be somewhat frightening because you do not know what will happen as you become this new person.

One way to overcome this roadblock is to recognize what is going on and make a conscious choice: "Do I want to stay where I am and hold on to predictable and familiar thinking patterns and behaviors even though it means experiencing all of the pain that goes with them?" *Or* "Do I choose instead to try new behaviors and thinking patterns that, although they may be somewhat uncomfortable and frightening at first, offer a life of increased joy and fulfillment—a more effective way of living?"

When making this choice, it helps to remember that after you have mastered the new behavior or thinking pattern, if you choose to, you can always go back to your old ways. Once you really experience the increased joy and fulfillment that positive changes bring, though, it is doubtful that you will choose to return to old self-defeating ways of thinking and behaving.

Another way to overcome this roadblock is to remind yourself that the period of discomfort experienced while learning new behaviors is usually short. The unfamiliar quickly becomes the familiar. Events that are frightening at first can quickly become old friends. It also helps to relabel the anxiety caused by your fear of the unknown as excitement. Develop the attitude that the task of changing your behavior is an exciting adventure—that the unknown is a birthday gift waiting to be explored.

Learning Requires the Use of an Effective Method

The old saying *Practice makes perfect* is not true. *Practice makes permanent.* Consider a person trying to learn to play the guitar. If this person holds the guitar incorrectly and uses improper fingerings for the chords and notes, intense practice will only make these poor habits automatic and hinder this person's ability to play well. Likewise, when you are trying to change self-defeating patterns, you need to use an effective approach to be successful.

This roadblock is one of the easiest ones to overcome. The activities described in these lessons have proved to be an effective approach for overcoming anxiety-related problems. They are useless, however, if they are not used. If you have not been making much progress, it may simply be because you have not been following the directions in the lessons carefully. If this is the case, continue on through the rest of the lessons but do the Recommended Activities more carefully. When you reach Lesson 15, go back through the earlier lessons again. As you repeat the earlier lessons, do the Recommended Activities you either skipped or did in a haphazard manner again, only this time do them as instructed.

Changing Behavior Takes Work

It takes time and effort to change the way you think and act. This is especially true for behaviors that have been repeated so many times that they are now automatic. Consider the way you brush your teeth.

This is a simple habit pattern, but since it has become so automatic and unconscious, like most habit patterns, a considerable amount of effort is required to change it. Before beginning to brush, you would have to remind yourself about the new method you plan to use. While brushing, your mind would wander and you would catch yourself returning to your old method. After a second reminder you would start using the new method only to forget and have to catch yourself again. And so it would go until enough time and energy had been spent to make the new method as automatic and as much a part of you as was the old one.

The key to overcoming this roadblock is to make a firm commitment to do the work required for change. During the process of changing a behavior, periodically recommit yourself to the work you are doing. It also helps to realize and accept that any major accomplishment requires a certain amount of tedious work. Dull work is more enjoyable if you focus on the results you have already accomplished, and remind yourself often of the benefits your continued efforts will bring.

Self-Defeating Behaviors Often Provide Important Secondary Gains

Painful behaviors often help satisfy—either directly or indirectly—one or more important needs. When a need is satisfied in this manner, it is called a secondary gain. The term *secondary* is used because it indicates that this method of satisfying needs is usually not arrived at through a deliberate, conscious process. Instead, it is the result of stumbling onto advantages and using them in an unconscious manner.

To understand how this occurs, recall a time when you had an injury or illness, such as a broken leg or a bad cold. Recall the benefits you received as a result of being injured or ill that you normally did not have—receiving extra sympathy or attention, avoiding an unpleasant task or situation, or receiving time off from work. You probably did not hurt yourself or become ill in order to obtain these benefits. Still, even though the secondary gains may have been far outweighed by the negative aspects of the situation, human nature is such that you probably found at least some ways to benefit from your misfortune.

The longer an unwanted event or condition persists, the more likely it is that you will learn how to obtain secondary gains from it. Sometimes a secondary gain becomes so important that it can cause you to maintain a painful condition or behavior in order to continue to receive the secondary gain. This is especially true if the need is an important one and you have few or no other ways to meet it.

There are two questions you can ask yourself to identify secondary gains you may be obtaining from a problem behavior or situation. First, "What benefits do I gain from my problem behavior or situation?" Identify ways in which your anxiety or the behaviors associated with it might help you gain attention, security, or some other benefit. Then ask yourself, "How would my life be different if this problem behavior or situation just magically disappeared?" Be aware of any feelings of regret, loss, sadness, or anxiety triggered by things that would be lost. In addition, note any feelings of anxiety or fear triggered by thoughts about things that would be gained. These types of feelings usually indicate that a secondary gain is present.

When you identify a secondary gain, develop a positive method for obtaining the same benefit currently being obtained through the problem behavior or situation. For example, Frank was a very nervous person who had many aspirations but did little to achieve them because of his anxiety symptoms. Frank also dwelled on "catastrophes" he had experienced and used them as a method for receiving attention from others.

As Frank explored how his life would be different if he were "strong," he realized that the thought of being independent and assertive made him very anxious. As he thought further, he identified two things that made him anxious. One was the thought of achieving some of his dreams. The other was a sense of doubt about whether people would be friendly and spend time with him. This helped Frank realize that one benefit of being nervous was that it allowed him to avoid taking risks. He could remain "safe" and blame his lack of effort on his anxiety symptoms.

Frank overcame his tendency to use anxiety as a means of avoiding risks by telling himself he could choose to either take a risk or remain safe. He did not have to use his anxiety to do this. Furthermore, he reminded himself that whichever choice he made was fine. He bolstered this type of rational self-talk with the rational arguments given in Lessons 6 and 7. He used this approach whenever he noticed himself blaming his failure to take a risk on his anxiety symptoms. This helped him make much progress in overcoming his anxiety symptoms.

Frank used three different approaches to overcome the anxiety associated with his fear that people would no longer take an interest in him when he was no longer anxious. First, he used rational self-talk to convince himself that the "poor you" and "how terrible" type of attention he was currently receiving with tragic stories was not really all that desirable. Even worse, people soon tired of his negative tales and began avoiding him. Next, Frank began developing social skills that allowed him to develop friendships and receive positive attention. Finally, Frank realized that underneath these fears was the belief that he was not a likable person. He found that the exercises in the next lesson helped him overcome these fears by developing a more positive self-image.

Whenever a secondary gain is identified, you can always find more effective and positive ways to obtain the benefits a problem behavior provides. While this takes effort on your part, doing so removes one of the more troublesome roadblocks to change. The previous lessons have already described many approaches that can be used in this way. More are described in the lessons that follow.

Irrational Thinking Is Still Exerting a Major Influence

It is impossible to change self-defeating behaviors when the irrational beliefs and distorted thinking supporting them are exerting a major influence on your life. Identifying and challenging irrational thinking that causes you to avoid the work necessary to change can be done in the following manner. First, look back and identify several occasions when you used rationalization or denial to sabotage or avoid the work required for constructive change. As you do this, examine your self-talk and actions. Identify irrational thinking, then develop and practice rational challenges you can use to combat it. One of the best ways to do this is to use the Block Method described in Lesson 5. In addition, identify words, actions, feelings, or situations associated with times when you are avoiding the work that needs to be done to change. Once you identify these thoughts, feelings, and actions, they can be used in the future to alert you to times when you are avoiding change.

While studying this lesson, Pam realized that she often avoided the work that needed to be done to change. During times like these, she would spend much of her day watching television or staring into space. She would also dwell on the past or worry about the future. Pam listed the nonproductive activities she would do during times like these along with the thoughts and self-talk she used. Next, she reviewed Lessons 4 and 5 and identified the main types of distorted thinking she used during these times: should/must thinking—especially in the form of all-or-nothing thinking, overgeneralization, magnification, minimization, and fortune-telling. She then wrote out rational challenges for the various types of distorted thinking associated with avoiding change and practiced them. Here is an example from her journal:

> It was time for me to practice going to the store and I thought: "What if I fall down in the supermarket now? There are so many people here. There may be someone I know there and that would be so embarrassing. I probably shouldn't go now."
>
> Here I am fortune-telling and magnifying again. I've already thought through the fear that I might faint or fall down while at the store. This is an old lie that has no basis in reality. I've tripped on things, but I've never fainted or fallen down because I've suddenly become weak. It isn't going to happen. As for someone seeing me, so what? Others usually don't notice my anxiety, and if they do, it's not important to them. I'm magnifying my fear of embarrassment and using it to avoid doing the practicing I need to do to get better. I don't like embarrassment, but I can handle it. I'm an adult, not a child, and I need to get out and practice if I'm going to get better.

As Pam spent time skimming through the lessons and working with the Block Method, she identified negative anticipation and thinking like a victim as two major problems for her. She found it useful to return many times to Lesson 7, where these two problems are discussed. She also found the section in Lesson 7 titled "Develop a Strong Belief in the Power of the Present" to be helpful. She had not really worked on this section during the week when she originally studied this lesson. So she went back and took this opportunity to work on it in conjunction with the current lesson. Later, Pam identified two other helpful sections that she had skipped in her earlier studies—Develop a Process Orientation and Schedule Activities in Lesson 6. Additionally, Pam made the following list and posted it in her bathroom:

Things I Do When I'm Avoiding Change
• Watch lots of TV.
• Sit and stare into space dwelling on how helpless I am or thinking about terrible things that might happen.

Distorted Thinking I Use When I'm Avoiding Change
• Fortune-telling and negative anticipation, especially about the awful things that will happen when I practice.
• Magnification—I exaggerate the discomfort I feel when I practice and forget that I only need to do what I feel I can do. I need to remind myself that even a little practice is always better than nothing.

In the weeks that followed, Pam found that when watching television or sitting and staring into space became a major daily activity, it was time to examine her thoughts and feelings. These two behaviors became powerful signals that alerted Pam to times when she was finding change difficult. She would then use the Block Method and review her notes on how she had challenged the irrational beliefs and distorted thinking that were associated with these times in the past.

Recommended Activities for Lesson 10
Continue Working with the Behavioral Approaches in Lesson 9

Continue to apply the behavioral approaches you learned in Lesson 9 to the self-defeating behaviors you want to overcome. If you are working on many problem behaviors, review Lesson 9 occasionally. Continue this work throughout the rest of this program.

Recognizing Times When You Avoid Change

This lesson points out that avoiding change is a natural part of human nature. This activity will help you understand how commonplace it is. Begin by listing at least two ways in which your mother, father, and the people close to you have avoided something new or different. Then spend time during the coming week observing how people around you avoid change. Do not say anything about what you see or try to determine why they are behaving in that way. Your goal is simply to notice how common it is for people to avoid change. Understanding how common it is for people to avoid change and seeing it in the people around you helps take away any shame or other negative feelings associated with the avoidance of change. This makes it easier to be more objective about times when you find yourself avoiding constructive change and use the ideas in this lesson to overcome this normal human tendency.

Learn to Release

One of the keys to success is the ability to release old, nonproductive patterns and adopt new, productive ones. Spend time this week considering what negative behaviors or habits you might need to release from your life in order to overcome your anxiety-related problems. Begin by considering the following list:

- Old attitudes that are not productive.
- Worry about your condition.
- Negative language and thinking patterns.
- Old "should" and "must" rules that do not reflect reality.
- Thinking in terms of "can't" and "have to" instead of choices.
- Distorted thinking patterns such as fortune-telling and magnification.
- Relationships that are not productive.
- Worry about what others might think.
- The need to be perfect or better than you are.

Go back through the list and put a check by any of the above items that either make you feel uncomfortable or that you know you need to continue working on. Add new items that come to you as you do this exercise. Chances are, the items you checked or added are ones you have already worked on in earlier lessons. If this is the case, review the notes and exercises you have done in your journal related to your checked items. If you've not yet worked on one, look it up in the index at the end of the book and locate the section in the lessons that addresses it. Then spend a few days working on the recommended activities for that particular section.

Identify and Challenge the Ways in Which You Avoid Change

The following questions focus on common ways that people avoid using this program effectively. Consider each one carefully and answer it with Yes, Sometimes, or No. As you read through the questions, if any make you think of a way in which you avoid change that is not listed, write it down in your journal.

Yes	Sometimes	No	
❑	❑	❑	Have I avoided the work involved in overcoming my anxiety-related problems by simply reading through the lessons once or twice without doing the recommended activities?
❑	❑	❑	Instead of thinking in terms of choices and focusing on what actions would be best to choose, am I still thinking in terms of unrealistic "shoulds" and "musts" and refusing to accept reality as it is?
❑	❑	❑	Instead of accepting anxiety for what it is—a set of automatic conditioned response patterns that are maintained by repeating lies to myself lies about what the unpleasant symptoms mean over and over—am I still telling myself lies about what it is: —a "mental illness," part of my nature that will never be changed, or my cross to bear?
❑	❑	❑	Has my fear that I will never overcome my anxiety-related problems caused me to get into the habit of just wishing things were different; and has this fear caused me to avoid making a firm commitment to working with these lessons as instructed?

Yes	Sometimes	No	
☐	☐	☐	Has my identity become so interrelated with my anxiety and am I so accustomed to feeling anxious and limited that any other feelings just do not seem "right"?
☐	☐	☐	Does my anxiety give me a special place with special treatment in my family, in my job, or among my friends that I would lose if I overcame it?
☐	☐	☐	Am I receiving attention from others because of my anxiety or limitations that I might not receive without those limitations (even though this attention is of a negative type)?
☐	☐	☐	Are there responsibilities or difficulties that others take care of for me because of my anxiety, thus making anxiety something I use to avoid them?
☐	☐	☐	What would my life be like if my anxiety suddenly just disappeared forever? Do these things somehow frighten me?
☐	☐	☐	Does the fear of failure cause me to stay the same and not try?

If you answered yes or sometimes to any of the above, review the section Six Roadblocks to Change. Then start to use the recommended approaches listed in that section to overcome any tendency to avoid change you may have.

Begin to Normalize Yourself

One common obstacle to overcoming anxiety-related problems is the tendency to view everything about yourself and your reactions as abnormal or sick. Every trait that humans have, both physical and psychological, can exist across a broad range. For example, some people are short, some tall, and some in between. If you happen to be short, you probably just see it as a normal variation. In the same way, it is important to see your traits and reactions as simply normal variations on what is typical of people.

One way to do this is to use labels for yourself and your reactions that are positive rather than negative. For example, if you are the type of person who is more excitable than the average person, see yourself as being dramatic or having lots of energy rather than as too sensitive. In essence, you are choosing to look at your traits from a healthy as opposed to a pathological point of view. This is not just a mental trick. Every trait you have has a positive as well as a negative side. While your traits have sometimes created problems, they have also served you well in many situations. For example, people who have a very reactive body are often highly intuitive because more information is being taken in. This heightened sensitivity often allows them to tune in to others and notice things that most people miss. It can also make them more empathetic and good listeners. All these qualities are often the ones that others like best.

During this week, identify aspects about yourself that you have considered abnormal or sick in the past. List ways in which each negative trait you identify has benefited you in the past. Also, take time to consider how this trait is expressed in others and how your expression of them is simply a variation. Finally, identify a positive term you can use to describe this quality.

Weird or Unusual Thoughts

In the section on OCD in Lesson 2 it was pointed out that most people *without* OCD experience thoughts that have no basis in reality, and that they are most likely due to automatic associations produced in the brain. These automatic and unconscious associations can take the form of weird or unusual thoughts that can range from a fear of tearing off your clothes and going crazy to having everyone you know laugh at you. Sometimes they can even be morbid or grotesque. These types of thoughts most commonly occur when you are tired, hungry, ill, or in some other way stressed or fatigued. In fact, they are one of the symptoms listed in the Troubleshooting Checklist in Lesson 5 that indicate you are tired or stressed.

These types of thoughts usually disappear on their own when you are feeling better physically and mentally. If you sometimes experience weird or unusual thoughts, recognize them for what they are: the workings of a tired and stressed mind. Do not blow them out of proportion. Just keep substituting positive thoughts for the unpleasant ones and using your rational self-talk. Also remember that your body is a machine with a limited supply of energy and take care of yourself. Do this and these types of thoughts will probably disappear as soon as you are feeling better physically.

If you suffer from OCD, keep in mind that this section is meant for people who do not have OCD. Eliminating obsessions usually requires the more structured approach described in Lesson 9. However, the fact that people without OCD experience thoughts that have no basis in reality can be used to help you reattribute and revalue obsessive thoughts as described in Lesson 2.

Challenging the tendency to avoid constructive change is an important part of overcoming anxiety-related problems. Spend at least one week with this lesson.

LESSON 11

Feeling Good About Yourself

Have you ever wondered why one person with only average ability is successful and happy while another person with exceptional ability is unsuccessful and unhappy? Perhaps you are this second person. A part of the answer can be found by examining the difference in each person's level of self-esteem and self-acceptance. This lesson explores these important parts of your self-concept and shows you how to increase your level of self-esteem and self-acceptance.

Self-Esteem and Self-Acceptance

As you matured into an adult you developed a complex set of attitudes and beliefs about who and what you are and your place in the world. These attitudes and beliefs make up what is usually called the self-concept. Your self-concept includes beliefs about your strengths and abilities, your weaknesses and shortcomings, and those personality traits you use to distinguish yourself from and identify yourself with the rest of humanity. Your self-concept influences all your hopes, aspirations, moods, and actions. Self-esteem and self-acceptance are two different but complementary parts of your self-concept. Self-esteem is the value and respect you hold for yourself. People with a high level of self-esteem see themselves as valuable. As a result, they treat themselves with respect, tend to their needs in a positive manner, and stand up for their rights. People with low self-esteem see themselves in a negative light. They do not value and respect themselves. This tends to cause them to ignore personal needs and put themselves down. There is often the tendency to put the needs and wishes of others first. When a very negative self-image is present, they may feel that they have nothing to offer others or that others can do nothing for them because they are so hopeless. Sometimes this may even cause them to retreat from the world. Any of these tendencies, when present, will inter-fere with their ability to give and receive love and can generate anger or resentment.

Self-acceptance is the ability to acknowledge and own all your parts, both desirable and undesirable. To understand self-acceptance fully, consider our acceptance of the sun and the moon. We do not try to hide or ignore the existence of the sun and the moon. Neither do we dwell on or exaggerate their good or bad qualities. The sun and the moon simply are, and we accept them as a natural part of life. This acceptance allows us to minimize the negative qualities of these heavenly bodies and more effectively utilize their positive qualities. In a similar manner, people with a high level of self-acceptance con-sider all their many characteristics and aspects—physical, mental, emotional, and spiritual—as simply a natural part of being human. This objective acceptance allows them to make the most of strengths and minimize weaknesses. You cannot have a high level of self-esteem without self-acceptance.

Self-esteem and self-acceptance have sometimes been overem-phasized as the key to mental health. A member of a street gang may have a high level of self-esteem and self-acceptance as a result of his or her membership in the gang. Yet because of a distorted worldview and unhealthy beliefs about relationships, this person will usually not have what most would consider a productive or satisfying life. So while developing a high level of self-esteem and self-acceptance will not solve all your problems, if you have low levels, working to improve in this area will enable you to use the various skills you are learning more effectively.

The Development of Low Self-Esteem and Self-Acceptance

Your first beliefs about your value or worth developed during early childhood. People with low self-esteem and self-acceptance usually experienced a real or perceived lack of acceptance during childhood. This rejection could have involved parents, siblings, teachers, peers, or relatives.

The most powerful rejection occurs when parents are so caught up in their own pain and inability to cope effectively with life that they are incapable of providing the warmth, love, and acceptance their children need. This is often the case when one or more of the various forms of abuse described in Lesson 1 is present. Children growing up with this type of rejection usually have significant problems in the areas of self-esteem and self-acceptance.

Another powerful form of rejection occurs when one or both parents have unrealistically high expectations concerning their children. This is sometimes due to the parent being a perfectionist; it can also stem from simple ignorance of what is appropriate for children of various ages. Regardless, children who are continually asked to perform at a skill level beyond their capability often develop a negative view of themselves.

Another possible source of low self-esteem and self-acceptance is the excessive use of negative labels, comparisons, humiliation, or criticism by adult caregivers. Sometimes this is done with good intentions even though it can be very discouraging. Consider the following types of comments, which are heard all too frequently wherever there are adults and children.

- Suzie is such a klutz.
- Ronald is the slow one.
- Why can't you be good like Mary?
- Sean did such a nice job; why don't you ever do that?
- Look at all the merit badges Betty has! I bet if you work hard, you can do that, too.
- Even though Edward is eight he still wets the bed almost every night (said to a casual acquaintance while Edward is listening).

- What a turkey! You've got your sweater buttoned up all wrong.
- You're so lazy you'll never amount to anything.

Negative labeling, comparisons, humiliation, and negative criticism such as the above are usually used by parents in an attempt to teach children important skills or lessons. Often they reflect cultural and family traditions rooted in the past, when people lived in a harsh, unyielding world. Unfortunately, these types of discouraging comments usually do the opposite of what is intended. Young children are not miniature adults. The section in Lesson 4 on needs and beliefs notes that children lack many of the higher reasoning powers of an adult, have limited experience, and are egocentric. Because of this, they tend to accept the labels and judgments of adults without question. When exposed to excessive negative labeling, comparisons, humiliation, and negative criticism, the result is usually low self-esteem and self-acceptance.

Low self-esteem and self-acceptance can also begin with rejection by other children. This is often due to a physical or mental disability, or to a child's race, religion, or social background. Children can be very cruel and frequently delight in teasing a child who is different.

Repeated rejection during childhood, whether the rejection is real or a misinterpretation of events, usually leads to the mistaken belief that one is in some way unacceptable, unlovable, or of less value than others. This generates a low level of self-esteem and self-acceptance as well as an excessive need for approval. In fact, the issues and behaviors associated with an excessive need for approval discussed in Lesson 8 are closely related to, and intertwined with, those generated by a low level of self-esteem and self-acceptance.

Low self-esteem and self-acceptance can also be the result of a childhood during which there were few experiences of success or mastery because a child was struggling with a learning disability or physical handicap. In addition, they may simply be due to the presence of a parent with low self-esteem and self-acceptance. As a child models after the parent, he or she begins to mimic the parent's words and behaviors, causing the child to mirror the parent's sense of inadequacy.

The Fear of Being Incompetent

Low levels of self-esteem and self-acceptance are often generated by the mistaken belief that one is in some way incompetent and does not measure up to others. When present, this belief can be a major source of anxiety, which is usually generated by any one or a combination of the childhood experiences described above.

People who fear being incompetent often feel like phonies or impostors when talking to someone they consider competent. This could be an employer, supervisor, peer, or stranger. There is often the fear that their incompetence will be exposed when dealing with authority figures or people who are very successful in life. As a result, many keep a constant lookout for signs that others are noticing their incompetence. The fear that they will be unable to reach their goals is also common and can cause a problem with procrastination, the avoidance of risks, or an excessive dependency upon others. Sometimes the fear of being incompetent causes people to interpret statements intended as humorous to be literal, causing them to become anxious or upset. They may even have images of themselves as small children in a world of giant adults or imagine themselves as frightened animals, such as a scared rabbit or dog.

If any of the above characteristics describe you, overcoming the fear of being incompetent will probably play a part in your full recovery from anxiety-related problems. In addition to learning to develop true self-acceptance, you need to separate your worth from your achievements. Lesson 6 discusses ways to challenge the mistaken belief that achievement determines worth. If you have not already begun working in this area, return to the section that describes how to challenge thoughts and behaviors that overemphasize the importance of achievement and work on this important skill while you are working on the ideas and skills presented in this lesson.

Eight Approaches for Increasing Self-Esteem and Self-Acceptance

Eight methods for increasing your level of self-esteem and self-acceptance are described below. It is impossible to work effectively on all of them at once during a one- to two-week period. So, after you read through all of them, put a check by the two or three areas that would be most important for you to work on at this time. As with earlier lessons, the easiest way to determine this is to decide which activities would be the most difficult for you to do. As mentioned previously, the more difficult a suggested activity seems to be, the more important it is to do. The easy activities usually involve beliefs or skills that are already a natural part of who you are. As you work through the various suggested activities, you will find they often refer to work you have already done. This is because they build on and reinforce work you did in earlier lessons. Keep in mind that you are working to overcome deeply ingrained behaviors and thinking patterns. Thus, it is often necessary to rework lessons that deal with your problem areas several times to overcome your anxiety-related problems.

Increase the Number of Compliments You Give Yourself

The continued repetition of an idea tends to make it a part of your belief system. This is how most of your beliefs, both conscious and unconscious, were acquired. What you heard and thought over and over when young eventually became part of your belief system and is now what you tell yourself over and over. This principle often works in a self-defeating manner. An example of this is the tendency to dwell on negative evaluations. By selectively remembering a criticism, exaggerating it to monstrous proportions, and repeating it over and over, you make it part of your reality. This lowers self-esteem and self-acceptance and causes you to miss valuable opportunities for growth and joy.

Increasing the number of compliments you give yourself uses this principle in a positive, self-enhancing manner. Here are three ways to do this.

Focus on Small Successes and Positive Experiences

Whenever you do anything, no matter how small, take a moment to find something about it that was done well and focus on it. If your tendency in the past was to focus on small errors and flaws, this may be difficult at first; however, with practice, it becomes easier.

Identify and Remind Yourself of Your Strengths Regularly

Develop a list of qualities or skills you possess which you consider to be positive. These need to be specific qualities you feel are accurate. Here is Ruth's list:

- I have a nice smile.
- I am well informed about current affairs.
- I am an excellent cook.
- I am a skilled pool player.
- I am very friendly.

People with low levels of self-esteem and self-acceptance often have difficulty thinking of even two or three items. If this is true for you, spend several days developing your list until there are five to ten items on it. You might find it helpful to have a friend or relative assist you. Often others can note positive things about you that are difficult for you to see or acknowledge.

After you have completed your list, recite it two or three times a day for three weeks. This works best if you make it a regular part of your day. For example, you could recite your list while driving to and from work or while you are getting ready in the morning. If you have difficulty remembering the items on your list, carry a copy with you or post it on a wall. Whenever you think of an additional positive quality, add it to your list. After a few days of practice, begin adding successes, even tiny ones you had during the day, along with examples of things you have done that demonstrate the positive qualities you have listed. Eventually, you will be able to list many positive qualities, skills, and successes without the need for your list.

Practice Mirror Talk

Practice reciting the list of positive qualities you developed once a day while looking at your image in the mirror. This is easiest if it is done while you are doing a regular daily activity such as combing your hair, shaving, or putting on makeup. As you say each item on the list, add, "And I like me." This is how Ruth recited the list she developed.

- "I have a nice smile. And I like me."

- "I am well informed about current affairs. And I like me."
- "I am an excellent cook. And I like me."
- "I am a skilled pool player. And I like me."
- "I am very friendly. And I like me."

Many people feel silly or find it difficult to face themselves with their good points and say them out loud. The more difficult this exercise is for you, the more important it is to do it until you can think of many positive qualities, skills, and successes; you can easily and comfortably face yourself in the mirror; you sound and look like you really mean the things you are saying as you recite your list; and you actually *enjoy* doing it.

Decrease the Number of Negative Things You Say to Yourself About Your Weaknesses

Answer each of the following questions on a piece of paper.

- What kinds of situations make me feel bad about myself?
- What kinds of activities have I wanted to undertake but did not try because I feared I might not do them well?
- What interactions between me and another person or persons during the past few weeks or months left me with negative feelings about myself?

Next, list as many negative labels or self-statements as possible that you said or thought to yourself about you and your behavior during or after the above events. Phrase them so they are short declarative sentences such as the following:

- I'm weak.
- I'm too passive.
- I can't do anything right.
- I'm so thoughtless.

Now review the section on labeling in Lesson 5. Add any of the negative labels that you checked there to your list. Once you have completed your list, go back through and change every negative label or statement into its positive opposite. Use phrases that begin with "I am," "I am becoming," "I am learning how," or "I can be." Here are examples that use the first two sentences on the above list.

CHANGING NEGATIVE STATEMENTS	
If You Say or Think:	Restate or Rethink It As:
"I'm weak."	"I am strong."
	"I am becoming strong."
	"I am learning how to be strong."
	"I can be strong."
"I'm too passive."	"I am assertive."
	"I am becoming assertive."
	"I am learning how to be assertive."
	"I can be assertive."

From now on, whenever you notice yourself making negative statements about yourself, stop and substitute new, positive labels for your actions or characteristics. To be effective, these positive statements need to be something you believe is true. It may seem dishonest to say "I am strong" when you are feeling weak. Statements such as "I am learning to be strong" or "I can be strong" usually feel more truthful. You may use statements other than the ones suggested. The only rule is they need to be positive and something you can believe.

Practice Giving Genuine Compliments to Others

Giving genuine compliments is an easy way to increase your level of self-esteem and self-acceptance. When you give genuine compliments, others usually feel better about both themselves and you. This in turn makes you feel better about yourself. A genuine compliment is different from praise that is general or excessive. The difference becomes clear when you examine the following examples.

Examples of Praise
• You're the greatest cook in the world.

- I just don't know what I'd do without your help.
- You're the best-dressed person I know.
- You're always so kind and generous.
- You're so good.

Consider how you would feel if the above statements were made about you. On one hand, they do feel nice. However, this sort of praise is so absolute you know it's not completely true. The high standard of performance implied by these types of statements can also feel like a burden. In addition, praise like this is so vague that it does not really tell you what you said or did that was appreciated. In contrast, the following examples of genuine compliments deal with small, specific actions. You know exactly what was appreciated. This makes them easier to accept than the examples of praise.

Examples of Genuine Compliments
- I really enjoyed that spaghetti.
- Your mowing the lawn helped me a lot.
- The color of that shirt really looks good on you.
- Thank you for the flowers yesterday; I enjoyed them very much.
- I appreciated your spending time with me.

Many people feel uncomfortable when complimented. This can be caused by compliments that are hard to live up to or seem insincere, such as the examples of praise. Sometimes the person lacks experience with compliments and does not know how to respond. Often, however, discomfort with compliments is due to low self-esteem and self-acceptance. The person receiving the compliment feels unworthy, as if somehow he or she is not "good enough."

If you have difficulty accepting compliments, decide which of these causes applies to you. Use rational self-talk to convince yourself that you deserve compliments. Whenever you receive a compliment, practice saying "Thank you," and nothing else. While this may be difficult at first, with time and practice it becomes easy. Eventually, compliments become enjoyable.

The ability to give and receive compliments brings several benefits. As you become more observant about what is positive in others, your ability to notice positive aspects about yourself increases. Noticing positive aspects of your environment also makes you more optimistic. All of this increases your level of self-esteem and self-acceptance.

Develop a More Realistic View of the World and Your Place in It

Becoming a positive realist is a major theme running throughout these lessons. Four ways to develop this orientation are listed below, along with the location in previous lessons where each is discussed in detail. If you have a negative outlook on life, this is an area you will probably need to return to several times.

Develop an Appreciation of Your Own Worth

You are a unique individual with a unique gift for the world. No one else has your experience or can see the world as you do. Develop an understanding and acceptance of this fact through positive self-talk, by reading encouraging books, by attending inspirational talks, and by listening to audio recordings such as those described in the back of this book.

In addition to the above, take time to review and clarify your spiritual or philosophical beliefs. How do you see yourself within the context of the world around you? What is the meaning of life? What is it that truly makes a person happy? This type of reflection is often ridiculed and seen as unimportant in a modern world that worships immediate self-gratification and the accumulation of personal possessions. Yet it is an essential activity that, when done periodically, helps give meaning to all of the other areas of your life.

If you already have a strong set of spiritual or philosophical beliefs, you know the power it has to help you see your value. If you have beliefs that helped you in the past but that you have not thought about at this point in your life, renew your connection to them. If you have never considered this side of yourself, begin to identify how you can feed your inner need for personal meaning.

Accept That You Are Not Responsible for the Emotional Reactions of Others

The reactions others have to you and to the events around them are the result of their beliefs and interpretations. You do not make them happy or cause them to become upset. They make themselves happy or cause themselves to become upset. You are responsible only for your own feelings and actions. If you are having trouble accepting this, review the section in Lesson 4 that discusses how emotions are generated. Remind yourself of the points it makes until you accept them.

Look for Facts Rather than Opinions

What matters is not who's right, but what's accurate. Make an effort to obtain accurate information about yourself, your problems, other people, and the various situations around you. Take time to think about your problems in a rational and logical manner. Do not accept the opinions and beliefs of others unless you have taken time to consider them carefully and they seem rational and realistic. If you continue to automatically accept the negative remarks from others as true, review the section on adopting an objective, problem-solving approach to criticism in Lesson 8.

Accept Your Weaknesses and Mistakes

Whenever you condemn yourself because of a personal weakness or mistake, remind yourself that you are not your mistakes. There is a difference between your self and your behavior. Also remind yourself that your worth is not determined by your achievement. Use the ideas in the section on dealing with mistakes objectively in Lesson 6 to remind yourself that mistakes are a natural part of being human.

In addition, learn to laugh at your errors and silliness. Humor is one of your greatest allies in learning to love and accept yourself. Increasing your ability to use humor in a positive manner increases your ability to use errors and mistakes as a source of wisdom. After they have served this purpose, humor then makes it easier to dismiss and leave these experiences in the past where they belong.

Learn to Refrain from Comparing Yourself to Others

People often feel miserable and second-rate because they habitually compare themselves to others. Underlying this tendency is the mistaken belief that worth is determined by achievement. When this is coupled with the tendency to minimize your own achievements and magnify those of others, the comparisons usually confirm your inadequacy. Review the section on magnification and minimization in Lesson 5. Then review the section titled The Irrational Belief That a Person's Worth Is Determined by Achievement in Lesson 6. Use the ideas in this section to develop rational self-talk reinforcing the belief that your worth as a human is a separate issue from what you do. For example, being an inferior dancer or an inferior cook does not make you an inferior person. In addition, memorize the following statement: *I am not inferior. I am not superior. I am simply me.*

Whenever you notice yourself comparing yourself with others, recall this saying. Then use the rational self-talk you have developed to remind yourself that your value as a human being has no relationship to others. You are unique, and because of this uniqueness it is impossible to do anything exactly like someone else. You can only do things in your own style and to the best of your ability. That is good enough. If someone else does not appreciate your value and uniqueness, that is his or her problem and loss.

Work at Reducing Indecisiveness

Indecisiveness is often the result of excessive concern about what others will think about your decisions. When an excessive fear of failure is present, avoiding decisions also helps you avoid making mistakes. Here are some ways to become more decisive:

- Develop a realistic view of mistakes. Use the ideas in Lesson 6's The Irrational Belief That All Mistakes Are Terrible to challenge any mistaken beliefs you still possess about the meaning of mistakes and their relationship to your worth as a person.
- If you usually rehearse your responses to others, practice

improvising. Just say the first thing you think. Begin this exercise with people you find safe and in situations you find comfortable. Then gradually expand it to other areas of your life.

- Work at reducing self-criticism and adopt the attitude of "what is, is." If this is difficult, review the section on distinguishing between responsibility and blame in Lesson 7.
- If others have commented that you tend to speak softly, practice speaking a little louder than usual. This may seem strange at first; in the beginning you may even feel like you are yelling at people. However, most people won't notice what you are doing. As you practice speaking in a louder and more decisive tone, you will find yourself acting more decisive.
- Tell others when you feel good or bad and let them know you appreciate things they have done. Appropriate self-disclosure and the giving of genuine compliments helps to make you more aware of your feelings and increases your self-acceptance.

Limit the Number of Commitments You Make

People with an excessive need for approval often fall into the habit of saying yes to almost every request made of them. Then they either cannot keep all the commitments they have made, or they sacrifice their own needs and wants in order to meet them. This leads to self-condemnation and further loss of self-esteem and self-acceptance.

If you frequently overcommit yourself, limit the number of commitments you make. Make a commitment only if you are certain you are able to keep it, you are willing to make a strong effort to keep it, and you actually want to keep it. Instead of automatically saying yes to requests from others, practice saying, "Let me think about that," or "I need to check my calendar. I'll get back to you later." When you are alone ask yourself the following questions: "Is this something that I'm actually able to do?" "Do I really have the time and energy to do this?" "Is this something I really want to do?" and "Is this something that would be good for me to do?"

If you have a very strong tendency to overcommit yourself,

limit yourself to one commitment a day at first. Continue limiting your commitments until you are keeping commitments without resentment or regret. Then gradually increase the number you make until you reach a level that is both comfortable and enjoyable. Some find it helpful to write the four questions listed above on a card that they can carry with them. They then read the card two or three times a day to remind themselves to take time to think before making commitments.

Use Your Imagination

Frequent repetition of positive experiences can alter your self-concept in a dramatic and positive manner. One major difference between people with a low level of self-esteem and self-acceptance and those with a high level is the types of memories they choose to recall. People with a low level usually dwell on negative experiences and failures while people with a high level spend their time recalling and enjoying positive memories. Set aside five to ten minutes a day to recall positive things you have done and success you have achieved. Re-create these memories in as much detail and as often as possible. As you recall each positive experience, compliment yourself on your success using genuine compliments as described earlier in this lesson. Continue with this exercise until it is easy to recall success and you feel good about your self-compliments.

Recommended Activities for Lesson 11

Develop Beliefs that Build Self-Esteem and Self-Acceptance

As you review the lesson, make a list of those ideas that reinforce self-esteem and self-acceptance and summarize them on cards. Review these cards once a day until you have memorized them. Here is a card that one person made:

Self-Esteem and Self-Acceptance

- I am not inferior. I am not superior. I am simply me. And that is good enough.
- This is my world. I deserve to be here.
- I take responsibility for and own all of myself—the good and the bad.
- I work to improve myself because of the joy and fulfillment it brings—not because it will somehow make me a better person.
- I was put down a lot when I was little—those were lies from parents who loved me but who were warped by their own childhood. I am a good and decent person who deserves the best in life.
- I have often felt incompetent. Actually, I am a very competent person. All of my evaluations at work and comments from others clearly show that I am good at many things.

Notice that the last two items on the above list address personal issues. If you have identified specific events or people in your past that influenced your life in a negative way, create powerful, direct statements that challenge negative beliefs that developed in response to these people or events.

Review Rational Challenges Developed in Previous Lessons

This lesson discussed how irrational beliefs discussed in previous lessons often contribute to low self-esteem and low self-acceptance. Review cards you prepared for Lessons 6, 7, and 8. Identify those ideas that you feel will help you with this lesson and review them along with the ideas you are memorizing from this lesson.

Work at Increasing Your Level of Self-Esteem and Self-Acceptance

As mentioned previously, you will not be able to work effectively on all the activities in this lesson at once. Do as many of the eight activities described in this lesson as possible. Focus on the two or three you checked as the most important for you at this time. Many find it most beneficial to focus on the first two: Increase the Number of Compliments You Give Yourself and Decrease the Number of Negative Things You Say to Yourself About Your Weaknesses. If you feel others are more important, however, focus on them. After you have completed the lessons, you can return to this one and work on the skills you don't have time for now.

Since low self-esteem and self-acceptance are usually accompanied by an excessive need for approval, spend thirty minutes this week reviewing Lesson 8. Many of the activities in that lesson can be combined with those in this one. If low self-esteem and low self-acceptance are problems for you, spend two weeks with this lesson.

Continue to Work with the Block Method

Continue taking five to ten minutes two or three times a week to use the Block Method. As you analyze your thoughts, look for expressions of any of the irrational beliefs that have been discussed in this and previous lessons. Review the directions in the Recommended Activities of Lesson 5 if you are still having difficulty using the Block Method.

Continue Working with the Behavioral Approaches in Lesson 9

Continue to apply the behavioral approaches you learned in Lesson 9 to the self-defeating behaviors you want to overcome. If you are working on many problem behaviors, take time to review Lesson 9 occasionally. Continue this work throughout the rest of this program.

Consider Your Progress

Take a few minutes this week to consider how you have changed since you began these lessons. Do this when you are feeling good so you are reasonable and objective. Always avoid evaluating your progress when you are sick, hungry, tired, or experiencing excessive stress. As you consider your progress, answer the following questions:

- How have my attitudes toward people, life, and myself changed?
- How has my approach to life and problems changed?
- Is there anything I am doing now that I was unable to do four months ago?

Congratulate yourself on any positive changes you identify!

Develop the Ability to Recognize and Accept Normal Anxiety

One of the keys to managing anxiety effectively is learning to recognize and accept "normal" anxiety. People with anxiety-related problems often fear anxiety so much that all anxiety is considered abnormal. Much of the anxiety you experience in life is an appropriate response to real-life situations; it has nothing whatsoever to do with your old self-defeating patterns. When you become anxious, remind yourself that anxiety is an inherent part of life. It is simply a response to a threat, and there are many real threats in life. Your goal is *not* to eliminate all anxiety. Your goal is to eliminate excessive anxiety and manage the normal, everyday anxiety you encounter effectively so you can live the life you want to live.

During this week, notice how often people around you become anxious. Whenever you find yourself becoming anxious, notice how much of it is normal and healthy. This is an important part of the process of "normalizing" yourself that was discussed in Lesson 10.

Continue to Use the Troubleshooting Checklist

It has been mentioned several times in the previous lessons that you may occasionally experience yourself falling back into old patterns. When this happens, refer to the Troubleshooting Checklist in Lesson 5. Then recall how you handled these situations before and do what was successful in the past. Remember—it takes work to develop new patterns, but with time and practice they eventually become automatic. At this point in the lessons you have spent only a short time working to change thinking and behavior patterns you spent a lifetime developing. It is reasonable and probable that sometimes you will slip back into old patterns. Expect to cycle between good and bad times. This is normal. When you do slip back into old patterns, often it simply means you are overly sick, hungry, tired, or stressed and need to take better care of yourself.

What Does It Mean to Overcome Anxiety?

There is much talk in the psychological community about the need to "resolve" issues and problems. What does this mean? The common impression is that the process is somewhat like going to a medical doctor with a minor injury or illness. The doctor dresses the wound or gives you medication, and after a while it is as if the injury or illness never occurred. This is not how psychological issues are usually "resolved."

Everyone has individual psychological issues that recur during his or her lifetime. For example, it is common for individuals raised with violence or poverty to have a heightened concern about security and lots of should/must rules. These issues will be theirs for life. Still, these issues can be moderated so they do not interfere with their ability to have happy and successful lives.

If you have been working through the lessons as described, you have already identified many of your issues. These might be a body that reacts strongly to stress, wiring in the brain that causes you to sometimes have obsessive thoughts, a heightened need for approval, perfectionistic tendencies, a tendency to use certain types of distorted thinking, or any of the other issues discussed in the previous lessons. You will probably never eliminate these tendencies completely. You don't have to. While they will occasionally affect your life in an adverse way, this will usually be during times when you are ill, hungry, tired, or experiencing unusual stress. They may also be triggered by people or events that resemble your past in some way as a result of conditioned response learning, discussed in Lesson 2.

The fact that this occurs occasionally is unimportant. What is important is to become skilled at identifying your issues, developing signals that alert you to when they are affecting your thoughts and behavior, and developing a set of skills that keeps them from interfering with your life in a negative way. It is similar to a popular carnival game where the player faces a platform with several holes. The heads of little mechanical gophers pop up out of the holes at random. The player is then supposed to hit the gopher back into the hole before others pop up. Your personality traits and personal issues are yours for life. Events will occur periodically that trigger old feelings and responses. The trick is to be like the person who becomes skilled at anticipating where gophers will pop up and hitting them back down into their hole.

Your goal is to become skilled at knowing when your "buttons" are being pushed and training yourself to respond in a way that manages your issues effectively and brings you what you want in life.

Self-esteem and self-acceptance are key issues not only in anxiety-related problems but in a wide variety of self-defeating behaviors as well. Spend at least one week with this lesson.

LESSON 12

Making Anger Your Friend and Ally

W hat do you think of when you think of anger? For most people this question brings a host of negative associations, such as frustration, hurt, loss of control, and fear. This is unfortunate since anger can be a positive, constructive force in your life when channeled appropriately. This lesson shows you how to make anger your friend and ally.

What Is Anger?

Lesson 4 describes in detail how emotions are generated through the following process:

$$\text{Event} \longrightarrow \text{Interpretation} \longrightarrow \text{Emotion} \longrightarrow \text{Action}$$

Emotions generate actions that satisfy needs and protect us from threat and loss. They do this in three ways: First, emotions activate the body and prepare it to take action. Second, emotions focus our attention on the perceived danger and produce an urge to take action. Third, emotions communicate our perception to others automatically through body language and facial expressions. As emotions become more intense, the activation of the body increases and we have an increasing desire to take action. At the same time, it becomes easier for others to see what we are feeling.

Anger is the emotional response triggered by the interpretation that a threat is or may be present. Once triggered, anger activates the fight or flight response that prepares the body for action. This physical response is accompanied by a desire to eliminate the source of the threat.

Like all emotions, anger can exist at many different levels of intensity. Unfortunately, many people fail to recognize annoyance, irritation, or displeasure as simply low-level anger. They only think of anger in terms of its higher levels of intensity, such as rage. Because undesirable actions often accompany more intense forms of anger, anger is often considered an undesirable and negative emotion. In fact, anger is often the driving force behind positive actions. When you ask a person to stop an activity that is annoying you, for example, it is low-level anger labeled as annoyance that is driving your actions. Whenever you assert yourself, it is anger—usually at a low level of intensity—that is providing the energy and motivation for your actions.

Anger is closely related to fear in that both are triggered by a perceived threat and both activate the fight or flight response. Anger produces a desire to meet and eliminate the threat, while fear produces a desire to escape from or avoid the threat. Because anger and fear are closely related, some people find that converting feelings of anxiety (low-level fear) to anger helps them overcome self-defeating behaviors associated with anxiety. When used in this way, anger provides increased motivation to meet and overcome the threat associated with the self-defeating behaviors. Relabeling the physical symptoms generated by anxiety as anger also enables these people to view their physical symptoms as a source of strength instead of as a sign of weakness.

The Threats That Generate Anger and Fear

Lesson 4 described in detail how human beings are unique in that they have no instinctive fears. By the time you are an adult, everything you identify as a threat is something you have learned. Furthermore, once a threat is identified, the key that determines whether you respond with fear or anger is your perception of how well you can meet the threat. This is also based on beliefs and thinking patterns you have learned. If a threat seems unmanageable, it triggers fear. If it seems manageable, it triggers anger. Sometimes, you will alternate between fear and anger as your perception of both the situation and your ability to cope with it changes.

One notable exception is a situation where the threat seems unmanageable and from which escape seems impossible. One person will experience paralyzing fear, and another intense anger. No one knows exactly how or why these reactions occur, although it probably has deep biological roots in our evolutionary past. In this sense we respond like a cornered animal: We either freeze or attack.

Another interesting aspect of the interpretation process that generates anger is the nature of threats in our modern world. In ancient times most threats involved physical needs and were concrete—you could see, touch, smell, or feel them—such as a wild animal, a hostile neighboring tribe, or a long drought. Concrete threats such as being fired from your job or threatened on the street still exist, but most of the everyday threats we experience in our modern, technological society involve psychological needs. These needs are usually partially or totally abstract, such as a sense of personal power, pride, love, self-respect, or a sense of belonging and significance. This aspect of anger is dealt with more thoroughly later in the lesson when inappropriate anger is discussed.

Actions Generated by Anger

The various responses people have when angry are summarized below. This list starts with what are usually the most undesirable response patterns and ends with what is usually the most productive one in everyday life. As you read through the list, remember that all anger patterns are learned. Because these patterns become automatic, they often seem unchangeable. However, because they were learned, they can be replaced with new patterns if you use an effective method and are willing to do the work required to bring this about.

- Violent, destructive and/or harmful actions.
- Tantrums—verbal and/or physical.
- Hurtful or critical remarks, sarcasm, or teasing.
- Sulking/pouting.

- Passive-aggressive behavior—behavior that causes problems for the person you are angry with but seems unintentional, such as forgetting something important or being late.
- Hurtful or destructive fantasies—daydreaming about what you would like to do to the person you are angry with.
- Repression—being angry but being unaware of your anger.
- Suppression—knowing you are angry but pretending not to be.
- Constructive action—action that reduces the threat with the least amount of harm or discomfort to both yourself and others.

The energy and motivation generated by anger and expressed through the actions listed above can be focused in one or more of the following directions:

- It can be ignored through suppression or repression.
- It can be turned inward and directed at a real or imagined personal weakness or inadequacy.
- It can be directed at someone or something unrelated to the threat that generated the anger.
- It can be directed at an identified external threat.

An example of each of the above is given in the following situation. Four different people have lost their money by putting it into a faulty candy machine. Don never allows himself to become angry and thus suppresses his anger and walks away, trying to be calm even though he is very irritated. Mark turns his anger inward at his perceived inadequacy and begins to put himself down with comments such as, "I'm so stupid. These things never seem to work for me." A few minutes after losing her money, Linda directs several harsh comments toward a co-worker, who does not deserve them. Deborah first directs her anger at the machine and kicks it. Then she directs it at the fact that she has lost money and goes looking for someone who can refund it.

Appropriate Versus Inappropriate Anger

Anger is an appropriate response when a real threat exists. The action it generates is appropriate when that action brings about the reduction or elimination of the threat with the least amount of discomfort or harm to yourself and others.

Anger can be inappropriate in two ways. The first is when anger is felt even though no real threat exists—for example, a person with good intentions says in a positive manner that your shirt looks nice and you become angry. The second is when anger is felt at a level of intensity too high for the threat that is present. An example of this is a person who goes into a rage when a shoelace breaks.

Anger felt when there is no real threat or at an excessively high level is usually the result of irrational thinking. This can be due to irrational beliefs that are part of a person's basic belief system or to a temporary reduction in the person's ability to think in a logical and rational manner. Both of these issues are discussed further in the next section. The actions generated by anger are inappropriate when they bring unnecessary harm to yourself or others.

Minimizing Inappropriate Anger

This section presents six approaches you can use to minimize the amount of inappropriate anger you experience. Once you have done this, you will have taken a major step toward the goal of making anger your friend and ally.

Protect Your Ability to Think in a Logical and Rational Manner

A major source of inappropriate anger is the loss of your physical ability to think rationally. Remember, the brain is a physical organ. Anything that interferes with its ability to function interferes with your ability to interpret events accurately. Common factors that interfere with the brain's ability to function are hunger, fatigue, illness, injury, excessive stress, and drugs. Inappropriate anger is much more likely when one or more of these factors are present. In fact, Lesson 3 pointed out that increased irritability and emotionalism are often early warning signs that you need to use stress management principles. A discussion of these principles along with suggestions for staying functional during times of high stress are given in Lesson 3.

Setting priorities and taking care of yourself as suggested in that lesson help to maintain your physical ability to think and assess possible threats accurately.

Challenge Mistaken Beliefs About Anger

There are two common mistaken beliefs about anger: the idea that anger is in some way a bad emotion, and the idea that it always results in undesirable behavior. Sometimes these mistaken ideas are the result of direct instruction. Children are often told very directly that anger is not an acceptable emotion. Here are some common examples:

- Don't get angry at me! (a command from a parent or adult).
- You shouldn't be angry at your brother or sister.
- Only dogs get mad.
- A lady/gentleman never gets angry.

Sometimes a child's anger is ignored or discounted with comments such as, "You're not really angry." A child may also come to the mistaken conclusion that anger is bad or dangerous if a parent always suppresses anger and rarely expresses irritation. Sometimes a child learns this lesson by living with an adult who is very explosive. In this case the child may need to stay calm in order to be spared the adult's wrath. A child might also make a conscious decision never to be like the explosive adult, and thereby develop the habit of suppressing anger.

If any of the above describes your childhood and you rarely or never allow yourself to experience anger, review the following ideas daily until they become a firm part of your belief system.

- Events will occur every day that cause you to become angry. This is normal.
- Anger is an appropriate response to a situation when a real threat exists.
- Emotions are often triggered by unconscious associations from the past. It often takes a long time to desensitize to these conditioned emotional responses.
- What is important is not what you feel but *how you respond*.

- Anger can be controlled and directed to become a positive force behind constructive actions.

Minimize Distorted Thinking and Irrational Beliefs

All the forms of distorted thinking and irrational beliefs discussed in the previous lessons can cause you to feel threatened when no threat exists and generate anger. This is especially true for events that violate your should/must rules. Roy is a good example of this. He had a rigid belief that people should always be fair. Whenever Roy was in a situation where someone acted unfairly, he would become extremely angry even when the situation was trivial. As Roy learned to challenge this rigid rule, he was able to focus on how he would respond when events were unfair instead of becoming angry and reacting to the fact that something wasn't fair. In a similar manner, as your ability to challenge distorted thinking and irrational beliefs increases, the amount of inappropriate anger you experience will decrease.

Build a High Level of Self-Esteem and Self-Acceptance

If you find it difficult to accept your human weaknesses and limitations, personal weakness and limitations become a threat and generate inappropriate anger. The best way to overcome this type of inappropriate anger is to use the approaches described in Lessons 8 and 11 to develop a high level of self-esteem and self-acceptance. People with a high level of self-esteem who accept their human frailties are not threatened when their limitations are noticed. As a result, they concentrate on what they can do, and feel no remorse or anger over what they cannot do.

Identify Sensations and Emotions That Have Been Taboo in the Past and Deal with Them More Directly

A taboo sensation or emotion is one you believe you must never experience. Often this is an unconscious belief. For example, Janet had a strong need to be in control of herself and any situation she was in. The experience of being weak or helpless was taboo. Whenever she perceived herself as being helpless or out of control, Janet found herself becoming angry. This did not help the situation. However, the physical feeling of strength generated by the anger created the illusion that she was powerful and in control. She could also ignore her weaknesses and inadequacies because she was busy being angry. Other emotions and sensations that are frequently covered by anger include fear, guilt, shame, embarrassment, confusion, and sexual feelings.

Emotions other than anger can also be used to hide taboo sensations. Anxiety and depression are two common ones. For example, John had strong sexual taboos and became very anxious whenever forbidden sexual feelings were experienced. John's anxiety helped distract him from the feelings he was experiencing.

Whenever an experience, emotion, or sensation is hidden by anger or any other emotion, it interferes with your ability to think rationally. Since most of your energy is used to generate and maintain the secondary emotion, little mental energy is left to deal with the world in a realistic, here-and-now fashion. This usually causes you to act in an automatic, self-defeating manner.

Identify any recurring situations in which you usually react with inappropriate anger. These are situations in which you hurt someone you love, damage or destroy something you value, find it difficult to explain yourself or understand what you are experiencing, or in some other way act in a self-defeating manner. After you have identified this type of recurring situation, the next step is to identify the forbidden emotion or sensation beneath the anger. Here are two ways to do this:

- Look at the recurring situations you have noticed in an objective manner and complete the thought, "I am acting as if . . ." This may suggest possible emotions or sensations. You might even pretend you are watching an actor in a movie and try to guess at what the character might be feeling in that situation.
- Identify the feeling you experienced just before the anger. You can do this either during or after one of the recurring situations you identified. The emotion or sensation just before the anger probably is not the forbidden feeling you are seeking. It can, however, help you identify the taboo feeling. Ask yourself, "What does

this feeling remind me of?" This question may trigger a memory of a painful experience in your past. The emotion or sensation felt during this past experience is probably the one you are avoiding.

Craig was living in a foreign country with his wife. During the first few months he noticed that he would become angry and sarcastic whenever they went shopping together. Using the above techniques Craig looked at his behavior and found he was acting as if his wife "should" know the local customs. He also found that the feelings he experienced just prior to his anger reminded him of times when he was very embarrassed as a child and young adult. Craig realized he was embarrassed because he did not know the local customs. After this realization, Craig only had to become aware of the embarrassment he felt when shopping with his wife and his anger would leave. He still felt embarrassed, but he was now able to respond in an appropriate manner. With time, the embarrassment faded.

You will know you have succeeded in identifying a hidden feeling when your anger vanishes. The emotion or sensation hidden beneath the anger simply replaces it. While this feeling may be uncomfortable, you are now able to utilize all your mental abilities to deal with the situation more effectively.

Whenever you uncover a taboo emotion or sensation underneath inappropriate anger, identify the threat and corresponding irrational beliefs that cause it to be taboo. As you become more aware of taboo emotions and challenge the irrational beliefs that make them unacceptable, they lose their power and become easier to experience. With practice, you stop converting the "forbidden" feeling into anger. In the previous example with Craig, he eventually found it easy to admit when he was embarrassed because he didn't know what to do. The fear of making a mistake no longer controlled him.

Learn to Release Resentments

Resentment is a re-stressing process where a past hurt is recalled and you tell yourself things about that event that make you angry over and over. Gaining skills in releasing resentments allows you to free tied-up energy so it can be used constructively. You also cease to be victimized by negative feelings and gain a sense of accomplishment,

freedom, and control. Whenever you find yourself nurturing a resentment, explore each of the following areas. One or more will probably
provide the key for releasing the resentment you are experiencing.

Weigh the Seriousness of the Offense and Ask Yourself, "Is Holding on to This Resentment Really Worth It?"

No matter how justified a negative feeling is when first experienced,
continuing to nurture and reexperience it has tremendous physical and
emotional costs for you. When carrying a resentment, you are the ultimate source of your own misery and stress. Resentment rarely affects
the object of the resentment. It is the person carrying the resentment—
you—who suffers the negative consequences of resentment.

Identify Actions You Can Take to Improve the Situation or Satisfy the Unmet Need That Is Generating the Resentment

Resentments involving someone you deal with regularly indicate that
a need is not being met. Identify the need and decide what action would
be appropriate. Can you approach this person and discuss ways to improve
the situation? If not, is there a symbolic way in which you might vent your
feelings, such as writing a letter that is never sent? Consider each action
that occurs to you and weigh the risks and benefits each offers. If any seem
promising, make a decision as to when and where you will carry it out.

Examine the Situation or Event from the Other Person's Perspective —There May Be a Very Good Reason for This Person's Behavior

Was the other person physically ill or tired? Did this person have
important concerns or problems that had nothing to do with you but
prevented the person from dealing with you in a more rational way?
Is it possible this person was busy *re*acting to events and people from
the past that had nothing to do with you but made it impossible to
deal with you in a rational manner? Does this person have irrational
beliefs and expectations that generate irrational behavior?

Examine Your Beliefs and Expectations and Determine If They Are Rational and Realistic

How "should" this event have taken place? Create the proper or
ideal situation or sequence of events and interactions. As you do this, use

the following questions to identify irrational beliefs and expectations. Do you have an exaggerated need for people to act "correctly" or for events to be "fair"? Perhaps you have an excessive need for approval, a perfectionistic tendency, or some other exaggerated personal need that has been frustrated. Are you accepting people and events as they are and deciding how best to respond to them, or are you refusing to accept reality and demanding that people and events somehow be different from what they are? Are any of the forms of distorted thinking or irrational beliefs discussed in this or previous lessons still playing a role in your resentment?

Identify Secondary Gains You May Receive from This Resentment

Does this resentment allow you to continue punishing someone or to receive some special reward, benefit, or attention you either do not know how to obtain or are afraid to ask for directly? Perhaps you have difficulty accepting responsibility for your feelings—that you are the ultimate source of your stress and misery—and rather than accept and acknowledge that the anger or hurt you felt was the result of your expectations and beliefs and your responsibility, you play the role of a victim. Does this resentment allow you to feel sorry for yourself without having to take responsibility for changing the situation as you continue to resent the other person for "making" you feel that way?

A Four-Step Approach for Dealing with Anger

The following four-step approach can transform anger into a friend and ally. In most situations it takes less than a minute to use. If you have difficulty responding in a positive manner when angry, identify the step or steps you fail to use. Then review the steps daily until they become an automatic part of your behavior.

Step 1: Stop and cool down. When anger first flashes, you lose much of your ability to reason logically and rationally. The first response you choose is often an ineffective one. In addition, taking action when anger first flashes usually makes you angrier. The ancient advice of counting to ten when angry has stood the test of time. Fortunately, in most situations it takes only a few seconds to regain your ability to reason. When you are very angry, take a time-out and excuse yourself. Take as long as you need to cool down so you can think rationally.

Step 2: Identify the source of your anger. Ask yourself, "Why am I angry?" Usually, this is all it takes to identify the source of your anger. If this doesn't work, ask yourself, "How am I threatened by this?" or "What do I want?"

Step 3: Check to see if your anger is appropriate. Most anger is a mixture of appropriate and inappropriate anger. The easiest way to determine whether your anger is mostly appropriate or mostly inappropriate is to ask yourself, "Is my anger appropriate for this situation?" Asking yourself this question allows you to become aware of times when there is no real threat or when the intensity of your anger is too high for the threat that is present. As discussed earlier, this is most often due to illness, fatigue, hunger, or excessive stress. When you are overreacting and your anger is mostly inappropriate, delay all action until you have time to cool down and identify the source of the inappropriate anger. When you are sick, hungry, tired, or stressed, it is often good, when possible, to wait until the next day. Things often look very different after a night's sleep. If your anger is mostly appropriate, go on to the next step.

Step 4: Take positive action. When deciding what to do, remind yourself that your goal is to minimize or eliminate the threat you are facing with the least amount of harm or discomfort to yourself and others. Most people already have many skills they can use to take positive action. This might involve taking action to protect yourself, resolving a conflict you have with someone, or developing an alternate plan that will satisfy the need or want that is being threatened. Each of these and other possible actions that you can take are explored in detail in the two lessons that follow.

Suggestions for People Who Habitually Suppress Anger

Anger has two important functions: It tells you when needs are threatened or unfulfilled, and it provides energy and motivation for overcoming threats and satisfying needs. If you habitually suppress anger, you have a reduced awareness of when needs are threatened or unfulfilled. This makes it difficult to take actions that satisfy your needs. As was discussed in Lesson 3, when important needs are denied, they generate stronger and stronger emotions that can trigger physical reactions, inappropriate emotional responses, or self-defeating behaviors.

One common self-defeating behavior associated with the habitual suppression of anger is periodic blowups. When you suppress anger, you are ignoring important needs. Eventually, the emotions generated by the ignored needs become so strong that you explode. Unfortunately, this type of anger usually causes you to act ineffectively. If you don't blow up periodically, the ignored needs may generate resentment, anxiety, depression, or passive-aggressive behavior.

Recurring anger that is continually suppressed can keep the fight or flight response activated. When this response is kept activated for prolonged periods of time, the muscle tension and overproduction of hormones associated with the fight or flight response can interfere with normal body functions, such as digestion and your ability to fight disease. Shoulder, head-, and backaches can also occur.

It might seem that the habitual suppression of emotions is always undesirable. This is not so. Throughout human history the ability to ignore certain basic needs and suppress emotions has helped people survive harsh environments. Since most people in the past died relatively young and were primarily concerned with physical survival, the negative effects of suppressing emotions were of little importance. A pioneer family living on the prairie, peasants farming a king's estate, or a group of nomadic hunters needed to put most of their time and energy into physical survival. Sharing work and meeting physical needs were far more important than meeting emotional needs.

It has only been in recent times and in select countries that most of the people in a society have enjoyed increased health and longevity along with a large degree of economic and political freedom. People in this environment do not spend as much time and energy meeting physical needs as their ancestors. This allows the satisfaction of emotional needs and quality-of-life issues to become more important. The result is that the habitual suppression of emotions now interferes rather than helps.

Do not misinterpret what has just been said to mean that today all suppression of emotions is undesirable. It is often important to suppress emotions temporarily in order to deal effectively with a pressing situation, such as a medical emergency or an important business meeting. Situations like these require immediate decisions and actions. Usually, the feelings generated by these events are best dealt with later. This type of occasional, temporary suppression of emotion is often appropriate. As previously mentioned, when you are sick, hungry, tired, or stressed, it is also often best to avoid reacting until you feel better. However, the constant, habitual suppression of emotions such as anger usually becomes self-defeating.

People who habitually suppress anger usually have difficulty in the following three areas. If this is true for you, spend extra time developing these skills.

Increase Your Ability to Identify Your Emotions Accurately

During the day, ask yourself periodically, "What emotion am I feeling?" Do this until it becomes easy to identify the various emotions you experience. As you do this, avoid using words that describe your situation or mental state, such as *frustrated, helpless, confused,* or *stressed.* Instead, identify the emotion that is being triggered. Several examples are listed below.

Words That Describe Positive Emotions

at ease	delighted	happy	pleased
calm	excited	joyous	proud
comfortable	exhilarated	loving	relieved
content	glad	passionate	satisfied

Words That Describe Negative Emotions

afraid	depressed	frightened	irritated
angry	disappointed	guilty	miserable
anxious	discontented	hate	repulsed
bored	embarrassed	hurt	sad

If you find it difficult to identify what you are feeling, develop physical or behavioral indicators you can use. A physical indicator can be any recurring physical response triggered by an emotion. Common examples for anger include tight shoulders, a clenched jaw, and increased agitation. Behavioral indicators can be identified by recalling how you have acted in the past when angry—for instance, not talking to loved ones, isolating yourself, and becoming busy with something that is really not important. Make a list of your indicators and memorize it.

Increase Your Ability to Identify Accurately Your Needs and Wants

Habitual suppressors often find it difficult to know what they want when confronted with a request or the need to make a decision. If this is true for you, delay making decisions. Take time to ask yourself, "What do I want?" If you are not sure, list the choices you have in your mind or on a piece of paper and tune in to the emotions each choice generates as you consider it.

Increase Your Ability to Develop and Carry Out Plans That Enable You to Satisfy Your Needs or Wants in an Appropriate and Realistic Way

When habitual suppressors identify what they want, they often find it difficult to take positive action. For many, this is because they lack skills in assertiveness. If this describes you, take extra time with the following two lessons, which describe assertiveness skills in detail. The other major forces that can help maintain the self-defeating behaviors characteristic of habitual suppressors are excessive need for approval, low self-esteem, and low self-acceptance. If this is true for you, review Lessons 8 and 11 where these issues are discussed in detail.

Suggestions for People Who Anger Easily

The tendency to anger easily is a learned behavior that helps people gain social power. People try to avoid upsetting a person with a quick temper, so this person often gets his or her way. At the same time, a quick temper makes it difficult to have healthy relationships. Most people try to avoid a person with a quick temper. This usually lowers self-esteem and increases the need for control in the quick-tempered person. This can cause other types of self-defeating behaviors.

A quick temper usually comes from growing up with a quick-tempered adult. The adult's behavior is passed on to the child by way of example. Sometimes a child is taught to be aggressive directly by parents who see life as a win–lose proposition. A quick temper can also develop in a child with weak or overindulgent parents. This child learns that throwing temper tantrums is an effective way to get what is wanted. As the tendency to throw a temper tantrum continues into adult life, it becomes self-defeating. Sometimes having a quick temper helps a child survive a harsh environment or a social setting where such a temper is valuable.

If you anger easily, work in the following three areas.

Learn to Delay Action When Angry

People with quick tempers often find this the most difficult habit to develop. It is, however, the key to regaining your perspective on things and choosing more appropriate responses. If you are quick-tempered, remind yourself daily, for as long as it takes, that you need to stop and cool down when you become angry. Then go through the four steps for dealing with anger described earlier in this lesson. The angrier you are, the longer you need to take. Remember, you can control your temper if you choose to. Choosing to let your anger run wild guarantees that you will act inappropriately.

Develop a Wider Range of Emotional Responses and Identify Taboo Feelings

The section titled Increase Your Ability to Identify Your Emotions Accurately, above, is just as important for people with a quick temper as it is for people who habitually suppress anger. Situations or emotions that are considered signs of weakness often generate anger. When you perceive yourself as being weak or helpless, anger makes you *feel* strong. Unfortunately, anger usually does not help and often makes matters worse. Being confused, helpless, embarrassed, and sad are common triggers of anger. Spend time doing the activities recommended in the section on taboo emotions earlier in this lesson. Use positive self-talk to convince yourself that any taboo feelings you identify are normal and healthy.

Develop Skills at Assertion

There is a big difference between being assertive and being aggressive. If you anger easily, you probably confuse the two. If you often rely on aggressive behavior to resolve conflicts, you need to develop a wide range of assertiveness skills that can replace your aggressive behaviors. These skills are described in detail in the two lessons that follow.

Dealing with Anger Directed at You from Others

The first and most important step in dealing effectively with anger directed at you from others is training yourself to avoid taking their anger as a personal attack. Most of the anger you encounter has little, if anything, to do with who you are or what you have done. Anger from others is usually due to one of the following factors:

- A temporary reduction in the angry person's ability to think rationally and increased emotionality due to hunger, fatigue, illness, or stress.
- The angry person's deep-seated irrational beliefs and expectations.
- Displaced anger being directed at you from a source that has nothing to do with you.

The best approach to use with displaced anger is often to distance yourself from the angry person so you will not be an easy target. Another approach is to describe in an assertive but tolerant manner what you perceive. For example, you could say to a co-worker who had a difficult meeting and who is now acting aggressively toward you, "I know Bob gave you a hard time this morning, but now it seems like you're taking it out on me even though I'm on your side." At this point most people back off. If they don't, distance yourself from them.

In the occasional instances where you have actually done some-thing that is a real threat or hardship for the other person, separate your behavior—what you did—from who and what you are. This enables you to remain more objective and problem-centered. Silently acknowledge and identify your needs but put them on hold temporar-ily until the other person has cooled down. Remember, an angry per-son is usually an irrational person.

The following approach is usually effective in turning the anger and attack from another person into a problem-centered discussion. It works equally as well for when you have actually done something to anger someone as for when displaced anger is being directed at you from an unknown source. Again, the key to making it work is to avoid taking the other person's anger personally.

Step 1: Begin by allowing the other person to express anger freely. Adopt an understanding and nonjudgmental attitude. Avoid interrupting or contradicting the sender. Do not defend, jus-tify, or rationalize your actions or position. Concentrate on reflect-ing the other person's concerns. This helps to dissipate the intense energy of "hot" anger so the other person can become more rea-sonable. As you do this, begin to ask for the specifics of legitimate problems or criticisms.

Step 2: As the angry person becomes more problem-centered and calmer, become more focused in your questioning. The clarification skills described in Appendix 5 are the most effective way to do this. If you are unskilled with them, develop skill by practicing clarification skills in friendly situations with people you know.

Step 3: Once the angry person has calmed down, if it is appropriate, begin legitimate problem solving. Once a person calms down, there is often no need for further problem solving. This is especially true when the other person's anger was trig-gered by something that had little or nothing to do with you. If a problem does exist and the other person is very angry, break off your discussion until a later time. This gives the person time to cool down and become more rational.

The above approach works well for the occasional angry con-frontations we all encounter. It does not work well if you are also very angry or easily intimidated by anger. When this is the case, it is often best to distance yourself from the angry person until he or she calms down.

If you are in an ongoing relationship at work or home with someone who constantly uses an angry or aggressive style, you may also want to consider the following:

- How important is this relationship to you? Do you have other alternatives?
- Is there any way you can minimize my contact with this person?
- If there is no way to avoid this person, a "walk-away" strategy may be appropriate. Simply walk away whenever this person becomes aggressive. Deal with this person only when he or she is relatively calm and rational. With some people it is best to just walk away without saying anything. With most, however, it is best to make a short statement such as, "I'm not willing to talk with you when you're so angry. I will discuss this with you later after we have both calmed down."

If you are in a relationship with someone who may become violent, do what is necessary to ensure your safety. If you have an immediate need for help, call the police. There are also many excellent shelters and crisis intervention centers around the country. They are usually listed in both the white and yellow pages of your telephone book. If you cannot find one, call either a local hospital or your county's mental health service and ask for help in locating one. These agencies can also recommend support groups and counseling resources where you can receive individualized help for dealing with your situation. Seek help if you need it.

The Fear of Losing Control

The fear of losing control can take many different forms. Since an authority figure may dominate you or make you do something you do not want to do, the fear of losing control is sometimes expressed as a fear of authority figures. Occasionally it even generates a master–slave mentality in situations where there is a hierarchy. For example, a supervisor or teacher may be viewed as an unfriendly master who needs to be either placated or overthrown. Other common forms for this fear include a fear of losing control to illness, relationships, or financial problems.

The fear of losing control is a major contributing factor in the development of both the anxiety/panic cycle and many avoidance reactions. It is usually not the panic attack that is feared, but the consequences of losing control during the panic attack. Likewise, when a place or situation is avoided, it is usually not the specific place or situation that is feared but the consequences of losing control of oneself or events in that place or situation.

Excessive concern with control is usually the result of growing up in an environment where helplessness and lack of control were major issues. Often this involves a domineering parent. Another frequent pattern is a child who has been unable to get a consistent response from parents and therefore lives with constant ambiguity. This often involves parents who are chemically dependent. As adults, children from this type of environment usually find uncertainty and ambiguity very difficult. The sense of helplessness or lack of control can also be due to physical, sexual, or mental abuse as well as growing up where there is war or social upheaval.

Anger is only one response people have to the fear of losing control. Many people simply avoid situations where they feel they have no control. Others follow a rigid set of rules for how they should behave and how tasks should be performed. Some make excessive requests when in social situations such as adjusting lighting and heating or putting limitations on what can be discussed or done. Such actions often cause people like this to be seen as controlling and manipulative. A small number gain a sense of control by giving up all control.

Many different types of irrational assumptions can generate the fear of losing control. Examples of self-talk that reflect these irrational assumptions are listed below. Place a check by any that are similar to how you think or talk.

- I have to be my own boss.
- Rules and regulations imprison me.

- I have to be free.
- I can't stand it when others tell me what to do.
- I have to do what is right (which means be perfect) in order to maintain control.
- Asking for help is a sign of weakness and loss of control.
- If I let someone get too close, he or she may come to control me.
- Others are always trying to control me.
- If I give in to others, they win and are controlling me.
- Conforming means losing control.
- I must remain independent in order to avoid losing control.

Study the following list of rational arguments and select those that best challenge the irrational beliefs you checked. List the arguments you select on a card and memorize them. Be sure to add any others you may think of in addition to those listed.

- There is nothing over which you have absolute control. The universe is such that every event is affected by many different factors. While some factors may exert a greater degree of influence than others, no one factor is totally responsible for any one event.
- Reasonably healthy adults who are thinking rationally can easily resist the influence of other people in normal situations if they so choose.
- Using rational self-talk skills and facing life as a positive realist allows you to stop and look at the people and events you encounter and make choices. This is the most effective way to exert control over your life.
- True freedom requires structure and an ability to work within the rules and limitations of nature and society. For example, a skilled musician practices the basic skills of his instrument and learns the rules of music so well he can freely improvise on any song; a skilled politician knows how to work within the system to achieve her goals.
- Every human has limitations and weaknesses. Knowing how to ask for and accept help when it is needed is the most effective way to get what you want.

- Acknowledging and accepting limitations is the first step in minimizing their influence on you.
- Blind rebellion against rules or social convention actually limits your freedom and the amount of control you have over your life.
- Rules and social conventions are simply a means for allowing people to coexist and achieve their life goals. For example, traffic laws are simply rules that allow many people to use public roads and drive safely.
- Conforming to social norms is often an effective and convenient way to achieve what you want.
- Giving up the illusion of control is the way to freedom.
- Compromising with others is often the best way to fulfill your needs.
- True intimacy requires you to be vulnerable at appropriate times with the appropriate people. If you refuse to be vulnerable, you will never experience true intimacy and doom yourself to a life of loneliness.

After you develop rational arguments that challenge your irrational beliefs, identify triggers—specific actions, words, phrases, or situations you can use to know when the fear of losing control needs to be challenged. Here are some examples of triggers Laura identified:

Phrases
- I should be able to do it myself.
- I can't get too close.
- Who do they think they are by telling me how to do things.
- I have to do this right.

Situations/Behaviors
- Inappropriate anger and condemnation toward myself or others when I am not completing a task as I think it "should" be done.
- Anxiety and a feeling that I need to get away when talking about personal matters or when in intimate situations.
- Anxiety, anger, or resentment when I do not know something and need to ask for help at work.

Laura recalled her rational arguments whenever she caught herself saying the above phrases, in the above situations, or doing the above behaviors. She found this helped reduce both the anxiety and inappropriate anger she experienced. It also helped her accept limitations and events over which she had little or no control.

Recommended Activities for Lesson 12
Examine the Roots of Your Anger Patterns

The following exercise takes ten to twenty minutes. Use paper and pencil when you do it.

- List the ways in which your parents expressed anger.
- What did your parents say and do to you when you became angry as a child?
- Were your siblings told the same things and treated in the same way when they became angry? If not, what did you think and feel when they were treated differently? Did you make any resolutions as a result of this different treatment? If so, are those resolutions still valuable today or are they interfering with your life?
- What made you angry as a child? What did you do when you became angry?
- What makes you angry as an adult? What do you do when you become angry?
- Is there anything about your present anger patterns you would like to change? If so, how will you do this? (You will find it easier to answer this final question after you have studied this lesson. You can then select, from the activities it describes, those that would be most appropriate for reaching your goal.)

After you have answered the above, consider how these patterns are still affecting you today. Then review this lesson and identify those specific ideas and skills that could be used to change these patterns.

Use Rational Self-Talk to Minimize Inappropriate Anger

The following exercise takes about ten minutes. Use paper and pencil when you do it.

- Recall a time recently when you experienced what you believe was mostly inappropriate anger—anger that was too intense for the threat that triggered it or anger that was occurring when no real threat was present. Describe the event briefly.
- Recall and list as much of your self-talk that occurred just before and during this event as you can.
- After you have listed all the self-talk you can recall, identify any distorted thinking or irrational beliefs that were present. Then develop a rational response for each one.
- List any additional things you could think or do that would help minimize this type of inappropriate anger.
- Take a moment to imagine yourself using the rational self-talk and new behaviors you listed in a future situation similar to this one. This final step is most important. Rehearsing desired behaviors greatly increases the chance that you will use them in the future.

Special Issues

This lesson addresses three special issues: the tendency to suppress anger, the tendency to become angered easily, and the fear of losing control. If any of these issues is a major problem for you, be sure to spend time studying the section that applies to you and do the exercises it recommends.

Spend at least one week with this lesson. If inappropriate anger or suppression of anger is a major problem for you, spend an extra week with this lesson.

LESSON 13

Standing Up for Yourself

Conflict arises whenever the satisfaction of your needs and wants interferes with those of someone else. Since everyone's needs and wants are different, conflict is a natural and healthy part of all human relationships. If you find this type of normal conflict difficult, it can be a major source of anxiety. This lesson shows you how to resolve conflicts in a way that is both effective and satisfying. Gaining skill in resolving conflicts positively reduces the anxiety associated with them and produces more enjoyable relationships.

Three Basic Types of Behavior

There are three basic ways to resolve conflict: You can become nonassertive, aggressive, or assertive. Understanding the differences among them is the first step to effective conflict resolution.

Nonassertive Behavior

The goal of nonassertive behavior is to avoid conflict. When you are nonassertive, you place the needs and wants of others ahead of your own. You allow others to make choices for you and take advantage of you. When most or all conflict is approached nonassertively, it is called general nonassertiveness. When nonassertiveness is restricted to a limited number of situations, it is called situational nonassertiveness. Situational nonassertiveness is much more common than general nonassertiveness. Situational nonassertiveness usually involves authority figures, such as supervisors, teachers, and parents, or people you are close to, such as a friend or spouse.

One common myth is that nonassertive people are always passive. While passive people are usually nonassertive, people who are active and enjoy interacting with others can also be nonassertive. Whenever you do not stand up for your rights or do not work to satisfy your needs and wants because they conflict with the rights or needs of others, you are being nonassertive. While this is appropriate in some situations, the frequent, habitual use of nonassertive behavior usually causes loss of self-respect and self-esteem. It is difficult to think well of yourself when your needs are not being met and others are trampling on your dignity and disregarding your rights.

Nonassertiveness sometimes results in passive-aggressive behavior. This is getting back at someone indirectly such as by forgetting an important commitment or being late. When people are unable to fulfill needs and wants in a direct manner, they sometimes resort to sulking or crying. Others develop a seesaw pattern in which they swing back and forth between nonassertive and aggressive behavior. People with a general nonassertive pattern often blame others for their problems and refuse to take responsibility for the quality of their lives. They may even play the role of martyr.

Whenever you choose nonassertive behavior, you choose definite irritation within yourself instead of possible irritation to others. Because a nonassertive response encourages unwanted behavior from others, it blocks improvement in undesirable situations. In fact, it usually guarantees that relationships and events will remain the same.

Aggressive Behavior

The goal of aggressive behavior is to gain control or power. When you are aggressive, you express needs and wants freely but in a hostile, tactless, or angry manner. You stand up for your own rights and work to satisfy your needs and wants; however, the rights, needs, and wants of others are ignored whenever they interfere with what you want.

In harsh conditions, aggressive behavior can often aid in survival. In modern, stable, democratic societies, though, aggressive behavior can be as self-defeating as nonassertive behavior. People who are the object of aggressive behavior usually feel as if they are being attacked. Sometimes this intimidates them and they do what the aggressive person wants. Other times, aggressive behavior causes others to become hostile and resist cooperating with or helping the aggressive person. In either case, aggressive people are usually avoided. As a result, aggressive people are often as troubled about their inability to make or keep friends as are shy people. Sometimes, after mistreating others or failing to solve an interpersonal conflict in a satisfying manner, they feel guilt and dejection.

Assertive Behavior

The goal of assertive behavior is to resolve conflicts in a way that is satisfying for both you and others. When you are assertive, you express problems, feelings, needs, and wants in a way that is both self-satisfying and socially effective. You respect the rights and dignity of both yourself and others. There is a personal focus on reasonable compromise rather than on winning. Solutions are sought that everyone can agree on.

Many people think that aggressive and assertive behavior are the same. The confusion may derive from the fact that much is said in books and workshops about changing nonassertive behavior into assertive behavior, while little is said about changing aggressive behavior into assertive behavior. Assertive and aggressive behavior both involve expressing yourself freely, standing up for your rights, and working to satisfy your needs and wants. However, an aggressive approach ignores the rights, needs, and wants of others, while the opposite is true of an assertive approach.

One common roadblock to being assertive is anger. The angrier you are, the more aggressive you will be. Another common roadblock to assertiveness is irrational thinking. There are many irrational beliefs about assertiveness that can keep you from asserting yourself. These are explored in the next section. Irrational thinking that blocks assertiveness can also be generated by an excessive need for approval, a fear of being incompetent, or a fear of losing control.

Two common myths often associated with assertiveness are that being assertive is always the best way to resolve a conflict, and that assertive people can get whatever they want. While an assertive approach is usually best in social situations and societies where people have equal rights and have similar power, it is not always the most appropriate or most effective way to resolve a conflict. There are occasional situations where aggressive behavior is appropriate, such as when there is imminent danger to life or property, or when a person or group will respond only to an aggressive approach. There are also occasional situations where nonassertive behavior is appropriate— usually those where the cost of asserting yourself in terms of time, energy, or resulting negative consequences outweighs the benefits you would receive. This is especially true for people who live in societies where there are large discrepancies in rights between socioeconomic classes.

As you become more assertive, you find assertiveness occasionally makes situations worse. At other times it has no effect. In most situations, however, an assertive style is the most effective and gratifying way to bring about positive change. Even when no change takes place, you usually feel better for having spoken up. The main question to consider when deciding whether you want to be assertive is, "Do I wish to risk the possibility of irritating others, or do I choose to definitely irritate myself by holding my feelings in and doing nothing?" In making that choice it helps to remember that when you use a truly assertive style, those who matter won't mind, and those who do mind seldom matter.

Common Irrational Beliefs About Assertiveness

Many different types of irrational beliefs can keep a person from being assertive. These irrational beliefs are usually concerned with the "worst possible" outcomes of being assertive. Several common ones are listed below. The first set generate nonassertive behavior; the second, aggressive behavior. Check any that reflect how you have felt during conflicts.

Beliefs That Generate Nonassertive Behavior

- If I assert myself, others will become angry or upset with me.
- If I assert myself and people become angry or upset, I may not be able to handle the situation.
- It is wrong and selfish to refuse the requests of others. If I allow myself to be selfish in this way, it makes me a bad person.
- I must avoid asking questions or making statements that might make me look stupid or ignorant.
- Assertive people are cold and selfish. If I'm assertive, I'll be so unpleasant that people will not like me.
- I prefer others to be open and straightforward with me. If I'm straightforward and open with others, though, I will hurt them.
- If what I do hurts others, I am responsible for their feelings regardless of my intentions and how I acted. (Common variation: I should be able to find a way of acting that will not hurt others.)

Beliefs That Generate Aggressive Behavior

- If I "give in" in any way, it means the other person has won and is taking advantage of me.
- My solutions and methods are best. If they are not accepted, I am a failure.
- In many ways people are my adversaries. They are trying to take away what is mine.
- I must always be on guard and fight or I'll lose what is mine.
- I must always be strong. If I compromise, it means I am weak.
- I always need to be in control. If others get their way, it means I am not in control.

As you work through this lesson, record any irrational beliefs about conflict you identify in yourself and develop rational self-talk responses you can use to challenge them.

Your Rights and Responsibilities

To be assertive, you need to believe in both your individual rights and the rights of others. People who grow up in families or societies

278 / Anxiety, Phobias, and Panic

that teach them that they have few rights usually find it difficult to assert themselves. The key for them to become more assertive is to develop a belief in their rights. Likewise, people who do not value others and who are self-centered usually find it easy to be aggressive. They need to develop an active belief that others deserve to be treated with dignity and respect.

This balance between rights and responsibilities is summarized below. Rights are shown in standard type; responsibilities in italic. As you read these rights and responsibilities, check statements that make you uncomfortable or do not reflect your normal behavior.

- I have the right to be treated with dignity and respect.
- *I have the responsibility to treat others with the same dignity and respect I desire from them.*

- I have the right to decide what is best for me.
- *I have the responsibility to allow others to decide what is best for them.*

- I have the right to have and express my own feelings and opinions.
- *I have the responsibility to express those feelings and opinions in a way that does not insult or put others down.*

- I have the right to ask for what I want and need.
- *I have the responsibility to allow others the right to refuse my request even though I might not like being refused.*

- I have the right to say no without feeling guilty.
- *I have the responsibility to allow others the right to say no.*

- I have the right to be listened to and taken seriously.
- *I have the responsibility to listen to others and take them seriously.*

- I have the right to make mistakes.
- *I have the responsibility to accept the consequences of those mistakes.*

- I have the right to all of my human weaknesses and limitations without guilt or shame.
- *I have the responsibility to allow others their weaknesses without ridiculing or resenting them.*

- I have the right to do what is necessary to protect my physical and mental health even though this sometimes requires nonassertive or aggressive behavior and discomfort in others.
- *I have the responsibility to do this in a way that causes the least amount of harm to both myself and others.*

If you checked any of the above statements, identify the irrational beliefs you hold that makes them difficult to accept. Then develop rational self-talk you can use to challenge your irrational thinking. If you are frequently nonassertive, practice reciting the rights you checked until they become comfortable and are reflected in your behavior. If you are frequently aggressive, practice reciting the responsibilities you checked until they become a firm part of your belief system and are reflected in your behavior.

The DERN Approach: An Effective Assertive Method for Resolving Conflicts

The DERN approach is an effective four-step assertive approach you can use to resolve most conflicts. *DERN* stands for "describe, express, request, and negotiate." These words describe each of the four steps used in this approach:

- *Describe* the problem behavior or situation.
- *Express* your thoughts or feelings.
- *Request* the changes or actions you want.
- *Negotiate* for a mutually satisfying solution.

Before you assert yourself, ask yourself "What do I want?" and "What is keeping me from getting what I want?" After you answer these questions, you are ready to use the DERN approach.

The first step in the DERN approach is to develop a short script that includes the approach's first three parts. This will be called a DER script. Your DER script is a simple and effective way to tell another person what you see and want in an assertive manner. Detailed guidelines that describe how to create each part of a DER script are given below.

D: DESCRIBE the problem behavior or situation.

- Describe the other person's behavior or actions objectively. Example: "You have been late three times this week."
- *Avoid vague words or descriptions. Example: "Sometimes you are so irresponsible."*

- Focus on one well-defined behavior or problem that you want to deal with now in specific, simple terms. Example: "The car needs a tune-up."
- *Avoid generalizing for all time. Example: "You never take care of the car."*

- Describe specific times and places where the problem occurs in a short, clear manner. The description should clarify the situation, not complicate it. For behaviors that have occurred repeatedly, focus only on the last two or three specific times they have occurred. Example: "I have asked three times during the past week to be shown how to operate the duplicator, but I still have not been shown."
- *Avoid mind reading or psychoanalyzing the other person by guessing at motives, goals, attitudes, or intentions. Example: "You seem to be afraid of teaching me how to operate the duplicator. You must want to be the only one who knows how to do it."*

E: EXPRESS your thoughts or feelings.

- Express your thoughts or feelings as your own without blaming or putting the other person down. Examples: "I'm concerned because my supervisor has commented about my being late." "I am really frustrated when this happens."
- *Avoid denying or holding your feelings in.*

- Keep your wording low-key and aim for emotional restraint rather than dramatic impact. Example: "That really annoys me."
- *Avoid unleashing emotional outbursts. Example: "I'm truly outraged at such behavior. People like you should be shot!"*

- Express your thoughts and feelings in a low-key, positive manner. Example: "It makes me angry when you refuse to speak to me. I feel like you don't care."
- *Avoid words that ridicule or shame, along with swearwords and labels such as dumb, selfish, and idiotic. Example: "You're cruel and heartless to treat me like this."*

- Stay focused on the specific offending behavior rather than on the whole person. Example: "It really annoys me to find a mess in my work area. It means that I have to take time to clean it up before I can start and that makes it more difficult for me to finish on time. "
- *Avoid attacking the character or personality of the person. Example: "If you were capable of organizing your time, you'd be able to get things done and things wouldn't always end up in my work area."*

R: REQUEST the changes or actions you want.

- Make a direct, clear and explicit request for a change or action. Example: "I need you to be here no later than three fifteen today."
- *Avoid only implying or hinting that you'd like a change. Example: "It would be nice to be surprised today."*

- When dealing with behavior, request only a small change. "I need this area to be kept clean."
- *Avoid asking for major changes in a person's character or personality. Example: "You need to learn how to be more organized."*

- Request only one or, at most, two changes or actions at one time. Example: "Would you give me a five-minute warning before you want to leave?"

- *Avoid demanding many changes or actions. Example: "I want you to stop asking me to leave at the last moment. And don't be so picky when we're out in public. That reminds me, I've been meaning to tell you . . ."*

- Describe the specific actions you want stopped and those you want to see performed. Example: "Please keep the door closed and be as quiet as you can in the morning."
- *Avoid asking for changes or actions in vague or general terms. Example: "Please be more considerate in the morning."*

- Consider whether the other person can meet your request without suffering large losses. Can you reasonably expect the other person to agree to your request? Example: "Please do not smoke in the car while we drive to work."
- *Avoid asking only for your own satisfaction while ignoring the other person's needs. Example: "You need to stop smoking and air out this car."*

A DER script is usually most effective when each part is only one or two sentences long. While your goal is to describe your perceptions and feelings accurately and make a clear request, this is best done with as few words as possible. If your script is too long, the other person usually stops listening and begins to rehearse a response. The following three examples show how this can be done using the above guidelines.

Example 1: Asking for Help

Situation: Sophia had just returned to work after a period of unemployment. During this time she assumed a major portion of the household chores. These chores were too much to continue doing after she returned to work. Sophia's goal was to have her spouse assist her more.

DESCRIBE the problem behavior or situation: "Since I returned to work two weeks ago, you have continued to do the same amount of work around the house that you did when I was out of work."

EXPRESS your feelings: "I am feeling overwhelmed and cannot continue to do all of the chores I did when I was not working."

REQUEST the changes or action you want: "I would like you to help me with the daily dishes and watering the yard. Will you help me and do these chores?"

Example 2: Saying No to Unreasonable Behavior

Situation: Ramon had a friend who was constantly dropping by without first calling despite many hints that he would like the friend to call first. This occurred two or three times a week, and the friend would stay for two or three hours each visit.

DESCRIBE the problem behavior or situation: "For the past month you have been dropping by two or three times a week to visit without calling me first. You then stay for two or three hours to visit."

EXPRESS your feelings: "I value our friendship but am becoming frustrated and annoyed because I never know when you are coming and there are things I want to finish that are being left undone."

REQUEST the changes or actions you want: "I would like you to call before you drop by."

Example 3: Asking for Understanding

Situation: Mia was recovering from panic disorder with agoraphobia. She was working on a regular basis with gradual in vivo exposure and had overcome most of the avoidance behaviors that had developed during the time she was agoraphobic. She was feeling very good about her progress but still had one major goal left: driving by herself. Mia's spouse wanted her to start driving by herself as soon as possible and was beginning to become very critical about the amount of time it was taking for Mia to reach her final goal.

DESCRIBE the problem behavior or situation: "During the past few weeks you have asked me at least once a day, 'When are you going to start driving by yourself?'"

EXPRESS your feelings: "I feel that I am under a lot of pressure whenever we talk about my driving. I also feel hurt because it seems like I'm not given any credit for all the effort I've put forth and all the progress I've made in other areas."

REQUEST the changes/actions you want: "I would like you to stop asking me when I will start driving by myself and let me follow the exposure plan I've developed at my own pace. This will help me reach this goal more quickly and make it more enjoyable to talk with you."

A complete DER script is often used to set the stage for the final phase of the DERN approach—negotiation. This is illustrated in Examples 1 and 3 above, where the DER scripts used by Sophia and Mia flowed into a negotiation phase. Sometimes, however, a DER script is used to set limits as was done by Ramon in Example 2. Ramon was not willing to negotiate on his need to have his friend call before visiting. Even when this is the case, a DER script is usually the best way to state your perceptions and needs clearly and objectively.

When dealing with simpler problems, it is often only necessary to use one or two parts of the DER script. Often a simple and direct description of a problem is all that is needed when the solution to a problem is obvious. For example, saying, "That cup leaks," will prevent most people from using a defective cup. If you have a specific action you want taken, add a request such as, "That cup leaks. Please use the blue one instead." The combination of a clear description with a direct but polite request can be used to resolve many simple everyday situations. Here are two more examples:

- This shirt was not sewn properly (describe). I would like to return it (request).
- Greenback Lane is under construction and the traffic is backed up (describe). Let's go by way of Madison Avenue (request).

The best way to become skilled with DER scripts is to create written scripts and rehearse them. The advantage of a written script is that you can check it against the guidelines given earlier and revise it if it doesn't follow them. When you recite a script, pretend that you are actually talking to the person for whom it is meant. Try to look and sound assertive as you rehearse your script. Continue practicing like this until it is easy for you to create effective DER scripts. With time and practice, DER scripts become your normal way of stating your perceptions and making requests.

The main roadblock to using DER scripts is strong emotion. Whenever you are angry or upset, take time to regain control of yourself so you can think rationally. If you are extremely upset, you may have to go someplace where you can be alone in order to cool down. As you cool down, you will find the creation of a DER script helps to focus your thoughts on constructive actions.

The Final Step: Negotiate

The fourth step of the DERN approach, negotiation, is usually required when you are working with complex or persistent problems. When this is the case, you will be a more effective negotiator if you consider the following before you begin negotiating:

- *How important is this issue?* Decide what a specific change in the other person's behavior or a specific action is worth to you. How much discomfort will you experience if the situation continues unchanged, and what benefits will you experience if your request is met?
- *What am I willing to do?* In most situations it is unreasonable to demand that only one person change or act. The concessions you are willing to make are your "bargaining chips" during a negotiation session.
- *What might this person ask for?* Most of the time you know the person with whom you will be negotiating. Considering this person's past behavior and what he or she might request reduces the chance of being caught off guard by surprise maneuvers.
- *Will the other person be willing to negotiate with me in good faith? If not, what negative consequences (punishments) can I use?* Fortunately, most negotiations do not require the use of negative consequences. When they *are* required, however, it is important that they be something you are both willing and able to carry out. Exaggerated or unrealistic threats you can't or won't carry out usually backfire.

Once you have considered the above, you are ready to negotiate. Negotiations are essentially a five-step problem-solving session:

Step 1: Describe the problem or difficulty you are having and state your request. The best way to make your needs and wants known in a way that causes the least amount of resistance is to use a DER script.

Step 2: Identify the other person's perceptions, needs, and wants. As soon as you finish delivering your DER script, others usually state their perceptions, needs, and wants. It is essential to take time for this before you begin negotiating. People are usually not willing to negotiate until they believe you have heard their position. The best way to understand others and convey to them that you have heard and understand them is to use active listening. Active listening is different from passive listening, where you just listen to a person without much response. With active listening, you reflect feelings, clarify points that are unclear, and periodically paraphrase what was said. If this is difficult for you, Appendix 5 describes how to develop three basic active listening skills. These skills are easy to learn and promote successful negotiations. They also prove beneficial in many other areas of life.

Shifting between stating your ideas and listening to the other person usually continues throughout the entire negotiation process. The better you are at shifting between these two opposite but complementary activities, the more successful you will be at negotiating.

Step 3: Generate possible solutions. After everyone's needs and wants are identified, it is time to generate possible solutions. One way to do this is brainstorming—a technique used by government and business professionals as well as by scientists. Everyone involved in the negotiation session offers as many potential solutions as possible. Avoid evaluating solutions while you are in the process of generating alternatives. Evaluating solutions as they are suggested stifles the creative process of thinking up new and different ways of resolving a problem.

Step 4: Evaluate possible alternatives and agree on the best solution. After several possible solutions have been suggested, evaluate them for practicality, the degree to which they satisfy everyone's needs, and the degree to which they are agreeable to everyone involved. During this phase, avoid focusing only on your needs. Keep both the other person's and your own needs in mind. At the same time, avoid feeling responsible for taking care of the other person's needs to the exclusion of your own.

The best solution is one that leaves everyone feeling satisfied. Avoid solutions that cause people to feel that someone has won and someone has lost. Your goal is to make everyone have a feeling of being a winner. While this is not always possible, the closer you come to reaching this goal, the greater the chances are that the solution you arrive at will work.

The best way to arrive at a solution agreeable to everyone is to think in terms of competing needs rather than competing solutions. Sometimes a person has already decided upon a correct or best solution before negotiating. This person then tries to use the negotiation session to sell this solution. This usually doesn't work. One way to avoid this trap is to remember that there are usually many different solutions for a given problem that would satisfy everyone's needs and wants. The challenge is to identify them.

If none of the proposed solutions is adequate, do more brainstorming. If everyone is stuck, take a break; then start again. Taking a break is especially helpful when strong emotions have been generated.

It is sometimes necessary to encourage a person to cooperate and negotiate in good faith. Usually, the best way to do this is to concentrate on positive things the other person will enjoy when the problem is resolved. In a business setting you might stress the increased savings or productivity that will result. In personal relationships you might stress increased closeness, additional free time together, or your personal appreciation for the other person's consideration. In some cases you may even want to offer rewards for the changes or actions you want—for example, doing some of the other person's work in exchange for help with your project. If you offer rewards, select ones that are appropriate for the person with whom you are dealing. Avoid rewards that only you would find desirable or that you can't deliver. If you decide to try rewards, you may even want to ask what this person would find valuable.

Only resort to negative consequences when positive ones have failed to win cooperation. If you decide to use negative consequences, be sure they are ones you are both willing and able to carry out. If none is available and the other person remains uncooperative, an assertive approach may not be appropriate for this problem.

Step 5: Restate the agreement and, if appropriate, formalize it. Once an agreement has been reached, restate it so everyone understands what they have agreed to. Do not let embarrassment or discomfort over an emotionally sensitive problem pressure you into ending your negotiation session too quickly. If you fail to restate your agreement, you and the other person may walk away with different understandings of the agreement.

If you think the other person may try to back out of the agreement later, formalize it in writing. In counseling this is often done when working with couples or with parents and children. Even when you trust the other person, it is usually best to formalize business agreements in writing. This can be done through a simple memo, an exchange of letters, or a formal contract.

Whenever you reach a mutually satisfying solution through a negotiation process, thank the other person for agreeing to change or take action. If you have been negotiating with a person who has been difficult to deal with in the past, suggest that future conflicts or problems be handled in a similar manner. Avoid bringing up new problems at this time; this could jeopardize the gains you have just secured.

"I Language"

When you review the various examples in this and the following lesson, you will find that assertive people usually speak using "I messages." An "I message" is a statement that tells the listener what you see, think, feel, or want in an objective manner that does not assign blame or put the listener down. A statement that assigns blame or puts the listener down is often referred to as a "you message." Here are some examples of each.

> *You message:* "You're making so much noise it's driving me crazy. Why can't you be more considerate?"
> *I message:* "I would really like some peace and quiet for a while. Would you do that in the other room?"

> *You message:* "Look at this kitchen. You're such a slob. When are you going to be more responsible?"
> *I message:* "I would like you to clean up the things you used in the kitchen so I can cook."

Recommended Activities for Lesson 13

Challenge Irrational Ideas About Being Assertive

Your beliefs about assertiveness and the behaviors you use to resolve conflicts developed during childhood. Before reading farther, take a few moments to answer the following questions:

- How did each member of your family handle conflict?
- How did the adults in your childhood train you to deal with conflict?
- What were you told about conflict (for example, don't rock the boat; people won't like you if you're nasty; ladies never yell; gentlemen don't fight)?
- Did your siblings receive the same training and the same messages you did? If not, what was different?
- How did you get what you wanted directly (for example, by asking or taking)?
- How did you get what you wanted indirectly (for example, by hinting, whining, sulking, or having someone else ask for you)?
- Did you learn how to get what you wanted in any other ways?
- Which of these methods do you use today to get what you want?
- What types of messages or statements do you repeat to yourself when you are in conflict with others?

As you review your answers, what beliefs about conflict stand out? Are any of these beliefs still influencing your life today? As you identify irrational ideas you have about conflict and being assertive, record them in your journal along with examples of when they influence your behavior. Then develop rational self-talk responses you can use to challenge them. Refer to earlier lessons if this is difficult. Once you have developed your rational responses, memorize them. Whenever you are in a situation where you are finding it difficult to assert yourself, recall the rational responses you developed.

Practice Reciting Rights or Responsibilities That Support New Behaviors

You can master all the assertive skills in this lesson, but you will not use them in your daily life if you do not believe in a balance of rights and responsibilities. Reread the list of rights and responsibilities and make a list of those that need to become a firm part of your beliefs. Recite them at least once daily until they are reflected in your behavior. If you tend to be nonassertive, you will need to focus on your rights. If you tend to be aggressive, you will need to focus on your responsibilities.

Practice Creating and Rehearsing DER Scripts

During this week, create and rehearse at least five different DER scripts. These scripts can be for current situations or for ones that have occurred during the past few weeks. Write out each script so you can compare it with the guidelines given in the lesson. If your scripts do not follow the guidelines, rewrite them so they do. If this is difficult for you, have someone you know and trust who is skilled at being assertive help you.

In order to develop skill in delivering your scripts, have practice sessions during which you pretend you are saying your script to the person for whom it is intended. The more difficult you find this sort of practice, the more you need to do it. You can practice creating and rehearsing scripts while driving, doing housework, or in any other private situation. Include practice sessions in front of a mirror so you can actually see what you look like as you deliver your script. The most powerful type of practice is to rehearse with a study partner you trust. During all your practice sessions, work at making your tone of voice and body language match the assertive words you are using. In essence, you are desensitizing yourself to assertive behavior so it does not seem strange or frightening.

Do not begin using your DER scripts in real-life situations just yet. Wait until after you have completed Lesson 14. In this lesson your focus is on learning how to create and deliver DER scripts. Lesson 14 teaches you how to respond to the resistance you will encounter when you assert yourself. During the time you are working with this lesson, create scripts for as many different types of situations as you can. Then rehearse them until it is easy to act in a confident, assertive manner.

Evaluate Your Negotiation Skills

Recall several situations where you negotiated for a change in someone's behavior or for something you wanted. Review the five-step negotiation process described in the lesson and identify actions you could take to improve your next negotiation session with some- one. Mentally rehearse those actions until you find them easy to use during actual negotiations. If you feel your listening skills are weak, read Appendix 5 and do the exercises it outlines.

Develop Skill with Simple Requests and Statements That Violate Your Rights and Dignity

There are many subtle ways in which a simple statement or request can violate your rights and dignity. People who are nonassertive often do not even recognize them. Many others recognize them but find it difficult to respond with an appropriate assertive reply. Seven common situations that violate your rights or dignity are listed below, along with possible assertive replies. As you read each one, notice that an assertive reply is one that is not angry or hostile. It is calm and polite but still shows the other person that you do not allow your rights or dignity to be disregarded.

Responding to Violating Statements

Type of Statement or Request	Example	An Effective Assertive Reply	Example
Being put on the spot	"Are you busy tonight?"	Answer with a question that requests the reason.	"What did you have in mind?" "Why do you ask?"
Receiving unwanted advice	"If I were you . . ." or "You should . . ."	Deny the "if" and affirm you are the one that has to make right decisions for yourself.	"That might be right for you but . . ."
Violation of privacy	"Maybe I shouldn't ask, but . . ."	Set your own limits; or answer with a question that requests the reason.	"I really don't care to say." "Why do you want to know that?"
Vague remarks or criticism	"You have been so defensive lately."	State your own opinion with a simple response; or ask for concrete examples.	"I don't think so." "Exactly what have I done that makes you say that?"
Insulting labels for your behavior	"That's a dumb thing to do."	Refuse to accept the label.	"I don't think so."
Having the worth of your choices questioned	"Do you really think that shirt suits you?"	Emphasize your right and ability to make personal judgments.	"Yes, I think it suits me just fine."
Negative predictions based on observations of your personality	"You're not assertive enough for the job."	Ask for clarification of the observation; or affirm your ability to judge your own strengths and abilities.	"In what way do you think I am not assertive enough?" "That may be how you see it, but I think I'll do just fine."

If you have difficulty in asserting yourself in these types of situations, do the following:

• Make a list of simple statements and requests you have encountered that violated your rights and dignity or which made you uncomfortable. Record the response you made to each statement.

• If you did not like your response, develop an assertive reply using the above suggestions. You can get many other useful ideas by listening to assertive people you know respond to similar situations. If you know someone with a positive assertive style, ask this person how he or she would respond to situations that are difficult for you. Record any responses you like. Remember that a given situation can have many different assertive responses that would be appropriate.

As you do this exercise, remember that it is meant only for situations where your dignity and rights have been violated by simple statements or requests. More complex conflict situations or problems require a DER script or the full DERN approach.

As with past lessons, take your time and do the exercises in this lesson as thoroughly as possible before going on to the next one.

LESSON 14

Staying on Track

The last lesson focused on expressing your thoughts and needs in an assertive manner using a DER script. This lesson shows you how to stay on track when others resist your assertive efforts. It also explores when and where it is more appropriate to be nonassertive or aggressive than assertive.

Seven Common Tactics That Can Sabotage Your Assertive Efforts

When you assert yourself and make a request, others often use one or more of the following tactics to resist your assertive efforts. Sometimes this is a deliberate effort to sidetrack your assertive efforts. More commonly, however, it is an automatic behavior learned early in life as a way to avoid doing something that they don't want to do or to avoid dealing with an issue they don't want to deal with. From time to time, you might also use these tactics yourself to resist the requests of others. There is nothing wrong with this reaction. It is a normal human response when faced with something you'd rather not deal with. However, the next time you notice yourself using one of these tactics, decide whether you could accomplish the same goal more effectively by using the assertiveness skills discussed in Lesson 13.

Avoiding Discussion of Your Request

The first and most direct way to avoid dealing with your request is to simply postpone the discussion. Two different approaches can be used to overcome this tactic: Push to discuss your request immediately, or have the other person specify a time and place where it can be discussed. If you push to discuss your request immediately, you may find an assertive approach called "yes, but" helpful. Acknowledge the other person's position, then say "but" to emphasize your need or perception. Occasionally, it is useful to specify the consequences of not discussing your request. Here are examples of each of these approaches.

Tactic	Response
"Some other time, I'm busy."	"I realize you're busy, but this is very important and won't take long."
"I'm too tired to talk now."	"I can understand that; however, before I let you go I need to know when we can talk and resolve this problem."
"I don't have time to think about that now."	"It really won't take long, and if we don't discuss this now much time will be lost because of the problems it will cause."

A second and more indirect method to avoid dealing with your request is to sidetrack the discussion with irrelevant comments or questions. There are three different ways to overcome this tactic: Ignore the distraction, dismiss the distracting comment with a short statement, or give a quick answer. After using one of these approaches, repeat your request and continue toward your assertive goal.

Tactic	Response
"You're lovely when you're angry."	(Comment is ignored) "What I need is . . ."
"By the way, Mr. Smith came by yesterday."	"That's not important now; however, as I was saying, we do need to decide on . . ."
"Don't you have work to do?"	"Yes, but it can wait until we're finished. As I was saying . . ."

Challenging Your Description

A person will sometimes try to sidetrack you from your assertive goal by challenging your description of the problem behavior or situation. Concentrating on specific behaviors and actions minimizes the chances of this occurring. If you have specified behaviors and actions and your description is still challenged, however, do not become sidetracked by arguing who is correct. Instead, turn the challenge aside by acknowledging that your perception is different from the other person's, then repeat your request. The "yes, but" approach is often an effective way to do this.

Tactic	Response
"That's not the way it happened."	"I can see that we have different ideas about what happened. In any event, I need . . ."
"You've got it all wrong."	"That may very well be how you see things. However, I still feel it is important to . . ."

Refusing to Accept Responsibility

Sometimes a person tries to avoid taking action or discussing a problem by refusing to accept responsibility for either the creation or resolution of a problem. Here are four common ways in which this is done.

Blaming

There are two types of blaming: You are blamed for the problem behavior or situation, or the problem is blamed on something other than you. Blaming is similar to challenging your description in that it centers on your description of the problem behavior or situation. Since the problem is seen as being caused by you or someone else, the other person views him- or herself as having no responsibility to take corrective action. The most effective way to deal with blaming is to avoid focusing on who is to blame and concentrate on your request.

Tactic	Response
"You didn't tell me to do that."	"That's true. However, I still need . . ."
"You forgot to remind me."	"That's not the issue. What I want . . ."
"The freight company always seems to mess up."	"I can see the problems that would cause, but I still need . . ."

"Everybody Does It"

Using the argument that "everybody does it" justifies a refusal to consider your problem seriously. The "yes, but" approach can be used to counter this tactic in either of two ways: Acknowledge this view without endorsing it then repeat your request, or redefine the situation in terms of your individual needs.

Tactic	Response
"Everybody drives fast."	"That may be; however, I am very uncomfortable when we are going this fast and I would like . . ."
"You're the first person to complain about my writing."	"That may be, but I find your writing very difficult to read and would like . . ."

Reinterpreting

A person will sometimes reinterpret the problem behavior or situation in such a way that there seems to be a misinterpretation or lack of information on your part. When this happens, a simple exchange of opinions or information often achieves your goals. However, people can also reinterpret their behavior as being based on good intentions and therefore excusable. When this happens, use "yes, but" to acknowledge the other person's stated good intentions and repeat your request.

Tactic	Response
"I wasn't really serious."	"That may be, but I feel . . ."
"I was trying to help you."	"That may have been your intention, but I think . . ."

Psychoanalyzing

A person may try to redefine the problem behavior or situation in terms of a psychological problem you possess. This is often someone who knows you well or who has some knowledge of psychology. Psychological explanations like these are usually inaccurate and often a subtle put-down. It is easy to become sidetracked by this tactic since the explanation offered may sound logical or deal with an issue that concerns you. Avoid becoming involved in an argument over the explanation. Simply affirm your own ability to assess your actions and personality then press on with your request.

Tactic	Response
"It seems you're becoming very paranoid."	"I think my behavior is perfectly normal. Now as I was saying . . ."
"You've been getting pretty uppity since that assertive workshop."	"I have been finding it easier to express myself. In any case, I need . . ."
"You've just got an inferiority complex."	"I can understand how you might feel that way, but I still feel . . ."

Triggering Guilt or Embarrassment

Here are four common tactics that can sabotage your assertive efforts by triggering guilt and embarrassment.

Tears

Tears can be very manipulative. Do not allow this form of "water power" to make you feel guilty about sticking up for your rights. If crying interferes too much with your DER scripts, write it out as a letter or memo that can be read in your absence.

Tactic	Response
"You're making me feel like an awful shrew."	"I'm sorry you choose to feel that way. However, I feel . . ."

Offended Martyr

Another guilt-producing tactic is to play the offended martyr. A martyr frequently makes accusations or describes your behavior as being "mean" or "cruel." Refuse to accept this interpretation and redefine your behavior objectively. Then persist in your assertive efforts. Avoid becoming sidetracked by arguments over your motives and remain focused on what you want.

Tactic	Response
"You're so mean to talk to me like that."	"I am not being mean; I am just describing what I see. Now what I want . . ."

Physical Symptoms

A person might use distressing physical symptoms as an excuse to avoid discussing your request. If you assume responsibility for causing this person's physical symptoms, your guilt can also prevent you from confronting this person in the future. Deal with this tactic in the same manner as you would postponing or sidetracking: Either negotiate a specific time to discuss the problem or press to discuss the matter now despite the physical symptoms. If the physical symptoms interfere too much with your DER script, send a letter or memo that can be read in your absence.

Tactic	Response
"Let's not talk now, I'm getting this terrible headache."	"When do you think you will be feeling better?" or "I'm sorry to hear that, but this won't take long."

Excessive Apologies

Do not feel guilty or embarrassed if a person begins to offer excessive apologies upon hearing your description of a problem. Simply accept the other person's apology and continue with your request.

Tactic	Response
"I'm so sorry! I should have never let that happen. How could I be so thoughtless."	"I'm glad you're sorry and I accept your apology. Now I feel we need to decide how . . ."

Intimidation

Intimidation is one of the more difficult tactics to overcome because it often triggers strong negative emotions inside you. This can cause you to either back away from your assertive goal or adopt an aggressive style that leads to a fight. In either case, you fail to get what you want. When you are going to deal with an intimidating person, take time before the meeting to do the following: Review both your rights and responsibilities, identify and develop effective rational challenges for irrational thinking associated with this person, develop and rehearse a DER script, and identify and practice the specific approaches described in this lesson that would be the most effective with this person. Here are five common types of intimidation.

Verbal Abuse or Name-Calling

There are many forms of verbal abuse, such as sarcasm, criticism, jokes, ridicule, insults, and swearing. The most effective approach to name-calling is to ignore it and continue pressing for what you want. If you do choose to redefine an inaccurate or slanderous remark, do so in a restrained way; you do not want to become involved in a fight that sidetracks you from your assertive goal.

Tactic	Response
"You must be losing your grip."	(Comment is ignored) "Furthermore, I think . . ."
"What makes a nitwit like you think you can tell me what to do?"	"I am not trying to tell you what to do. What I am trying to do is solve the problem of . . ."
"You're acting like Wonder Woman."	"You may think any way you want, but I need . . ."

Hostile or Negative Body Language

Sometimes people use their face, body, or tone of voice to convey the message that your assertive approach is angering, boring, or hurting them. Deal with this tactic by either commenting on the nonverbal message, or by ignoring it and continuing with your assertive efforts. If you comment on a nonverbal message, you may need to switch to your listening skills before continuing.

Tactic	Response
The other person looks very upset and unhappy.	(Nonverbal message is ignored) "Now about the problem of . . ."
The other person frowns and looks angry.	"You seem angry about what I am saying."

Interrogation

Some people are very good at bombarding you with questions that sidetrack you from your assertive goal. There are two ways to deal with this: Give a quick response, or dismiss the questions and requests for justifications as either irrelevant or unimportant. In either case you then quickly return to your request.

Tactic	Response
"Do you really think this is necessary?"	"Yes. What I want is . . ."
"Why is it so important to you?"	"I do not have to justify my feelings." or "That's just the way I feel."

Debating

Some people are very adept at using superior knowledge or logic to overwhelm others. When you are making a request, there is one thing that is always more powerful than knowledge or logic—your feelings. You do not need to justify or logically explain them. Simply state that while you understand they may seem illogical, it is the way you feel. Then proceed to press for your assertive goal.

Tactic	Response
"You are being totally illogical."	"I understand that it seems illogical to you. However, I still feel very strongly . . ."

Postponing a Decision

Sometimes a person appears ready to listen and agrees to negotiate but then postpones making a decision. This type of procrastination is actually a subtle form of non-negotiation. If you are not sure whether a postponement is sincere or merely a procrastinating tactic, grant one postponement before using one of the two following assertive approaches:

- *Set a deadline for making a decision without further delay:* If the person tries to put you off again when the deadline arrives, you are dealing with a non-negotiator. Approaches to use with non-negotiators are described in the next section.

- *Insist on a tentative immediate agreement with the provision for further negotiation:* Your basic message is, "I want a temporary agreement now. Then, unless you discuss and agree upon a different solution by _____, the agreement we make now goes into effect." A variation of this approach is the conditional contract. Use a conditional contract when the other person insists on a consultation for an expert opinion. Anticipate the possible opinions that might be obtained and plan your actions accordingly. Your basic message is: "If the expert's opinion is X, we will _____; if it is Y, we will _____." Make sure you agree on a specific time to obtain the consultation and set a deadline for the final decision. Remember, you have the right to be present at any consultation that affects you and to hear the consultant's advice directly rather than from the person with whom you are negotiating.

The Non-Negotiator

Most people respond positively to the approaches you are studying. However, anyone who continues to use the tactics discussed in this lesson to avoid or sidetrack your negotiation efforts is a non-negotiator. In addition to using the previous tactics, tough non-negotiators may also resort to one or more of the following.

"There Is No Problem"
With this tactic, the non-negotiator refuses to accept that a problem exists. If this person has some regard for your feelings, emphasize your feelings and how important the problem is for you.

Tactic	Response
"I just don't see what all the fuss is about."	"I know you don't believe there is a problem here, but I do and I feel very strongly about . . ."

"All Solutions Are Unacceptable"

Sometimes a non-negotiator continues to find all proposed solutions unacceptable. Try turning the task of developing an acceptable solution over to the other person. When you do this, set a deadline for this person to have one or more reasonable solutions ready to discuss.

Tactic	Response
"Frankly, none of these ideas seem workable."	"Well then, why don't we take a break and see if you can come up with some ideas which might be acceptable. How about meeting again after lunch to discuss them?"

"The Price for Change Is Too High"

Sometimes very aggressive or hostile people make unreasonable demands in order to meet your request. Try pointing out the unreasonableness of the demands. As you do this, emphasize both your feelings and the importance of the problem.

Tactic	Response
"That's what I need from you if this report is going to be on time."	"I feel that your request is unreasonable. This is a very important problem that requires us to cooperate in order for it to be resolved."

Refusal to Negotiate

Some non-negotiators refuse to even discuss your problem. If this occurs, focus on the other person's refusal to negotiate and use your assertiveness skills to get a commitment to discuss your problem.

If you have tried positive approaches and the other person continues to be a non-negotiator, two basic options remain: Use a more aggressive approach and specify the negative actions you will take if the problem is not resolved, or attempt to resolve your problem through one of the three nonassertive approaches discussed in the next section. If you decide to specify negative consequences, carefully consider your ability and willingness to carry them out. Failing to carry out a consequence that you have outlined usually makes non-negotiators even more unwilling to cooperate.

Five General Approaches for Resolving Problems and Conflicts

Lesson 13 stated that there were three basic ways to resolve conflict: You can become nonassertive, aggressive, or assertive. This section expands these three categories into five by describing three different nonassertive approaches: conform, withdraw, or select a substitute goal.

In order to be effective in life, you need to select and use the most appropriate approach for the situation you face. Sometimes a person will not use a particular approach because of a lack of skills. Other times a person has irrational beliefs that makes an approach unacceptable. Whenever an inappropriate approach is used to resolve a problem, the result is unnecessary stress and discomfort. For example, Judy refused to withdraw from a very negative job situation even though other jobs that paid equally well were available. For her, changing jobs was interpreted as failure and was totally unacceptable. She continued to try to change working conditions where she was even though improvement was hopeless and she experienced severe physical problems due to the stress.

As you read each of the following descriptions, be aware of any negative reactions you have. If you notice any, take a moment to identify the beliefs generating them. In addition, if you identify any approach you seldom or never allow yourself to use, list the beliefs that prevent you from using it. Whenever you identify irrational beliefs, develop rational self-talk responses you can use to challenge them. Be sure to record your work in your journal so you can refer back to it in the future.

Conform

The first nonassertive approach for resolving conflicts is to conform. You simply comply with the demands of others and go along with a situation without making any effort to change it. Conforming is often the best approach to use when the amount of discomfort you feel is small and the act of asserting yourself would either produce few results or result in more stress and conflict than is produced by having your needs and desires go unfulfilled. Three common types of situations where conforming is appropriate are: no-win situations involving inflexible bureaucracies such as the Internal Revenue Service, situations where you are in conflict with a person with higher rank or authority than you such as a judge or your boss, and situations in which you value another person's friendship and the issue involved is not very important to you.

When you choose to conform, you can reduce your discomfort by reexamining your beliefs and expectations about the situation and becoming more philosophical. This often requires you to identify and challenge should/must rules associated with the situation. While conforming is sometimes the best way to resolve a conflict, it is self-defeating when used as your main method of dealing with conflict. A person who continues to ignore needs and wants tends to experience more and more frustration, anger, and resentment. When not expressed directly, these feelings may be expressed inappropriately or create internal stress that slowly eats away at you both physically and mentally.

Withdraw

A second nonassertive approach for resolving conflict is to withdraw. You retreat from the problem situation and make no further attempt to resolve the conflict. This is an appropriate approach when other approaches are not working and you are experiencing stress and conflict that is or will become a destructive force in your body or daily life.

If you find it difficult to withdraw from no-win situations, use rational self-talk to convince yourself that withdrawal is often the best way to solve a problem that cannot be resolved through any other approach. Remind yourself that it is impossible to master every situation and successfully overcome every problem you face. As you use this type of rational self-talk, examine your beliefs. If you find it difficult to withdraw from no-win situations, it may be because you consider the act of withdrawing a sign of weakness or failure. This self-defeating attitude is often generated by a combination of perfectionistic, all-or-nothing thinking and the mistaken belief that worth is determined by achievement. A review of Lesson 6 will help you challenge this type of irrational thinking and convince yourself that knowing your limits and withdrawing when you have reached them is a sign of wisdom.

If withdrawal is one of your main methods for dealing with conflict, learn to be more assertive and stand up for your rights. Review the rights listed in Lesson 13 until they are a firm part of your belief system. Create and rehearse DER scripts until they become easy to create and comfortable to deliver.

Select a Substitute Goal

A third nonassertive approach is to select a substitute goal. When it is necessary to withdraw from a no-win situation or when an assertive goal is unattainable, you select a new goal. While this might seem like an obvious approach, many people find it difficult. This usually is because they have perfectionistic, all-or-nothing thinking patterns and should/must beliefs that cause them to consider anything less than their first choice as unacceptable.

Selecting a substitute goal is often the best approach to use when you are dealing with a non-negotiator and are either unwilling or unable to carry out negative consequences that would force cooperation. For example, Terry's co-worker had poor work habits that interfered with Terry's job. This person refused to recognize there was a problem or negotiate with Terry. Terry did not want to push the issue too hard since his supervisor did not want to get involved. Therefore, he decided to focus on a new goal of protecting himself from this fellow employee. Terry did this by reducing the amount of time he interacted with this person and by writing memos that put on record what was occurring whenever this person's poor work habits interfered with Terry's work. This minimized the effect this person had on Terry and his job.

The selection of a substitute goal can also be effective when personal goals are creating tremendous stress or disappointment. For example, Rose wanted very much to become a surgeon but did not have the grades or ability. She finally decided to satisfy her desire to be in medicine by becoming a physical therapist.

Become Aggressive

It is often appropriate to become aggressive when life or property is threatened or you are dealing with someone who is irrational or emotionally immature and will only respond to an aggressive approach. Unfortunately, this approach is either overused or used at inappropriate times by many people. Some use an aggressive approach as their main method for meeting everyday needs and resolving conflict. Others seesaw between an aggressive approach and one of the nonassertive approaches described above. This second group uses a nonassertive approach until the frustration and resentment resulting from denying needs and wants build to a point where they can no longer be denied. An aggressive approach is then used in an attempt to satisfy the needs and wants. The aggressive approach is also sometimes used to punish the person or persons viewed as being responsible for the deprivation.

If you use an aggressive approach as your primary method for resolving conflict, spend additional time developing assertiveness skills and learning to channel anger into constructive actions as described in Lessons 12 and 13. If you seesaw between nonassertive and aggressive behavior, spend additional time building self-esteem, becoming more in touch with your feelings, and developing assertiveness skills as described in Lessons 11, 12, and 13.

Become Assertive

In most situations it is best to ask for what you want in a polite, direct manner and resolve conflicts through the negotiation process described in Lesson 13. Working with the guidelines and exercises in these lessons is enough to enable most people to develop a more assertive style. If asserting yourself is very difficult, however, consider doing additional work with a book on assertiveness, attending one or more assertiveness workshops, or possibly even working with a therapist.

When Is an Assertive Approach Most Effective?

The best way to decide when an assertive approach would be effective is to think in terms of how much power you have. Power, in this sense, is the ability to influence others to act in the way you would like them to act.

Your assertive skills are most successful in situations where you have more power than the other person. This usually involves people who are providing a service or selling something such as salesclerks, repairmen, and waiters.

A more difficult type of situation involves people who have the same amount of power as you. Examples of these are friends, relatives, people who cut into line ahead of you, or people who are talking loudly on a phone in a public area. These types of people can sometimes be tough to deal with. Still, most will respond positively if you use an assertive approach.

The most difficult type of situation arises when the other person has more power than you. These types of people are usually authorities in law, business, or government such as judges, police officers, teachers, corporate bureaucrats, and doctors. While these types of people are often the most frustrating to deal with, they also usually respond positively when assertiveness skills are used.

If you are not sure about whether it would be best to assert yourself in a particular situation, ask yourself the following questions:

- *How irritating is this?* Take a moment to tune in to yourself and determine the amount of discomfort you are feeling. Remember, discomfort signifies that a need or want is being frustrated or threatened. The more discomfort you feel, the more important the need or want is and the more important it is to take action.
- *What is irritating me?* The next step is to determine what need or want is being frustrated or threatened, along with the source of this frustration or threat. If you are not sure, delay action; you may do more harm than good.
- *What can I do to satisfy that need or want or at least make it known?* Once you know what you want, decide who has the power to help you achieve it. Then identify the approach that has the greatest chance of success. This is the point at which many people become sidetracked by a desire to punish the person causing the discomfort or by a need to win. Winning

usually means proving you have more power and control than the person causing the discomfort. Both of these detours tend to be self-defeating exercises. Even when you succeed in winning or punishing the offending person, the victory is usually empty since you probably failed to satisfy your original need. You can help minimize the tendency to become detoured by keeping your assertive goal in mind. Keep asking yourself, "What do I want? What is the best way to achieve it?"

What to Do When People Fail to Keep Their Agreements

Sometimes you think you have resolved a problem with others; then they fail to keep the agreement. When this happens, consider the following:

- *Were the rewards or negative consequences you promised sufficient motivation?* If you only offered rewards, you may need to strengthen those rewards or consider negative consequences. If you said you would carry out negative consequences, do so. Some people need to know you are serious before they will act. Be willing to give people a second chance before considering them non-negotiators.
- *Are reminders needed because this person is naturally forgetful or very busy?* When you are dealing with issues that are important for you but unimportant to the other person, you may need to train this person to remember to carry out the agreement you made. This is especially true if this person is naturally forgetful or very busy with other activities. Since it is better to win cooperation than force submission, use cues or reminders in a friendly, encouraging manner rather than in a way that is felt to be a put-down or punishment. Also, remember that the closer the reminders are to the time the behavior or action is to be performed, the more effective they will be. While you may need to give several reminders at first, keep in mind that your

goal is to have the other person learn to keep the agreement without being reminded.

- *Are one or more automatic behaviors interfering with this person's ability to keep the agreement?* This is especially important if your request requires this person to change a deeply ingrained behavior such as smoking or swearing in your presence. When this is the case, adopt a tolerant attitude similar to what a sympathetic teacher has toward a struggling student. If the other person has made reasonable and well-intentioned attempts, reward this partial fulfillment of the agreement. Keep in mind how difficult it is to change many of the automatic behaviors you have been working on. If sufficient progress is not made after a reasonable length of time, decide whether the other person is willing to spend the time and energy needed to change and whether you have the time, energy, and willingness to continue assisting in this process. If not, consider an alternative solution.

- *Is there a factor you have overlooked that greatly influences this person's ability to keep the agreement?* Illness, work-related activities, and personal relationships are common factors that can prevent a person from keeping an agreement. If you identify a factor like this, reanalyze the problem, develop a new script, and try again. As you negotiate a new agreement, be sure to address the problem created by the factor you have identified.

If you have considered the above, made a reasonable effort to resolve your conflict assertively, and have made little or no progress, you are probably dealing with a non-negotiator. When evaluating behavior, *pay more attention to what a person does than to what a person says*. Past behavior is usually the best predictor of future behavior. The only exception is a person who is working in a systematic and dedicated manner to change old patterns as you are doing with this program. Be wary of entering into an agreement with someone whose track record indicates that he or she is untrustworthy and fails to keep agreements. If you make an agreement with a person like this, decide what you will do if the agreement is broken before you begin negotiating.

Resolving Conflicts with Businesses and Salespeople

If you use the following guidelines, you will find that your assertive skills will usually work well in situations where you receive defective merchandise or poor service:

- Identify the correct person to deal with—someone who has the power to help you.
- Lodge your complaint privately, or quietly if in a public setting.
- Register your complaint as soon after you notice the problem as possible.
- Be sure to have any and all receipts, supporting paperwork, or defective merchandise readily available for inspection.
- Keep in mind the various elements of the DERN approach. While all the guidelines are important, the four most essential ones to keep in mind are: make only one complaint at a time, avoid statements that may make the other person defensive, avoid apologizing for your complaint, and be specific as to what happened and what you want without generalizing with words like *always* or *never*. Remember: With simple problems, only the describe and request parts of a DER script may be required; with more complex problems, all four parts will probably be needed.
- Only complain about actions or defects that you think can be changed or corrected.
- Try to stay friendly as you register your complaint and say something complimentary about the other person or the situation. This helps minimize defensiveness in the other person.

Recommended Activities for Lesson 14
Continue Developing Basic Assertive Skills

Continue developing any of the skills presented in Lesson 13 that you feel are weak. These might include any of the following:

- Creating DER scripts.
- Responding to simple situations that violate your rights.
- Enhancing your listening skills.
- Developing negotiation skills.

If asserting yourself is difficult, continue reviewing the list of rights and responsibilities you checked in Lesson 13 each day. Also be sure to challenge irrational ideas you have about being assertive whenever you are using your assertive skills.

Practice the Skills Used to Overcome Sabotaging Tactics

Recall instances where it was difficult for you to assert yourself and identify the specific tactics other people used to sabotage your assertive efforts. Develop a DER script for each situation you recall and rehearse it several times. As you rehearse, imagine the other person interrupting you with the specific tactics this person used in the past. Then practice using one or more of the approaches suggested in this lesson for overcoming each tactic.

You can practice overcoming resistance from others in this way while driving, doing chores, or just about anywhere. If it is difficult for you to use the skills described in this lesson, however, spend time practicing with another person. As you do this, switch roles at times. Let your practice partner deliver your script as you pretend you are the person with whom you wish to be assertive. This allows you to see how your practice partner uses the skills you are studying. It also shows your practice partner how to role-play the person you have in mind when it's your turn to deliver your script. It is also effective to practice in front of a mirror. This helps you develop gestures and expressions that are assertive.

Begin Using Your Assertiveness Skills

Begin using the assertiveness skills you are developing. As you begin, remember to start with as many factors in your favor as possible. Learning to be assertive is similar to learning to play the piano.

Just as a piano student begins with easy pieces and gradually works up to more difficult works, start with small conflicts or needs, master them, and then go on to more difficult ones.

Have a Review Session of the Day's Problems and Conflicts

At the end of the day, spend a few minutes reviewing the problems and conflicts that occurred along with how you dealt with them. Do this daily for as long as you are working on developing your assertiveness skills. As you review your day, identify alternative approaches that might resolve similar conflicts or problems more effectively in the future. Practice skills you failed to use but would like to use in the future. You may even want to plan regular practice sessions for skills that are difficult. This type of review and practice increases your ability to use assertiveness skills in similar future situations.

Avoid using this review as an opportunity to condemn yourself because you "failed" to handle each situation in the "best" way or as it "should" have been handled. Remember that you handle each and every situation as best you can at the time it occurs. True, you sometimes forget to use some of your skills, but that is only human and is to be expected.

Developing assertive skills takes time and practice. Spend at least one week with this lesson—longer if asserting yourself is difficult.

Lesson 15

Continuing Your Growth

This is the final lesson in the program—but it is far from the end of your journey. As you choose and carry out one of the plans described in this lesson, you will probably find that your ability to manage anxiety effectively will continue to increase for many months to come. So you have not really come to an ending, but to the beginning of a new life.

Three Plans for Continuing Your Growth

The rate at which people working through these lessons overcome their anxiety-related problems varies greatly. By this lesson, some feel they have completely overcome their self-defeating behaviors and are managing anxiety effectively, while others feel they have only just begun. Most are somewhere in between. Read each of the following statements and place a check by the one that best describes your current progress:

- Plan A: The anxiety-related symptoms and self-defeating behaviors I was experiencing when I started these lessons are no longer a major problem in my life. Any remaining anxiety-related problems are now minor and do not seriously interfere with my ability to function effectively and enjoy life.

- Plan B: I have made progress in overcoming my anxiety-related problems. However, I still have self-defeating behaviors and reactions associated with anxiety that are interfering with my ability to function effectively and enjoy life.
- Plan C: I have made little or no progress in overcoming my anxiety-related problems, *or* I feel that I was making progress but am now "stuck" and making little or no progress.

Read the plan that corresponds to the statement you checked and follow the directions it gives. If you cannot decide which statement best describes you, read each plan and use the one that best fits your needs.

Plan A: For People Who Feel Anxiety No Longer Seriously Interferes with Their Lives

Some people reach this point after one time through the lessons; others after working through the lessons two or more times. Some need the help of a professional therapist to reach this point. It really doesn't matter how long it took or whether you worked alone or with a friend, a group, or a therapist. You have now reached the point where anxiety is no longer seriously interfering with your life. Stop and congratulate yourself! You have accomplished one of the most difficult tasks there is: changing the way you think and act.

As time goes by, the skills you have developed will become even more effective. This does not mean that you will eventually handle all problems and conflicts you encounter perfectly; no one does that. You now have a much greater understanding of yourself, however, and a much wider range of skills to deal with life than the average person. To ensure your continued growth, devote some time and energy to reinforcing the new behaviors, attitudes, and ways of thinking you learned while working through the lessons. This prevents stagnation and the possibility of slipping back into old patterns. Four different ways in which this can be done are described below.

- *Take time learning relapse-prevention skills:* In recent years, *relapse prevention* has become a popular term to describe knowledge and skills that help people who have experienced anxiety-related problems maintain their recovery. Before this term became popular, I used the term *long-term recovery* to describe this process. My second book, *Overcoming Anxiety: From Short-Term Fixes to Long-Term Recovery*, was written as a follow-up to this one and, like these lessons, guides you through a series of lessons that explain how to maintain the progress you have made. Many people have found *Overcoming Anxiety* to be an effective way to reinforce the lessons in this book and add new skills that ensure their continued recovery.

- *Schedule a monthly review of the lessons:* Spend at least one hour a month reviewing the lessons. Concentrate on only one lesson during this review. As you review the lesson, identify skills where further work is needed. Make a conscious effort to strengthen any weak areas you identify by following the exercises described in the lesson. Select different lessons for each review session so you eventually review the entire program. Continue this practice for at least six months.

- *Review your coping cards at the first sign of old behaviors:* Save the various summaries of key concepts and coping self-statements you made while working through the lessons. When you notice yourself returning to old patterns, review the cards that challenge those specific behaviors or thought patterns.

    Keep in mind that when old patterns return, they often are simply a sign that you are experiencing physical or emotional stress. Do not just focus on your symptoms. Instead, identify the sources of stress that have triggered your symptoms and develop a plan that addresses them directly.

- *Use classes, workshops, or support groups to reinforce and further the progress you have made:* As you worked through these lessons, you identified various areas that were especially important for you to work on in order to achieve recovery. Attending a class or workshop that addresses these specific areas is an excellent way to reinforce and extend the concepts and skills you learned. Personal growth classes and workshops are held at churches, hospitals, colleges, the adult education division of local school districts, and counseling centers. While many excellent programs are available throughout the country, some are of dubious quality. Therefore, it is always best to check the credentials and experience of the person presenting the workshop. It also is best to stay away from programs that promise a quick fix. If it sounds too good to be true, it probably is.

The time and energy needed to continue your growth will decrease as time goes by. Some people find they can keep their momentum going and continue progressing by doing two or three of the above activities. Others need to do all four. If you are doing well and continuing to apply your skills effectively, you are probably doing enough. If you are slipping into old patterns and failing to use the skills you learned from these lessons, you probably need to spend more time reviewing and practicing. Taking time for these activities becomes easier if you remember that the time and energy you spend with them is returned to you many times over as your ability to live more effectively and enjoy life increases.

Plan B: For People Who Have Made Progress but Still Have Important Anxiety-Related Problems

If you are feeling disappointed or consider yourself a failure because you have worked through the lessons and still have anxiety-related problems, stop and challenge the perfectionistic thinking behind these thoughts and feelings. Many people find that anxiety continues to seriously interfere with their lives after completing the lessons. Usually, this is simply because their anxiety-related problems are the result of many different deeply ingrained beliefs, thinking patterns, and behaviors. You spent years developing these self-defeating habits. It is unreasonable to believe that the short time it takes to work through the lessons once is enough to completely change a lifetime of learning. People with numerous deeply ingrained self-defeating beliefs and habits often require a year or more to internalize all the material presented in these lessons. Many find they need to work through the lessons two or more times. This is especially true for people who experienced physical, emotional, or sexual abuse as children.

As you challenge negative thoughts and feelings you have about your progress, be especially aware of should/must thinking, overgeneralizations, and magnification/minimization. Focus on the progress you have made and remind yourself that there is no one time when you "should" or "must" overcome all your problem behaviors. You are progressing at your own rate—a rate best for you. Keep in mind that it takes time to learn new concepts and skills. Change is usually a slow process. The process of change is illustrated in the following little story.

FIVE SHORT CHAPTERS ON CHANGE

Author Unknown*

Chapter I: I walk down a street and there's a deep hole in the sidewalk. I fall in. It takes forever to get out. It's my fault.

Chapter II: I walk down the same street. I fall in the hole again. It still takes a long time to get out. It's *not* my fault.

Chapter III: I walk down the same street. I fall in the hole again. It's becoming a habit. It *is* my fault. I get out immediately.

Chapter IV: I walk down the same street and see the deep hole in the sidewalk. I walk around it.

Chapter V: I walk down a different street.

* This version of the story appeared in the *ABIL Newsletter.* ABIL (Agoraphobics Building Independent Lives) is a large nonprofit organization headquartered in Richmond, Virginia.

Once you have developed rational self-talk that challenges negative thoughts and feelings, it is time to make a firm commitment to continue your journey. Plan B is simple: Start with Lesson 1 and work through the lessons again in order. As you do this, you have two basic goals. First, work at deepening your understanding of concepts you either missed or did not understand fully the first time through. Second, practice skills you either skipped or did not learn thoroughly due to lack of time, understanding, or commitment. The best way to reach these goals is to follow these suggestions:

• Take your time with each lesson. Spend two or three weeks on a lesson if you feel you need it.

- Be sure to read each lesson at least three times—more if you are having difficulty with the concepts.
- Do as many of the exercises you skipped as possible. Also be sure to repeat exercises which were a challenge for you when you did them previously.
- After working through the lessons in this book a second time, work through the lessons in *Overcoming Anxiety*. This book covers several new areas that supplement and extend the work done in these lessons.

Many people find it difficult to follow the above guidelines because they either are too busy or find it difficult to use written lessons. If this is true for you, put a check by any of the following ideas that could help you give the lessons the time and energy they deserve.

- Establish a regular time to work with the lessons. Make this scheduled study time as important as your regular meals. If you follow a written calendar, record your study times on the calendar.
- Remind yourself that you can make the most progress when you are feeling good and your life seems to be running smoothly. It is during these times that it is easiest to look at yourself objectively and do the activities listed in the lessons.
- Find a study partner or group that can help you keep motivated and use the lessons as they are intended to be used.
- Consider working with a therapist who is skilled with anxiety-related problems.

Most people who use Plan B are surprised at the amount of information that was missed on their first or even second time through the lessons. There are several reasons for this. The amount of information you can absorb and the number of skills you can master in a given amount of time is limited. The more anxiety is interfering with your life, the more difficult it is to learn the concepts and skills in the lessons. Because you have made progress in reducing the amount of anxiety you experience, you now have more energy available as you go through the lessons again.

Each lesson contains more information and describes more skills than can be mastered in one to three weeks. The lessons are intentionally written in this fashion, since the specific skills and information that are important differ from person to person. The information and skills important for your continued progress at this time are also probably different from those that were important when you first began.

Because the concepts and skills presented in the lessons are interconnected, it is easy to miss some or much of what is presented. Full mastery of a concept or skill in one lesson often requires the mastery of concepts and skills in others. Now that you have studied the ideas and practiced the skills in later lessons, you have an increased ability to apply the ideas and skills presented in earlier ones. Likewise, your increased understanding and skill with the earlier material helps you as you repeat the later lessons.

One final situation can occur where a specific situation, place, or memory triggers an emotional response that overwhelms your cognitive techniques. Examples would be an intersection where an accident occurred, speaking with a supervisor who is similar to an abusive parent, or memories of a rape, mugging, or childhood trauma that produce excessively high levels of anxiety. When this is the case, I have found an approach called Eye Movement Desensitization and Reprocessing (EMDR) to be very effective at reducing the conditioned response aspect of this type of emotional trigger. If you are interested in finding out more about this approach, see the address listed in Appendix 3, Guidelines for Selecting a Therapist.

Plan C: For People Who Have Major Anxiety-Related Problems and Feel They Are Blocked and Unable to Progress

If you have chosen this plan, you have either not made much progress since beginning the lessons or made some progress then became blocked and ceased progressing. Before going any farther, read and answer the following questions:

- Did you spend at least one week on each lesson?
- Did you work through the lessons in order, reading each one at least three times?

- Did you do most of the Recommended Activities for each lesson?
- When doing recommended activities, did you take care to do them in the way you were directed to?

If you answered no to any of the above, your lack of progress or feeling of being blocked is probably due to using the program incorrectly. If this is the case, do not feel bad or condemn yourself. Many people do this when they first work through the lessons. Many have never worked with printed lessons like these and lack the reading and study habits needed to use the lessons effectively. If you fit into this group, follow Plan B and work through the lessons again.

Another common reason for difficulty is the presence of a factor that causes you to resist change. If you think this might be the case, review Lesson 10 and identify the source of your resistance. Then follow the suggestions given in Lesson 10 for overcoming that particular source of resistance.

Often, anxiety-related problems are intertwined with other issues such as being raised in a dysfunctional family where there was physical or emotional abuse. When this is the case, there are often deep-seated core beliefs and unresolved hurts from the past that can interfere with your ability to use these lessons effectively. The companion to this book, *Overcoming Anxiety*, can help you identify areas that might be causing problems and provides tools for overcoming them.

If none of the above seems to apply to you and you are feeling that you are stuck and not progressing, seek help from a professional therapist who understands anxiety-related problems. Appendix 3 describes how to find one.

Appendix 1

The Six Basic Types of Anxiety-Related Problems

While there are many different diagnostic categories for anxiety-related problems, these problems can be grouped into six general types, most commonly used by mental health professionals.

Panic Disorder

The key feature of panic disorder is the presence of unexpected panic attacks that occur for no apparent reason. No reasonable external threat is present, nor are any medical causes of anxiety present. People with panic disorder often develop agoraphobia—the tendency to avoid places or situations where escape might be difficult or embarrassing or where help might be unavailable in the event of a panic attack. When this is the case, their condition is referred to as panic disorder with agoraphobia. While the types of places or situations avoided vary greatly from person to person and sometimes even from time to time, a definite pattern is usually present. A person with this condition may need a companion, called a support person, when traveling away from home or into new or frightening areas. A support person ensures that help will be available if a panic attack should occur.

A person's agoraphobic avoidance level can range from mild to severe. Agoraphobic tendencies can also subside and resurface.

Agoraphobics commonly avoid being outside the home alone, traveling beyond a "safe" distance from the home, crowded spaces, bridges, elevators, public transportation, driving on the freeway, making a left turn while driving, or standing in lines.

Obsessive-Compulsive Disorder

People with obsessive-compulsive disorder (OCD) experience unwanted thoughts, called obsessions or compulsive behaviors, that seem impossible to stop or control. An obsession is a persistent idea, thought, image, or impulse that is senseless or repulsive and intrudes on a person's consciousness. Common obsessions involve thoughts or mental images of violence, harming oneself or others, violating social norms such as swearing or exhibiting unacceptable sexual behavior, producing contamination or infection in oneself or others, and doubt about whether some action has been performed. Obsessions can also focus on symmetry, special numbers, colors, words, phrases, or even melodies.

A compulsion is an action repeated in a ritualistic fashion. The action may be done with the intent to produce or prevent some future event or situation, even though the compulsion has no realistic bearing on the event or situation it is meant to affect. Compulsions can also be normal, rational activities performed in a clearly excessive manner. Compulsions are usually done in response to an obsession. For example, a person fearing contamination (the obsession) might engage in ritualistic or excessive hand washing or cleaning (the compulsion). Common examples of compulsions include repeated hand washing or showering; constant cleaning of clothes, the home, and even groceries; counting, checking, arranging, or ordering things; and touching. Mild obsessions and compulsions are common and are only considered a problem when they interfere with normal activities, cause mental or emotional distress, or cannot be controlled.

Research has now shown that OCD has the largest physiological component of all the anxiety-related problems. A simple way of thinking of this is that a sort of neurological "hiccup" occurs where the brain becomes stuck while performing a normal activity. OCD is not caused by family problems or attitudes learned in childhood.

Brain imaging techniques that reveal the parts of the brain that are active when a person is thinking or doing something have shown that people with OCD often use different brain circuitry when thinking than people without OCD. In addition, specific types of illnesses or injuries can trigger the development of OCD. For example, a report by Robyn Smith of Penn State College of Medicine states that six out of ten patients studied developed OCD after suffering mild traumatic brain injury. Another interesting finding is that 20 percent of OCD sufferers also have motor tics, suggesting it may be related to Tourette's syndrome.

Post-Traumatic Stress Disorder

Post-traumatic stress disorder (PTSD) is severe stress resulting from a traumatic event such as rape, assault, a natural disaster, major surgery, wartime combat duty, experiencing a serious accident, or observing a serious accident. A person with PTSD can experience recurring images of the traumatic event, a feeling that the traumatic event is occurring in the present, recurring distressing dreams of the trauma, or intense physical discomfort when exposed to events that resemble some aspect of the traumatic event. A person with PTSD may avoid places or things associated with the trauma and may also experience a general numbing. This numbing can range from avoidance of thoughts or feelings associated with the trauma to a general feeling of detachment or estrangement from others. At least two of the following types of body arousal will also be present:

- Difficulty falling or staying asleep.
- Irritability or outbursts of anger.
- Difficulty concentrating.
- Hypervigilance.
- Exaggerated startle response.
- An excessive physical reaction when exposed to events that symbolize or resemble an aspect of the traumatic event—for example, a person who was rear-ended in an automobile accident becomes very anxious whenever a car approaches from behind.

Specific Phobia

There are two main types of phobias, specific phobia and social phobia. People with specific phobias experience extreme, disabling, or irrational fear of something that poses little or no actual danger. This fear usually causes the person to avoid the feared object or situation. While specific phobias often do not cause a major disruption in people's lives, many find that their lives are limited in significant ways.

Specific phobias can involve objects or situations such as animals, insects, flying, closed spaces, heights, darkness, or bridges. A specific phobia differs from agoraphobia in that anxiety is focused on a specific external object or situation and is present only when that object or situation is encountered. Specific phobias are common and do not usually create major problems in life since one simply avoids the feared object or situation. A specific phobia becomes a problem only when the feared object or situation cannot easily be avoided or is important to one's work or personal life.

Social Phobia

The second main type of phobia, social phobia is characterized by a fear of embarrassing oneself in social situations. As a result, a person avoids situations where he or she must "perform" and be under the scrutiny of others. In one sense, social phobia is an extreme form of performance anxiety. For some people, just thinking about feared situations can produce severe anxiety and even panic attacks.

Mild forms of social phobia are very common. The fear of public speaking, sometimes referred to as stage fright by actors and musicians, is probably the most common. Other common forms include difficulty in using public bathrooms, fear of writing or signing one's name in the presence of others, difficulty in eating or drinking in public, and the fear of blushing.

One common misconception about social phobia is that it is the same as shyness. While people who are shy can be very anxious around others, they do not experience the extreme anticipatory anxiety of people with social phobia. They also may have no tendency to avoid social situations. In contrast, people with social phobia usually aren't shy and can be completely at ease with people in many situations. However, specific situations where they feel they are being scrutinized, such as those listed above, can cause intense anxiety. They also tend to think about anxiety-producing circumstances beforehand and often avoid them. After being in a situation where they feel they were being watched, they will dwell on and worry about what others may have thought or observed about them.

Generalized Anxiety Disorder

A person with generalized anxiety disorder (GAD) has experienced six months or more of chronic, exaggerated worry and tension that is either unfounded or much more severe than the normal anxiety most people experience. Family, health, money, and work are common sources of worry. For example, a person might constantly worry about something bad happening to a child who is in no danger, or about finances when things are actually going well. In addition, at least six of the following symptoms are often present when anxious. These symptoms must also not be due to some medical condition such as hyperthyroidism or caffeine intoxication.

Motor Tension
- Trembling, twitching, or feeling shaky.
- Muscle tension, aches, or soreness.
- Restlessness.
- Easy fatigability.

Autonomic Hyperactivity
- Shortness of breath or smothering sensations.
- Palpitations or accelerated heart rate (tachycardia).
- Sweating or cold, clammy hands.
- Dry mouth.
- Dizziness or light-headedness.
- Nausea, diarrhea, or other abdominal distress.
- Flushes (hot flashes) or chills.
- Frequent urination.
- Trouble swallowing or lump in the throat.

Vigilance and Scanning
- Feeling keyed up or on edge.
- Exaggerated startle response.
- Difficulty concentrating or "mind going blank" because of anxiety.
- Trouble falling or staying asleep.
- Irritability.

APPENDIX 2

Methods for Developing a Relaxation Response

The term *relaxation response* was coined by Herbert Benson and is used to describe a state of deep muscle relaxation that is triggered by some set method. Many different methods can be used to trigger a relaxation response. They range from meditation and hypnosis to autogenic training and biofeedback. This appendix begins with a brief description of four of the most popular methods, followed by two detailed scripts that can be recorded and used for practicing the various methods. The two scripts include wording that show how to associate your relaxation response with a cue in order to develop cue-controlled relaxation. Information on obtaining professionally produced CDs that use these scripts can be found at www.rpeurifoy.com.

Progressive Relaxation

Progressive relaxation is the oldest of the "modern" approaches to deep relaxation. It was first formalized by Edmund Jacobson in 1908 and is based on the principle that a muscle will become more relaxed after it is first tensed. Progressive relaxation takes practice to master, so expect only limited success when you first begin. With regular practice, however, most people find they can eventually use it to relax their entire body fairly quickly.

1. Pick a time and place where you will not be disturbed and lie or sit in a comfortable position.
2. Close your eyes and breathe in a relaxed manner while you scan your body and notice how the various muscle groups and joints feel. As you do this, identify the parts that are most tense.
3. Tense and relax one muscle group at a time. Begin with the feet and slowly work your way up to your head and face. Before moving from one muscle group to the next, do a complete breathing cycle, breathing in and out in a relaxed manner. Use moderation as you tighten and relax each muscle group, especially neck and back muscles where excessive tightening might result in a strain or injury. Some people also find that overtightening the toes or feet can sometimes result in muscle cramps.

   The more difficult it is for you to relax, the more you need to take additional time and work with smaller groups of muscles. For example, tighten and relax the toes on the left foot first, then the right foot. As you become skilled with this process, you can shorten it by combining muscle groups, such as tightening the toes on both feet at the same time.
4. When you have completed tensing and relaxing the muscle groups in your entire body, stop for a moment to feel how much more relaxed you are than when you began. Identify those areas where tension remains. If you wish, you can switch to a counting or visualization process to deepen the relaxation you have produced.

Breath Counting

Counting backward is a common relaxation technique. It is found on many different types of audio recordings designed to produce a relaxation response as well as by therapists teaching relaxation response techniques to clients. Breath counting is an effective adaptation of this approach if you are working on your own.

1. Pick a time and place where you will not be disturbed and lie or sit in a comfortable position.

2. Close your eyes and begin counting backward from 50. After you exhale, notice that you don't have to breathe in again immediately and can rest comfortably for a few seconds. For some people this may only be one or two seconds. For others it may be as long as twenty seconds. Count during this peaceful time when the lungs have paused and the body is still. Count one number for each cycle of breathing in and out.

As you practice breath counting, you will probably find that you occasionally lose track of the number you are counting. This is normal. When this occurs, simply resume counting from the last number you can remember. If 37 is the last number you remember counting, resume your count with 36. If you wish to spend more time with this exercise, start counting at a higher number such as 75 or 100. One advantage to this method is that, with experience, you can estimate how long it will take depending on what number you begin with.

3. After completing your countdown, you can either return to your normal alert state or spend additional time developing your relaxation response by switching to one of the other methods.

As with progressive relaxation, breath counting often takes several practice sessions before it begins to produce results. Once you become skilled with it, however, it can be not only a good method for producing a relaxation response, but also an effective centering technique that can be used when your mind is whirling with many different thoughts or concerns.

Focal Point Technique

Numerous types of religious and secular meditation are practiced around the world. Many of them offer effective methods for producing a relaxation response. The following method is an adaptation of the one developed by Herbert Benson after he studied many different types of meditation.

1. Pick a time and place where you will not be disturbed and lie or sit in a comfortable position.

2. Close your eyes and choose a center of focus. This is a word or phrase that helps shift your mind from logical, externally oriented thought to an internal, passive center of focus and stops the mind from wandering when it occurs. The most common focal point is a word such as "one," "calm," or "relax." However, a short phrase can also be used, such as "Relax and be at peace." Many people like to use words or phrases that have a spiritual or religious meaning, such as "God is with me" or "I am being watched over."

   People who are very visual find it useful to develop a secondary focal point in the form of a mental image that forms a background for the use of the word or phrase that has been chosen. Examples include a mental image of a calm lake or a religious figure. Some people prefer a focal point that allows them to keep their eyes open, such as a candle, picture, or statue.

3. Repeat your word or phrase each time you exhale. As you do this, adopt a passive attitude. This is the most important element of this method. Avoid concern about how well you are performing the technique and adopt a "let it happen" attitude. Your mind will occasionally slip away from its concentration on the word or phrase you have chosen. When this happens, don't panic or abandon your practice. This is normal and to be expected. It does not mean you are performing the technique incorrectly. Simply redirect your mind to your breathing and continue repeating your chosen word or phrase after each exhalation.

4. Practice for ten to twenty minutes, then open your eyes and resume your normal activities. You may open your eyes to check the time, but do not use an alarm.

Fantasy

This is another technique that is widely used on cassettes presenting relaxation response techniques and in therapy. It is often referred to as imagery or visualization. These two terms are somewhat misleading, however, since they imply that you must "see" what you are fantasizing. This is unfortunate since many people who are poor visualizers incorrectly conclude that they cannot use fantasy techniques. Anyone who can imagine people, places, and events can use fantasy techniques whether they actually see anything in their mind or not. While the following fantasy procedure can be used by itself, it is frequently combined with progressive relaxation and counting techniques.

1. Pick a time and place where you will not be disturbed and lie or sit in a comfortable position.

2. As you breathe comfortably, close your eyes and imagine something peaceful and enjoyable. The types of places and activities you can use for a fantasy are limited only by your imagination. They can range from the seashore or mountains to a mythical garden. Be as creative as you want. Go on an imaginary journey or visit with real or imaginary friends. Recall a pleasant memory or do the impossible and fly on a cloud if the mood strikes you. This is your mind and your imagination. You have complete control and can make up any rules you choose. If unpleasant thoughts occur or your mind wanders, simply redirect them back to your chosen fantasy.

    When using fantasy, remember that it is based on a simple principle: Whenever you imagine an experience vividly, you trigger the physiological responses that accompany it in real life. A simple example of this is the tension you feel when watching an exciting movie. Since your goal is to have your muscles relax, choose something relaxing. Exactly what you choose to imagine is unimportant as long as it is relaxing and enjoyable, will hold your interest, and can be created in detail. The more vividly you create the situation, the stronger will be the physiological responses that are triggered. The best way to do this is to involve as many of your senses as possible. For example, if you are imagining a hidden beach, imagine the warmth of the sun, the sound of the surf, the taste and smell of the salt air, and as many other details as possible.

3. After ten to twenty minutes, open your eyes and resume your normal activities.

Relaxation Response Scripts

The following two scripts provide you with a detailed example of how the four methods described in this appendix can be used to produce a relaxation response. They also show how the different methods can be combined and associated with a simple physical cue to develop cue-controlled relaxation. Begin with the first script and record exactly as written on whatever recording medium you are comfortable using. If you prefer, you may have someone you know who has a soothing voice record it for you. When reading the script, use a slow, calm pace and pause where indicated by a series of three dots (. . .).

After you have recorded one of the scripts, pick a time and place to listen to it when you will not be disturbed. Sit or lie with your hands and feet uncrossed so there is free circulation of the blood and assume a comfortable position. It often helps to remove shoes or apparel that might interfere with your physical comfort. Then start the recording and follow the recorded directions. While many people like to work with one script at a time, others prefer to record a second script. This allows them to alternate between the two scripts for variety.

You will probably find your mind wandering while listening to a recorded script. This is especially true after you have used it several times and know what to expect. When this happens, do not be concerned. Your goal is to produce deep relaxation. Whether you stay focused on the words of the script or let your mind wander is unimportant as long as you are producing a relaxation response.

With time, you will find that simply recalling the different steps in the script will begin to produce a relaxation response. When you develop this ability, you will have a powerful tool for calming yourself in anxiety-producing situations.

Script 1: Progressive Relaxation and Fantasy Techniques

In this script progressive relaxation is used to start your relaxation response. Fantasy is then used to deepen your relaxation and create a "special place." Having an imaginary special place is a useful tool for many anxiety-producing situations. It not only provides you with an additional method for producing relaxation and calming yourself, but is also a valuable form of distraction.

Script

In just a moment, it will be time to begin developing your relaxation response through a process of progressive relaxation. By placing the first two fingers and thumb of either hand lightly together and keeping them in this position during this process, you will develop a very effective anchor, a simple physical cue or signal that can be used to activate your relaxation response whenever you feel yourself becoming anxious or tense.

Now take a moment to settle down into where you are sitting or lying and take a few relaxing breaths . . . Close your eyes as you take these relaxing breaths so you can experience more fully the sensation of the air moving in through your nose and traveling down deep into your lungs . . .

Let the muscles of your rib cage relax . . . as your diaphragm invites the air inside . . . and the area below your stomach lifts and expands gently . . . notice how the air seems to just trickle out . . . as the diaphragm releases and moves gently . . . and easily . . . back into its soft . . . relaxed . . . flattened position . . . then, after a brief pause, the whole process is repeated effortlessly . . .

As you continue to breathe in this soothing manner . . . take a moment to scan your body and become aware of any areas that seem tense and tight . . . notice also any areas that are relaxed and loose . . . after you have done this, move your attention to your left foot . . .

As you breathe in, tense the muscles in your left foot and hold both the breath and the tension for a few seconds . . . then, as you exhale, release the tension and allow your foot to relax completely . . . now do the same for the right foot . . . tense as you inhale and hold your breath for a few seconds . . . then exhale and release all of the tension . . .

Now allow yourself to breathe in . . . and out . . . as you relax and prepare to shift your awareness to your left leg . . . and when you're ready, tense the left leg . . . hold it a moment . . . then let go as you exhale . . . now do the same for the right leg . . . tense as you inhale and hold for a few seconds . . . then release as you exhale . . .

Now take time once again to breathe in . . . and out . . . in a relaxed . . . easy manner . . . taking the air way down deep inside . . . letting it flow out slowly . . . comfortably . . .

Now become aware of your buttocks . . . and as you inhale, tighten the muscles of your buttocks . . . hold a few seconds . . . and when you're ready to let go, exhale and release the tension there . . .

And when you are done . . . take time to become aware of little sensations that let you know you are beginning to relax as you breathe in and out in a way that is just right for you . . . taking in just the right amount of air . . . becoming more and more aware of the pleasure of deep relaxation . . .

Now become aware of your abdomen and stomach . . . as you inhale, tense this area and hold it along with your breath for a few seconds . . . then release as you exhale and note the pleasant differences you are beginning to experience . . . and when you are done . . . continuing to breathe in . . . and out . . . so peacefully . . . calm and controlled . . .

Now directing your attention to your chest and shoulders . . . tense this area where so much anxiety and stress is stored as you breathe in and hold your breath for just a few seconds . . . now let go and release as you exhale . . . and take time once again to breathe in . . . and out . . . gently . . . easily . . .

Now become aware of your left hand and arm . . . make a fist with your left hand as you breathe in and tense both the fist and arm . . . hold it a moment then release the fist and relax the arm and hand completely as you continue to breathe in . . . and out . . . peacefully . . . calmly . . . now direct your awareness to your right hand and arm . . . make a fist with your right hand and tense it along with the arm as you breathe in and hold it for a moment . . . and when you're ready . . . breathe out completely and release the fist . . . relaxing the hand and arm . . . letting go of all the tension . . .

And again taking time to breathe in . . . and out . . . as you now move your awareness to your neck . . . another area where tension is sometimes stored . . . and as you finish a relaxing breath, tense the neck as you breathe in and hold your breath for just a few moments . . . then exhale all at once and release the tension there . . .

Now resting again . . . taking another relaxing inhalation . . . breathing at the most comfortable pace you can . . . in the most comfortable way possible . . . and when you've completed taking this relaxing breath, move your awareness to your face and head . . . as you breathe in, tense all the muscles in your head and face and hold . . . and when you're ready, let go . . . let go of all the tension in your body and in your mind . . .

And as you continue to breathe easily . . . and relax more and more . . . take a moment to scan your body and become aware of how much more relaxed you are than when you started . . . and if your body wants to readjust, to settle even more deeply, just allow it to do so as you continue to breathe out tension . . . breathing it out through your fingers . . . through your toes . . . just like sand pouring out your fingers . . . out your toes . . . just letting go and allowing your body to settle even more easily . . . just like settling into a thick white cloud . . . allowing the cloud to carry you so comfortably . . . so peacefully . . . so securely . . . all of your body so loose and limp and relaxed . . . just like a rag doll . . . all that's important right now is your own increasing sense of relaxation and peace . . . your own feelings of comfort and safety . . .

And now, imagine and create in your mind a very special place . . . a place of your choosing . . . one where you can feel at peace and secure . . . where you can experience re-creation and renewal . . . this can be a place where you have been to before, or one to where you have always wanted to go . . . maybe a place you have read about or seen in a movie, or that someone has told you about . . . it can even be a place that only exists in your mind . . . your special place can be any kind of place you wish . . . one that is just right for you . . . where there is comfort and contentment . . .

And as you find your special place . . . a place that's security . . . comfort . . . and contentment . . . let yourself really take it in . . . whether it's the coolness of a breeze . . . the sounds of birds . . . clouds drifting by . . . the colors of sunlight filtering or sparkling . . . or whatever is there . . .

And you may find that you want to be the only one there; or you may want to have a special friend or relative there . . . you may even want to create a special person to share your special place . . . at times, you may want to change your special place in some way or even create a new one . . . and that is perfectly fine . . . this is your special place . . . you can do whatever you want to here . . . and as you take some time now to enjoy the comfort and peace and security of your special place . . . just let your mind wander and drift to wherever it wishes . . .

Allow one to three minutes of silence before continuing with the rest of the script. If you have the know-how, you can include some relaxing music during this portion of the recording.

Spending time in your special place brings an inner peace and strength that allows you to face the world with new energy and confidence. Anytime you wish to return to your special place, you can do so by simply closing your eyes and taking a moment to relax. You will then be able to return to your special place and renew your energy and confidence and replenish yourself. Knowing that you now have this special place allows you to face the world in a positive new way . . .

From now on, placing the first two fingers and thumb of either hand together signals your mind and body to relax deeply, calm and controlled, and to experience the same feelings of relaxation . . . peace . . . and security that you are feeling now . . . Your eyes may be open while you are experiencing these positive feelings, and you will be able to more effectively do whatever it is that you are doing . . .

Now in just a moment I will begin counting from one to five. With each count you will become more and more alert. At the count of five you will feel bright, alert, wide awake, and refreshed. You will have a feeling of well-being throughout your arms, your legs, and your entire body. I will now begin counting . . . one . . . just floating back so easily to this time and space . . . two . . . your muscles beginning to stir . . . three . . . move your toes and fingers slightly as you become more and more alert . . . four . . . your eyes getting ready to open . . . five . . . opening your eyes as you're ready, you

feel alert and rested as though you just awoke from a refreshing sleep
. . . now take a deep breath, fill up your lungs, and stretch.

Script 2: Variations on Breath Counting and Focal Point Technique

This script uses a combination of counting and focal point techniques. Since your rate of breathing varies depending upon how relaxed you are, the countdown pace on a script that is to be recorded needs to be independent of your rate of breathing. However, the idea of using a countdown to focus your attention and trigger a relaxation response is essentially the same as in breath counting. The initial spot on which you focus in this script and the word or phrase you repeat in the middle of the exercise are variations on the focal point technique. External focal points such as the spot teamed up with counting or breathing techniques are very useful in anxiety-producing situations.

Script

In just a moment, it will be time to begin developing your relaxation response through a process of progressive relaxation. By placing the first two fingers and thumb of either hand lightly together and keeping them in this position during this process, you will develop a very effective anchor, a simple physical cue or signal that can be used to activate your relaxation response whenever you feel yourself becoming anxious or tense.

Now take a moment to settle down into where you are sitting or lying and take a few relaxing breaths . . . Close your eyes as you take these relaxing breaths so you can experience more fully the sensation of the air moving in through your nose and traveling down deep into your lungs . . .

Make yourself comfortable and find a spot a little above your eye level to fix your attention on . . . it can be any type of spot . . . perhaps an interesting object . . . a shape . . . an area . . . a color . . . anything that appeals to you . . . now, as you continue to look at that spot, allow your eyes to go into a soft focus . . . not really concentrating hard, but rather just using the spot as a center of focus in a soft, easy way . . . now inhale deeply through your nose and hold it for just a moment . . . then exhale all at once through your mouth . . .

As you now take a second deep breath, notice the tension in your chest . . . and as you again exhale all at once through your mouth, feel the release as you start to really relax . . . now take a third deep breath . . . hold it a moment . . . then let it all out and notice how good your body is beginning to feel . . .

Continue to focus your attention on the spot as you now breathe in . . . and out . . . evenly . . . and regularly . . . relaxing more and more deeply . . . and as you continue to focus on the spot, your eyes may water a little . . . your eyelids may even flutter a bit as they begin to feel very heavy . . . and these are all good signs that you are ready to relax completely . . .

And as you continue to focus on the spot, your eyelids become increasingly heavy . . . so heavy that you want to close them . . . now, on a very comfortable . . . relaxing exhalation . . . just allow them to close . . . keeping your eyes closed now allows you to move into a deeper . . . and deeper relaxation . . . as you now move your attention to your hands and continue to breathe very easily and comfortably . . . calm and controlled . . . breathing all the way from your abdomen . . .

And as you focus on your hands, you begin to notice a very pleasant and interesting sensation . . . beginning maybe in your right hand . . . maybe in your left hand . . . perhaps even in both hands . . . you may feel this sensation in the back of your hands or perhaps in your fingers . . . a feeling of lightness . . . or increased warmth . . . perhaps a coolness . . . or a sensation of heaviness . . . very often a feeling of pleasant tingling . . . any one or combination of these feelings is a good sign that your muscles are relaxing and letting go . . . causing your blood vessels to expand a little and allow just a little more blood to flow to your skin as your entire body moves into deeper and deeper relaxation . . .

And you can just allow that pleasant sensation to begin to spread throughout your body . . . calm and controlled . . . more and more relaxed with every exhalation . . . breathing in comfort and peacefulness . . . breathing out all the tension as you allow a very natural process of deep relaxation to carry you deeper and deeper . . . very calm, pleasant feelings . . . nothing to do but allow it . . .

And you can go even deeper now as I count from ten to one . . . your relaxation doubling with every number . . . ten . . . just allowing a very natural process of deep relaxation to carry you even more deeply inside . . . even more peaceful and relaxed . . . nine . . . more and more comfortable . . . eight . . . relaxing, calm, and controlled . . . just allowing yourself to float and drift . . . seven . . . nothing is important but the increasing sense of comfort and peacefulness . . . six . . . even deeper . . . five . . . halfway there . . . continuing to go even deeper with every exhalation . . . four . . . and you can allow yourself to go deeper and deeper . . . drifting comfortably . . . three . . . so peaceful . . . so comfortable . . . so secure . . . two . . . relaxing deeply . . . nothing to bother . . . nothing to disturb . . . the deep relaxation proceeding on its own . . . completely relaxed right now . . . one . . .

And in just a moment you will have time to go even deeper into this pleasurable state of deep relaxation by using a word or phrase as a focal point . . . this can be any word you choose that is relaxing and comfortable . . . you might like the word "calm" . . . or the word "relax" . . . you might even want to use a short phrase such as "I am centered and calm" . . . it can be any word or phrase you choose . . .

And you will repeat your word or phrase once every time you exhale . . . and if you choose, you may also imagine a special place while you practice saying your word or phrase on every exhalation . . . and with every exhalation . . . and every repetition of your word or phrase . . . your relaxation will increase . . . deeper and deeper . . . and now you have time to say your word or phrase on each of your exhalations.

Allow one to three minutes of silence before continuing with the rest of the script. If you have the know-how, you can include some relaxing music during this portion of the recording.

From now on, placing the first two fingers and thumb of either hand together signals your mind and body to relax deeply, calm and controlled, and to experience the same feelings of relaxation . . . peace

. . . and security that you are feeling now . . . Your eyes may be open while you are experiencing these positive feelings and you will be able to more effectively do whatever it is that you are doing . . .

And now it is time to return to the outside world. In just a moment I will begin counting from one to five. With each count you will become more and more alert. At the count of five you will feel bright, alert, wide awake, and refreshed as if you awoke from a peaceful sleep. You will have a feeling of well-being throughout your arms, your legs, and your entire body. I will now begin counting . . . one . . . just floating back so easily to this time and space . . . two . . . your muscles beginning to stir . . . three . . . move your toes and fingers slightly as you become more and more alert . . . four . . . your eyes getting ready to open . . . five . . . opening your eyes as you're ready, you feel alert and rested as though you just awoke from a refreshing sleep. Now take a deep breath, fill up your lungs, and stretch.

APPENDIX 3

Guidelines for Selecting a Therapist

When seeking therapy, remember that a given therapist does not work effectively with every type of person or problem. In order to find a therapist with a personality and an approach that is effective for you, talk with at least three therapists before choosing one. There are several ways to obtain the names of therapists who work with anxiety-related problems. Several good sources for referrals are listed below. If you are unable to locate a suitable person from these sources, you might try encouraging a local mental health professional whom you like to develop a specialization in anxiety disorders. Many professionals working with anxiety disorders were recruited by people with anxiety-related problems.

Referral Sources
- Friends who have had therapy.
- Your family physician or health maintenance organization.
- The Internet. Many national organizations such as the Anxiety Disorders Association of America (www.adaa.org) or OC Foundation (www.ocfoundation.org) have lists of therapists and treatment programs along with the types of anxiety disorders they treat. Additional organizations can be found by typing the name for any of the anxiety-related problems described in Appendix 1 into any Internet search engine. You can also try

typing in your specific type of anxiety disorder as well as your location. For example, a search using the words "panic disorder Sacramento" yields several pages of results.
- Your local telephone book. Therapists who specialize in various anxiety-related problems often list these in their ads.
- Local professional societies such as organizations of psychiatrists, psychologists, marriage family therapists, and social workers.
- Medical schools, universities, and other major research and clinical centers.
- Local mental health associations.

After you have obtained the names of three therapists, give each one a call. When talking with each therapist, begin by describing as quickly and as simply as possible your symptoms and the behaviors you want to eliminate or change. Many people find it helpful to have written notes to keep them focused. Next, ask the questions listed below. A good therapist welcomes questions about his or her treatment approaches and understands the importance of finding someone who matches your personality and problem. As you talk with each therapist, be sure to ask for an explanation whenever you do not understand what is being said. Two qualities you definitely want in your therapist are a willingness to answer questions directly and the ability to explain things clearly.

Are You Licensed?

Licensing varies from state to state. In California, for example, there are four different types of state-licensed psychotherapists. They are:

- *Psychiatrists:* These are medical doctors (M.D.) who, after their basic training in medicine, specialized in psychiatry.
- *Psychologists:* These usually have a doctorate (Ph.D.) in psychology.
- *Marriage and family therapists:* These usually have a master's degree (M.A. or M.S.), or sometimes a doctorate (Ph.D.), in counseling or psychology.
- *Social workers:* Social workers who conduct individual therapy

APPENDIX 3 / 345

are often referred to as clinical social workers. They usually have a master's degree (M.A. or M.S.), or sometimes a doctorate (Ph.D.), in social work.

While licensing does not guarantee competence, it does indicate that the state's standards of education and training have been met. When discussing licensing with a therapist, it is a good idea to ask what requirements needed to be met in order to be licensed in your state. Since some states do not issue licenses in all of the above categories, you can also ask whether the therapist is a member of a professional association. If so, ask what requirements needed to be met in order to join the association.

How Much Experience or Training Have You Had with My Type of Problem?

If at all possible, try to find someone who has experience dealing with the type of problem you are experiencing. If the therapist has little or no experience with your type of problem, it is best if he or she at least has some specific training that deals with it.

What Is Your Basic Approach to Treatment?

This is probably the most confusing part of therapy since there are many different therapeutic approaches, each with its own set of terms. With anxiety-related problems, it is best to find someone familiar with both cognitive therapy and a form of behavioral treatment known as in vivo exposure (also called contextual therapy or exposure therapy). Cognitive therapy involves the learning of specific techniques for changing the way you think. In vivo exposure concentrates on going into difficult situations and using specific behavioral and cognitive techniques to cope with the frightening feelings and thoughts as they occur. The goal of in vivo exposure is for the anxious thoughts and feelings to diminish and finally disappear as experience and skill are gained. Cognitive and behavioral approaches are often combined with other forms of treatment such as psychopharmacologic treatment (the use of medications) and psychodynamic therapy. Therapists who use a combination of these approaches usually tailor them to the individual needs of a client.

Another exciting new approach that I have found very useful is called Eye Movement Desensitization and Reprocessing (EMDR). I have found EMDR especially useful when a straight cognitive–behavioral approach as described in this book is not working well with specific traumatic memories or anxiety-producing situations. EMDR also works well with emotional triggers associated with childhood abuse or trauma. Unfortunately, it may be difficult to find someone who is skilled in this method. While EMDR seems simple, it actually requires a high degree of skill and experience to use effectively. If you're interested in finding a therapist trained in this approach, information on EMDR can be found on the Internet at www.emdr.com.

Does the Standard Course of Treatment Have a Fixed Length? If So, How Long Is It and Are There Provisions for Follow-Up?

Many therapists who work with anxiety disorders have a basic program that lasts from eight to twenty weeks. This type of program may be a group or individual program or may combine both group and individual therapy. Programs like this often feature group or individual in vivo exposure with either a therapist or a trained paraprofessional.

What Is Your Definition of Success with My Type of Problem, and Based on That Definition, What Is Your Rate of Success?

With anxiety-related problems, two major areas of importance are the reduction of anxiety symptoms and the elimination of self-defeating behaviors such as avoidance patterns.

How Much Does Treatment Cost and Is Any of It Reimbursable by Health Insurance?

Once you have chosen a therapist and have had two or three sessions, you will want to decide whether the therapist's personality and style seem right for you. It is best if you can answer most of the following questions with a yes.

Do I feel:

- That it's safe to say whatever I want when I am with the therapist?
- More hopeful and positive about myself at the end of most therapy sessions?
- That what the therapist says makes sense to me and seems relevant to my problems?

Did the therapist seem:

- Comfortable with me?
- At ease rather than stiff and formal?
- Flexible and open to new ideas?
- Genuinely concerned about me?

During our sessions, does the therapist:

- Take time to establish a set of goals for my therapy that I am able to understand; and is the therapist willing to use these goals to make periodic evaluations (every four to six weeks) of how the therapy is going and to set new goals if it seems appropriate?
- Encourage the feeling that I am as good as he or she is and treat me with respect rather than as if I am sick, defective, or about to fall apart?
- Admit limitations rather than pretend to know things he or she does not know?
- Answer direct questions in a simple, straightforward manner?
- Find it easy to admit when he or she is wrong and apologize for making errors or for being inconsiderate?
- Welcome and encourage my viewpoint when I disagree rather than reacting negatively or telling me that I am resisting?
- Allow me to direct the conversation if I want to do so?
- Act as if he or she is my consultant rather than the manager of my life?
- Show empathy and caring and give value to my feelings and thoughts?

- Reveal things about him- or herself either spontaneously or in response to my questions and do this without bragging or monopolizing the conversation?

While it is important to find someone you are comfortable with, it is also important to remember that your goal is to eliminate or change behaviors that concern you. Do not allow therapy to drag on for months without any progress. While many problems do require long-term therapy, there is usually some sense of progress after four to six sessions. Of course, progress will be slower for a person from a dysfunctional family who experienced much physical, emotional, or sexual abuse than it will be for a person from a reasonably healthy family with only one or two issues that need to be addressed. If you do not feel you have made any progress after six sessions, however, you may want to consider changing therapists. Your time, money, and well-being are at stake. You are not obligated to a therapist simply because you started or have been with him or her for months or years.

When you feel that you want to either end therapy or change therapists, it is usually best to discuss this with your current therapist before you take action. The only exception to this would be if the therapist makes sexual advances toward you or does anything else that is clearly unprofessional. If this ever occurs, leave immediately and report what has happened to your state licensing agency. If there is no licensing of therapists in your state, report the incident to the professional organization to which the therapist belongs.

If you have changed therapists several times and have tried several different approaches with little progress, it may be that you have not made a real commitment to the therapeutic process or failed to give any one approach enough time. If this is the case, you may find it beneficial to resume work with the therapist who seemed most effective.

APPENDIX 4

Suggestions for People with Sleep Problems

I t is common for people with anxiety-related problems to have sleep issues. When such issues continue for a long period of time, they can increase your symptoms of anxiety and interfere with your health, relationships, and overall ability to function effectively in life. This can become a vicious circle in which poor sleep caused by anxiety-related problems makes the anxiety symptoms worse, and the worsening symptoms perpetuate sleep problems.

This appendix discusses what is commonly called sleep hygiene along with three common sleep issues associated with anxiety-related problems. It is important to note, however, that sleep problems can also be due to many other factors. For example, there are a variety of chronic health problems such as asthma, angina, chronic pain, acid reflux, and arthritis that can make it difficult to sleep. Chronic sleep disturbance associated with sadness can also be a sign of major depression. Because chronic sleep problems can be due to either a medication or medical problem, it is always best to discuss sleep problems with your physician.

Good Sleep Hygiene

For many people with anxiety-related problems, the path to better sleep is simply a matter of developing better sleep habits. This is usually referred to as developing good sleep hygiene.

- *Establish a regular time to go to bed and get up each day:* Erratic sleep habits interfere with your biological clock and are a common cause of poor sleep. Naps are all right if taken early in the afternoon and for less than an hour, but avoid late-afternoon naps. Staying awake after midnight can also make it more difficult to fall asleep, because many people get their second wind after midnight. During the evening, do not allow yourself to doze off while reading or watching television prior to bedtime. These brief periods of sleep can interfere with your regular sleep. If you have been going to bed and getting up at widely varying times, focus on getting up at the same time each day—this is when your biological clock is set. Getting fifteen minutes of natural sunlight soon after you wake up can also aid in resetting your biological clock. Avoid making up for lost sleep on weekends or holidays until your sleep cycle has become stable.
- *Ensure a comfortable environment:* Don't neglect the obvious. Sleep is easiest in a dark, quiet, and well-ventilated room. It is also important to wear something that is loose fitting and comfortable.
- *Follow an established routine for going to bed*: Having a set ritual such as brushing your hair and teeth, pulling down the sheets, and setting out clothes for the next day tells your body, "It's time to fall asleep now."
- *Do relaxing, calming, and soothing activities just prior to the time you are to go to sleep:* Warm baths, reading, watching television, praying, or meditating can all help settle you down for a good night's rest. Avoid anxiety-provoking activities such as balancing your checkbook, paying bills, or arguing.
- *Reserve your bed for sleep and sex:* Do not read, watch television, or do other activities in bed. The goal is to make a strong association between going to bed and sleeping. If sleeping is very difficult, make the entire bedroom off limits to everything except sleep and sex. Do not make it an all-purpose room where you do many activities such as watching TV, reading, balancing the checkbook, or exercising.
- *Use relaxation techniques*: Relaxation response techniques such as those described in Appendix 2 are usually very effective in

helping you fall asleep. It helps to record them so you can play them when you wish to sleep. If you do not want to record them yourself, professionally recorded versions are also available at www.rpeurifoy.com.

- *Reduce stimulants:* Caffeine is a stimulant found in coffee, tea, chocolate, and many over-the-counter medications. Nicotine is another common stimulant. In addition, many medications contain stimulants such as pseudoephedrine, a common decongestant. If a medication says "nondrowsy formula," it probably has something in it that is a stimulant. Keep in mind that substances such as caffeine that did not interfere with sleep in the past can sometimes become a source of poor sleep during times of stress.
- *Reduce sedatives*: Many different over-the-counter medications such as antihistamines can interfere with your ability to have quality sleep. In addition, many prescription drugs can alter normal sleep patterns and suppress deep sleep or REM (the time when you are dreaming) sleep. They can also leave you groggy the next day. Even sleeping pills will cause problems when used for more than a few days.
- *Avoid alcohol:* Drinking can actually make matters worse. Even moderate amounts of alcohol can disturb sleep or create a backlash of sleeplessness later in the night.
- *Exercise four to six hours before bedtime:* Exercise just before sleeping will interfere with sleep. Exercising in the late afternoon, however, increases the amount of deep sleep in the first half of the night. Even a brisk walk around the block may help.
- *Avoid large meals before bedtime:* While a glass of milk—which contains tryptophan—can help induce sleep, high-protein foods may induce wakefulness. Large meals and excessive fluids can also cause indigestion, heartburn, or frequent awakenings to urinate, all of which will interfere with your sleep.
- *Use sound screens:* If noise in your surroundings either makes it difficult to go to sleep or wakes you up, there are two common solutions: earplugs and sound screens. A sound screen can be tranquil music or devices that play soothing sounds such as the sound of a waterfall or the ocean. These soft sounds mask

noises in your environment and make it easier to sleep. You can also simply place a radio next to your bed and tune it between stations so you only hear the random static. This random noise is also referred to as white noise. Turn the volume down so there is only a low level of white noise in the background and it will serve as a cover for other distracting sounds. A fan can also be used in this way.

- *If you can't sleep, get up and do a relaxing activity:* Do not lie awake in bed for more than twenty minutes. If the relaxation response exercises in Appendix 2 do not induce sleep, get up and go to a different part of the house. Do a quiet, relaxing activity like reading a book or watching television until you feel tired. At first, some people who have had disturbed sleep for a long period of time find they spend much of the night out of bed and get only four or five hours of sleep altogether. This is continuous, sound sleep, however, and gradually expands to fill the night.

- *When productivity lags during the day, change your activity pace:* The most "natural" way to keep awake is to move: Get up from your chair, pace the room and stretch. Try light rests and creative breaks instead of alcohol, cigarettes, or coffee.

When You Find It Difficult to Fall Asleep Due to Worry

When worrying about problems prevents you from falling asleep, get out of bed and go to another part of the house. Then use the Four-Step Analysis described in Lesson 7 to develop a concrete plan for dealing with the problem. Summarize your plan into a simple coping self-statement as is described in Lesson 7. Then go to bed and use one of the relaxation techniques described in Appendix 2 to focus your mind on a neutral activity and relax your body. Many people find the technique called breath counting especially effective. When you begin thinking about the problem, repeat your coping self-statement and resume your relaxation exercise. If worry over problems prior to going to sleep is a recurring pattern, establish a regular time at least an hour before your bedtime routine when you can use the Four-Step Analysis to develop concrete plans for dealing with your concerns.

Awakening to Panic Attacks

Some people with anxiety-related problems find they are occasionally awakened by a panic attack in the middle of the night. This often leaves them in a state of high anxiety. Current research now suggests that panic attacks that occur during sleep are not due to dreams. Instead, it is thought that they are due to some neurological mechanism that is not understood at present. People who awaken with panic attacks probably have a genetic factor that, in some way, triggers the fight or flight response. If you are awakened by panic attacks but do not recall a dream, this is probably true for you. If you are being awakened by bad dreams, skip to the next section.

If you experience nighttime panic attacks but are able to return to sleep fairly easily, continue to do whatever you do to return to sleep. However, if you find that nighttime panic attacks trigger negative self-talk and high anxiety that makes it difficult to return to sleep, do the following:

- First, get out of bed and fully awaken yourself. This is easily done by washing your face. Once you are fully awake, use coping self-statements to state accurately what has just happened and calm yourself, such as, "This was just that neurological quirk that I have. It is *not* dangerous. These feelings are only uncomfortable and will diminish soon." If you have difficulty remembering your coping self-statements at night, write them on a card and post them in an easy-to-find place.
- Second, spend ten to twenty minutes with a distracting and relaxing activity such as reading or watching television. This is essentially a decompression period that allows your body to settle down.
- Finally, go back to bed. If you find it difficult to go to sleep, use one of the relaxation response techniques in Appendix 2 to help you get back to sleep.

Recurring Nightmares

People suffering from post-traumatic stress disorder sometimes experience recurring nightmares. The nightmares might involve scenes of abuse from childhood or pictures from a recent trauma such as a car accident or crime. The following three steps have been shown to be effective in helping people eliminate such nightmares:

Step 1: Write down the nightmare with as many details as possible. Spend ten or fifteen minutes and describe in writing the recurring nightmares you have been experiencing. Try to include as many details as possible. What exactly do you see? What are the feelings that are generated? Do the places, people, or things in the nightmare change from time to time? If so, how do they change? What is it that stays constant?

Step 2: Change the dream any way you wish, spelling out the details of the new dream. Now spend ten minutes and rewrite your nightmare so it changes into something that is no longer frightening. Pretend that you are a screenwriter who has been handed a movie script that has no ending. Your job is to complete the script in such a way that it has a happy ending. You may start at any point in the old script that you want.

Rosalyn was having recurring nightmares about a car accident she had been in where she was thrown out of the car. In her dreams she would be driving and begin swerving until she hit something and was thrown from the car. The roads would sometimes change, as would the object she struck. She decided to change the dream so that after she began swerving, she would regain control of her car and arrive at her sister's house. She would then go in and have a pleasant visit.

Isaac was having recurring nightmares about a vicious beating he had received during a robbery. In his nightmares the perpetrator would appear in various locations and begin beating him unmercifully. Isaac rewrote his dream so that he would see the perpetrator, then realize he had mistaken his friend for the offender. The two of them would go to Isaac's house and begin working on his car, something he enjoyed doing with this friend.

Step 3: Mentally rehearse the changed dream before you fall asleep. Once you have developed the new dream you want to have, take a few minutes just before you go to sleep and play it through in your mind. The more vividly you use your imagination to do this, the more effective it is. It may take several days for the nightmare to begin transforming, but eventually it will.

Sometimes people who have been having recurring nightmares will find that after using this technique to end them, they have a similar dream months or years later. Usually, this is because they have experienced something in their life that involves similar emotions to those experienced in the original trauma. These emotions can trigger dreams similar to the recurring nightmares. For example, Isaac was free from his recurring nightmare for many months when suddenly he had a dream similar to his old ones. When we discussed it, he realized that there had been an incident at work where his supervisor had verbally beat him up. The old image of being physically beat up was simply his mind's way of trying to process this new experience of being beat up emotionally. Isaac developed a plan for how he would handle his work situation and rewrote the dream so it reflected his plan. A couple of days later, he had the dream and it transformed as he had rewritten it. He did not experience it again.

APPENDIX 5

Developing Effective Listening Skills

In our modern, busy world, taking time to listen is one of the greatest gifts you can give to someone. Listening shows you care about another person and is the key to effective problem solving. Unfortunately, many people really don't know how to listen effectively. This appendix shows you how to use what is often referred to as active listening or reflective listening.

Acknowledgment Responses

The term *acknowledgment responses* refer to all the nonverbal and verbal responses you make that indicate to the speaker that you are listening. Common nonverbal responses include eye contact and nodding of the head. Common verbal responses include the various empathetic grumblings you make such as, "uh-huh," "yes," and "mmmm." Acknowledgment responses are the simplest of the four basic active listening skills. Since they are probably already a part of your automatic behavior, they will not be dealt with in detail.

Feeling Confirmation

Feeling confirmation is the process of making guesses about another person's emotional response and commenting on it. Feeling confirmation has many uses and benefits. It provides you with a method for dissipating a person's strong emotions so this person can utilize his or her rational abilities more effectively. This is useful with problem solving that involves emotionally charged issues. It also makes you more effective by increasing your understanding of the person you are listening to and increases the overall amount of communication that takes place. In addition, it's an effective way to convey understanding and empathy to a person.

The first step in giving feeling confirmation is to make a guess about what the other person is experiencing on an emotional level. Next, comment on what you believe the other person is experiencing using one of the following three approaches:

- *Personal statements:* Decide how you would feel if you were in the other person's situation and make a personal statement about it. This is the easiest approach for many people. Examples: "That would have really scared me." "I think I'd be angry if he said that to me."
- *"Seems" approach:* Use words like "seem" to indicate that what you are saying is your perception. This is seldom offensive to others. Never state how a person is feeling in a direct fashion ("You're angry")—the other person may resent it, especially if you're wrong. Examples: "You seem angry." "I'm guessing that really scared you."
- *"Soft" questions:* Comment using words such as "weren't," "didn't," or "aren't." Examples: "Weren't you worried?" "Didn't that make you mad?"

Clarification Skills

Clarification skills involve the use of questions or statements to obtain information from a person. The most common clarification approach is to use direct questions such as, "What do you want?" or "Where are you going?" While direct questions are fine in many situations, they tend to block communication and cause a person to become defensive or stop talking when the person is experiencing negative emotions. The stronger the emotions, the more this tends to be true. Any one of the following three approaches can be used to soften a direct question and obtain the same information.

- *Personal statements:* Use phrases such as "I'd be interested in learning" or "I'd like to know" to change your question into a statement that expresses your interest in learning more about the information you want. Examples: "I'd be interested in learning more about what you want." "I'd like to know how you do that."
- *Confusion:* State in a simple, direct sentence your confusion or inability to understand whatever it is you wish to learn. This is a very nonthreatening approach that can be used whenever there is a high risk of the other person becoming defensive. A person is rarely threatened by your confusion. This is one approach that can usually be repeated if the other person continues to be vague. The only problem with this approach is that some people will not allow themselves to appear confused. If your level of self-esteem is high enough to allow you to appear ignorant or confused, you will find this approach very useful. Examples: "I don't quite understand what it is you want." "Boy, how you do that is a real mystery to me." "I'm still confused as to how you . . ."
- *Incomplete sentence:* Use an incomplete sentence that requires the information you want in order to be complete. This approach is like the fill-in-the-blank tests you took in school. It works best when used in the middle of a conversation and you want specific information. It is also best to avoid overusing this approach. Examples: "So, what you want is . . ." "And you went to . . ."

Paraphrasing

Paraphrasing is summarizing key points and repeating them in your own words. This is different from parroting back the other person's exact words. The main purpose of paraphrasing is to verify that what you heard was accurate and to communicate your understanding to the other person. This allows the other person to correct any misunderstandings. This is extremely important when resolving conflicts, because people will usually not listen to you until they know you have heard and understood their position. Since paraphrasing can sound artificial and become distractive when only one form is used, become skilled with each of the following four forms.

- "I statement": Begin with a phrase such as "I hear you saying . . ." or "As I understand it . . ."

- "You statement": Begin with a phrase such as, "So you think/feel/want . . ." or simply, "You think/believe/are going . . ."

- Summary form: Begin with a statement indicating that you intend to summarize what has been said, such as, "Let me see if I'm following you . . ." or "So what you are saying is . . ."

- Question form: Any of the above forms can be transformed into a question by simply raising your voice at the end of the sentence. You can also use a direct question such as, "Are you saying . . ."

  While direct questions are often effective when commenting on implied messages or clarifying confused ideas, direct questions can make a person feeling strong negative emotions defensive if they are overused.

Below are some examples of the different forms of paraphrasing, all in response to the following statement:

"I've had this flu for the last few days and haven't been feeling like putting in any more time than I have to . . . I know the meeting at six is going to drag on and not get much accomplished. Plus, I probably won't be much good in the shape I'm in, anyway, and so I was kind of hoping I could stay home so I could take care of my flu and maybe even go to bed early.

- "I statement": "What I hear you saying is, you want to skip the meeting and stay home so you can take care of yourself."

- "You statement": "Because you're sick, you want to skip the meeting and stay home."
- Summary form: "So what you are saying is that you want to skip the meeting and stay home."
- Question form: "Are you saying that you want to skip the meeting and stay home?"

Exercises

Learning to develop the above listening skills is actually fairly simple. It is usually best, however, to practice them one at a time. Begin by spending two days practicing just the feeling confirmation skills. Whenever you are talking with someone who is expressing emotions, comment on them using one of the forms of feeling confirmation. You will be most successful if you start by commenting on strong positive emotions (example: "That must have really been exciting!"). After you have practiced feeling confirmation skills with positive emotions for two days, spend the next two days practicing clarification skills in neutral or positive situations. Then spend the next two days practicing paraphrasing skills in neutral or positive situations. If you feel you need more work, repeat the two-day practice cycles until you feel comfortable with each skill. Do not use your new skills in situations where there are strong negative emotions until you feel skilled in neutral and positive situations. In a fairly short period of time you will find that these skills have become a natural part of how you talk.

Supplemental Materials

Books

At the time of this publication, Mr. Peurifoy has written two additional books:

- *Overcoming Anxiety: From Short-Term Fixes to Long-Term Recovery:* This book was written several years after *Anxiety, Phobias, and Panic* as a companion volume. It focuses on additional skills and work that will help you maintain your recovery and prevent relapses.
- *Anger: Taming the Beast:* This book is unusual in that it is designed for people who find it difficult to express anger and assert themselves as well as for those who are explosive. It follows four people as they work through their anger-related issues.

Audio Programs

Mr. Peurifoy has produced a variety of audio programs that are designed to be used along with these lessons. They include the relaxation response scripts found at the end of this book as well as a variety of other audio programs. Information about what is currently available can be found on the Internet at www.rpeurifoy.com. You can also receive information by writing to:

LifeSkills
P.O. Box 7915
Citrus Heights, CA 95621-7915

About the Author

Reneau Z. Peurifoy, M.A., M.F.T., first specialized in anxiety-related problems in 1981 and managed a private practice in Sacramento, California, for twenty years. Mr. Peurifoy was selected to present his treatment approach at eleven National Conferences on Phobias and Related Anxiety Disorders presented by the Anxiety Disorders Association of America and co-sponsored by Massachusetts General Hospital and Harvard Medical School (1989–1999). He has spoken to groups and conducted training seminars on treating anxiety disorders nationwide. Most recently, he has returned to teaching psychology at a local college.

In addition to his work with anxiety-related problems, Mr. Peurifoy has worked with couples and school-age children and has designed and conducted educational programs on anxiety, anger, assertiveness, stress management, and other topics in a wide variety of settings. Feeling a special commitment to teaching effective parenting skills, he has helped more than two thousand parents through his classes.

Mr. Peurifoy spent five years as a teacher before deciding to go into counseling. Two of those years were spent in Japan teaching science at St. Joseph's College, an all-boys school in Yokohama. Mr. Peurifoy met his wife, Michiyo, in college. They were married in 1974 and together they have two children, Audric born in 1979 and Monique born in 1983.

Index

Abdominal distress, 3, 6, 37
Accepting questionable sources
    as authoritative, 114–15,
    119
Achievement and worth, 131-
    32, 143, 239
Acknowledgment responses.
    See Appendix 5
Active listening. *See* Appendix 5
    Social role playing, 207
Adrenaline, 6
Aggression. *See* Assertiveness
Agoraphobia, 21
    Definition. *See* Appendix 1
Alcohol, 4
All-or-nothing thinking, 104–5,
    119, 127, 162
Amygdala, 7, 21
Anger, 85, 249–67
    Appropriate vs.
        Inappropriate, 252–59
    Definition, 250
    Fear of losing control, 267–71

Four-step approach for,
    259–60
From others, 265–67
Mistaken beliefs about, 254-
    55
Quick temper, 263–65
Resentment, 257–59
Roots of anger, 271
See also Assertiveness
Suppression, 260–63
Taboo sensations and emo-
    tions, 255-57, 264
Threats that generate,
    250–51
Anticipatory anxiety. *See*
    Negative anticipation
Anxiety
    Anxiety/panic cycle, 20–23,
        39, 48
    Brain circuits, 7
    Childhood factors, 11–16
    Definition, 2
    Excitement, 197

Anxiety *continued*
  Helping others, 80
  Medical causes, 4, 18, 23, 28
  Negative self-talk, 41
  New activities, 196-97
  Nighttime panic attacks, 353
  Normal, 196, 197, 226–27
  Overcoming anxiety, 246–47
  Panic attack, 3–4
  Personality traits and, 8–11, 28
  Recognizing normal anxiety, 246
  See also Conditioned response learning
  See also Fight or flight response
  See also Relaxation response
  Skills checklist, 59
  Symptoms, 2–4
  Symptoms as messages, 67-68
  Time to overcome, 27–28, 98–99, 125, 144, 315
Anxiety disorders
  Depression and, 1
  Descriptions. *See* Appendix 1
  Eating disorders and, 1
  How common, 1–2
  Overcoming anxiety, 246–47
  Simple explanation for, 29–31
  Six basic types, 1–2
  Substance abuse and, 1
  Time to overcome, 27–28, 98–99, 125, 144, 315
Anxiety Disorders Association of America, 52
Anxiety/panic cycle. *See* Anxiety

Approval, 167–76
  Criticism, 172-77
  Criticism, four-step approach, 172–75
  Delaying decisions, 175
  Excessive need for, 9, 167–76
  Performance related, 14
  Rational challenges for rejection, 177
  Rejection and, 170, 177
  See also Self-esteem
  Worth, 170
Assertiveness, 273–312
  Aggressive behavior, 274
  Anger and, 265
  Broken agreements, 310–11
  Businesses and salespeople, 312
  Definition, 275
  DERN approach, 279–88
  Guilt and embarrassment, 299
  "I language," 288–89
  Intimidation, 300–302
  Irrational beliefs about, 276, 289
  Nonassertive behavior, 273
  Non-negotiator, 302–4
  Resolving conflicts, 305–8
  Rights and responsibilities, 277–79
  Sabotaging tactics, 295–304
  See also Anger
  Simple violations of your rights, 291–93
  When to use, 308–10
Asthma, 4

Autonomic nervous system. *See* Fight or flight response

Basic skills checklist, 59
Behavioral therapy, 181–208
  Definition, 181
  Exposure therapy, 185–200
  Goals, defining, 185
  Guidelines for practicing, 195–200
  Guidelines for support people, 209–11
  Identifying problem behaviors, 182
  Imaginal exposure, 204–6
  Rapid in vivo exposure, 203–4
  Response prevention, 200–203
  Social role-playing, 206–8
  Use an effective method, 218
Blaming, 159–63, 297
  Rational challenges, 164
Block method, 121–23, 144, 177
Body
  Body as a machine with limited energy, 65, 179
  Ignoring needs of, 10
  Indications your body is sick, hungry, tired or overstressed, 125
  Loss of ability to think rationally, 253
Body scanning, 20
Bottom-line technique, 142
Breath holding, 37–39

Caffeine, 4, 60
Can't thinking, 94–96, 119
Cardiovascular problems, 4
Catastrophizing. *See* Magnification/minimization
Change, 213–23
  Five short chapters on, 319
  Identifying ways you avoid, 225
  Learn to release, 224
  Recognizing avoidance to, 224
Checking. *See* Obsessive-compulsive disorder
Chest pain, 3
Child abuse, 12
Choking, 3. *See also* Dyspnea
Circular questioning, 93–94, 119
Clarification skills. *See* Appendix 5
Cognitive therapy, 87
  Three-step process, 120
Comparisons, 240
Compliments, 234–36, 237–39
Compulsions. *See* Obsessive-compulsive disorder
Concentration problems, 125
Conditioned response learning, 35, 196
Conflicts, 273–76
  Daily review of, 314
  Resolving, 305–8
  with businesses and salespeople, 312
Control, 9, 10, 20, 267–71

Coping self-statements, 40–47, 56–59
  Anger, 272
  Examples, 56–59
  Generalized anxiety disorder, 47
  Obsessive-compulsive disor-
    der, 43–46
  Panic disorder, 16–22
  Post-traumatic stress disorder, 46
  Social phobias, 47
  Specific phobias, 46
Cost-benefit analysis, 88, 91
Criticism, 172–75, 177
Cue-controlled relaxation, 35–36, 52–53, 78, 96, 120
  See also Appendix 2

DER scripts. *See* DERN approach
Decisions, 70–71
  Delaying, 175, 178
  Indecisiveness, 241
  Limiting commitments, 242
  Postponing with non-negotia-
    tor, 302
Decompression routines. *See* Stress
Denial, 214–16
Depersonalization. *See* Feelings of unreality
Derealization. *See* Feelings of unreality
DERN approach. *See* Assertiveness
Desensitization. *See* Exposure therapy

Diabetes, 4
Diaphragmatic breathing. *See* Hyperventilation
Diet and exercise. *See* Stress
Disapproval. *See* Approval
Discounting. *See* Magnification/minimization
Distorted thinking, 103–20
  Blaming, 161
  Change and, 221–23
  Definition, 103
  Habitual thinking patterns, 86–87
  Identifying, 120
  See also Block method
  Summary of different types, 118–20
  Three-step process, 120
Distraction, 47–50
Dizziness. *See* Dyspnea
Drugs. *See* Medications
Dry mouth, 6, 37
Dyspnea, 3, 37

Ego strengtheners, 88
EMDR. *See* Eye Movement Desensitization and Reprocessing
Emotional reasoning, 115–18, 120
Emotional support, 75–76
  Guidelines for support peo-
    ple, 209–11
Emotions, 82–86, 267
  Ability to control, 157
  Healthy management of, 116
  Identifying, 262

Increased emotionality, 125
Purpose of, 85
See also Anger
See also Emotional reasoning
Suppression of, 10, 14
Taboo, 255–57
Taboo sensations and, 264
Exercise. *See* Diet and exercise
Exposure. *See* Behavioral therapy
Externalization. *See* Distraction
Eye Movement Desensitization
 and Reprocessing, 321, 346

Faintness. *See* Dyspnea
Fear, 85
 Anger and, 250
 Definition, 2
 of becoming ill or dying, 3
 of being incompetent, 233
 of going crazy, 3
 of losing control, 3, 267–71
 of making mistakes, 133–34
 of rejection. *See* Approval,
  excessive need for
 See also Negative anticipation
Feeling confirmation. *See*
 Appendix 5
Feelings of unreality, 3
Fight or flight response, 4–7, 21
 Anger and, 250, 261
Five-step problem-solving
 approach, 154–55
Flashbacks. *See* Post-traumatic
 stress disorder
Flooding. *See* Rapid in vivo
 exposure

Flushes, 3, 37
Fortune telling, 113–14, 119
Four-step analysis for negative
 anticipation, 152
Four-step approach for criti-
 cism, 175
Four-step approach for dealing
 with anger, 260
Frustration, 159

GAD. *See* Generalized anxiety
 disorder
Generalized anxiety disorder,
 26, 47, 60, 165
 Coping self-statement exam-
  ples, 59
 See also Appendix 1
 See also Negative anticipation
 Simple explanation, 31
Goals
 Behavioral therapy and, 185
 Setting realistic, 138
Good day rule, 123–24
Guidelines for practicing. *See*
 Behavioral therapy
Guidelines for support people.
 See Emotional support

Habitual thinking patterns, 86–87
Helping others, 78
Hippocampus, 25
Hot flashes. *See* Flushes
Humor, 75
Hyperventilation, 5, 18, 21
 Diaphragmatic breathing,
  36–38, 53–56, 78
Hypothyroidism, 4

"I language," 288–89
Imaginal exposure. *See*
    Behavioral therapy
Indications your body is sick,
    hungry, tired or over-
    stressed, 125
Inner ear problems, 4
Internalization. *See* Body scan-
    ning

Journaling, 146

Labeling, 104. *See also*
    Overgeneralization
Learned helplessness, 213–14
Listening skills. *See* Active lis-
    tening
Locus of control, 96
Loss, 85, 159

Magnification/minimization,
    108–11, 119
Marijuana, 4
Massage, 145
Medical conditions, 4, 18, 23,
    28
Medications, 4, 19, 50–52
Memory deficiency, 125
Mind reading, 113, 119
Mirror talk, 235
Mistakes, 133–34, 240
    Problem-solving approach to,
    135–36

National Institute of Mental
    Health, 1, 52
Nausea. *See* Abdominal distress

Needs, 81–82
    Identifying, 263
Negative anticipation, 20,
    147–56
    Creativity and, 8
    Definition, 147
    Four-step analysis, 148–52,
    165
    Generalized anxiety disorder
    and, 147
    Past, separating from present,
    155
    Positive realist, becoming a,
    147, 165
    Problem-solving skills, 154–55
    Rational challenges, 164
    So what if approach, 152–53
    Uncertainty, 153
Negative friends, 100–102,
    162–63
Nightmares, recurring. *See*
    Appendix 4
NIMH. *See* National Institute
    of Mental Health
Normalizing yourself, 226–27
Numbness, 3, 37

OCD. *See* Obsessive-compul-
    sive disorder
Objective evaluation, 88, 91
Obsessive-compulsive disorder,
    23, 43–46, 60
    Coping self-statement exam-
    ples, 57
    Four step approach, 43–46
    Response prevention,
    200–203

See also Appendix 1
Simple explanation, 29
Weird or unusual thoughts,
228
Overgeneralization, 105–8, 119
Labeling, 106, 119

Palpitations. *See* Tachycardia
Panic attack. *See* Anxiety
Panic disorder, 16–22, 42–43
Coping self-statement exam-
ples, 56
See also Appendix 1
Simple explanation, 29
Paraphrasing. *See* Appendix 5
Parasympathetic. *See* Fight or
flight response
Paresthesias, 3, 37
Passive-aggressive behavior,
252, 274
Past
Power of present, 157–59
Separating present from, 155
What's happening? What's
real? technique, 166
Perfectionism, 9, 127–42
Beliefs that support, 130–34
Bottom-line technique,
140–42
But habit, 137
Challenges for, 143–44
Definition, 127
Experiencing pleasure, 139
Focus on positives, 136
Locus of control, 96
Perfectionistic self-talk,
128–30

Practicing and, 198
Problem-solving approach to
mistakes, 136
Process orientation, 139
Schedule activities, 142
Setting realistic goals, 138
Personality, development of, 11
Personalization, 112, 119
Phobic anxiety/panic. *See*
Situational anxiety/panic
Play, 50, 74
Pleasure, 139
See also massage
Positive realist. *See* Negative
anticipation
Post-traumatic stress disorder,
23-24, 46
Causes, 23-24
Coping self-statement exam-
ples, 57
Flashbacks, 24
See also Appendix 1
Simple explanation, 30
What's happening? What's
real? technique, 166
Practice guidelines. *See*
Behavioral therapy
Present, power of, 157–59
Problem-solving thinking, 89,
135–36, 154–55, 165
Problem-solving, five-step
approach, 154–55
Procrastination
Process orientation, 139
Schedule activities, 142
Progressive relaxation. *See*
Appendix 2

Psychotherapy, 31–32
  See also Appendix 3
PTSD. *See* Post-traumatic
  stress disorder

Questioning, 88, 91

Rapid in vivo exposure. *See*
  Behavioral therapy
Rational challenge, 88, 91
Rational self-talk. *See* Coping
  self-statements
Rationalization, 214–16
Redirecting statements, 88
Redirection. *See* Distraction
Relapse prevention
  Normalizing yourself, 226–27
  Overcoming anxiety, 246–47
  Recognizing normal anxiety, 246
Relaxation response, 31
  See also Appendix 2
  See also Cue-controlled relax-
  ation
Relaxing by tensing and relax-
  ing muscles, 208
Repression, 252
Resentment. *See* Anger
Response prevention. *See*
  Behavioral therapy
Responsibility, 160, 240
  Refusing to accept, 297
  Rights and, 277–79
Rights. *See* Assertiveness
Rituals. *See* Compulsions
Roadblocks
  Symptom reducing skills,
  33–34

Scapegoating. *See* Blaming
Schwartz, Jeffrey M., 43
Secondary gains, 219–21, 259
Self-acceptance. *See* Self-
  esteem
Self-concept. *See* Self-esteem
Self-efficacy, 213–14
Self-esteem, 229–43
  Self-acceptance, 229
  Self-concept, 229
  Threat and, 255
Self-talk, 87–89
  Keeping a record of, 97
  Perfectionistic self-talk, 128–30
  See also Block method
  See also various emotions
  See also various types of dis-
  torted thinking
  Types of, 87–88
Setbacks. *See* Two or three
  steps forward, one step
  backward
Shaking, 3, 37
Shortness of breath. *See*
  Dyspnea
Should/must thinking, 89–93,
  104–5, 118
  Evaluating should/must rules,
  98
  See also Can't thinking
  See also Circular questioning
Shyness, 25
Simple phobias. *See* Specific
  phobias
Situational anxiety/panic, 4
Sleep problems, 61. *See also*
  Appendix 4

Smothering sensations. *See*
Dyspnea
So what if approach, 152–53
Social phobia, 25-26, 47
Coping self-statement exam-
ples, 58
See also Appendix 1
Simple explanation of, 30
Social role-playing, 206–8
Social role-playing. *See*
Behavioral therapy
Specific phobias, 24–25, 46
Coping self-statement exam-
ples, 58
See also Appendix 1
Simple explanation of, 30
Spiritual support, 76–77
Spontaneous anxiety/panic, 4
Stress, 18, 20, 32, 61, 63–80
Body as a machine with limit-
ed energy, 65, 179
Decompression routines, 73
Definition, 63
Diet and exercise, 68–69, 78,
178
Early signs, 65–67
Emotional support, 75–76
Fight or flight response, 64
Humor, 75
Indications your body is sick,
hungry, tired or over-
stressed, 125
Managing periods of high
stress, 69–71
Physical, 64
Play, 74
Psychological, 64

Relaxation, forms of, 72
Spiritual support, 76–77
Traditions and routines, 77
Stress symptom inventory, 66–67
Study partner, 32
Substance abuse, 11
Substitution, 88, 90
Success
Rewarding, 99–100
Support people. *See* Emotional
support
Suppression of feelings, 10
Sweating, 3, 6, 37
Sympathetic. *See* Fight or flight
response
Systematic desensitization. *See*
Exposure therapy

Taboo sensations and emotions,
255–57, 264
Tachycardia, 3, 5, 37
Therapy. *See* Appendix 3
Threat, 6, 85
Anger and, 250–51
Distorted thinking and, 255
Tingling sensations. *See*
Paresthesias
Trembling, 3, 37
Troubleshooting checklist, 125
Two or three steps forward, one
step backward, 125, 198

Uncertainty, 153, 217–18
See also Negative anticipation

Victim thinking, 156–59
Rational challenges, 164

Weird or unusual thoughts, 228
What if thinking. *See* Negative
  anticipation
What's happening? What's real?
  technique, 166

Worry. *See* Negative anticipation
  Sleep problems. *See*
    Appendix 4
Worth. *See* Achievement and
  worth